# OUT OF THE
## *Ordinary*

RUTH SMITH MEYER

Printed in Canada

978-1-4866-0829-4

Word Alive Press
131 Cordite Road, Winnipeg, MB R3W 1S1
www.wordalivepress.ca

MIX
Paper from
responsible sources
FSC
www.fsc.org    FSC® C016245

Library and Archives Canada Cataloguing in Publication
Meyer, Ruth Smith, author
        Out of the ordinary / Ruth Smith Meyer.
Issued in print and electronic formats.
ISBN 978-1-4866-0829-4 (pbk.).--ISBN 978-1-4866-0830-0 (pdf).--
ISBN 978-1-4866-0831-7 (html).--ISBN 978-1-4866-0832-4 (epub)
        1. Meyer, Ruth Smith. 2. Authors, Canadian (English)--21st
century--Biography. I. Title.
PS8626.E9415Z463 2015        C813'.6        C2015-900283-4
                                            C2015-900284-2

If you have touched my life in any way over the years,
consider this book lovingly dedicated to you,
for you have helped me become who I am.

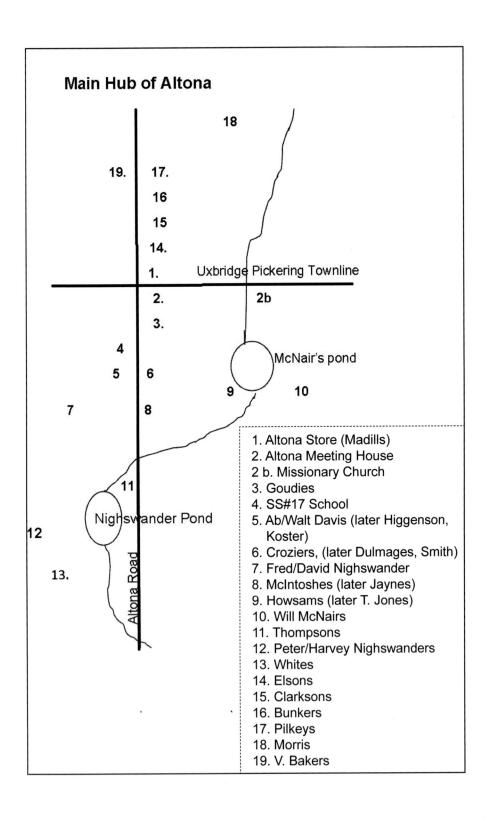

# Main Hub of Altona

18

19.    17.

16

15

14.

1.    Uxbridge Pickering Townline

2.    2b

3.

4

5    6    McNair's pond

9    10

7    8

11

Nighswander Pond

12

13.

Altona Road

1. Altona Store (Madills)
2. Altona Meeting House
2 b. Missionary Church
3. Goudies
4. SS#17 School
5. Ab/Walt Davis (later Higgenson, Koster)
6. Croziers, (later Dulmages, Smith)
7. Fred/David Nighswander
8. McIntoshes (later Jaynes)
9. Howsams (later T. Jones)
10. Will McNairs
11. Thompsons
12. Peter/Harvey Nighswanders
13. Whites
14. Elsons
15. Clarksons
16. Bunkers
17. Pilkeys
18. Morris
19. V. Bakers

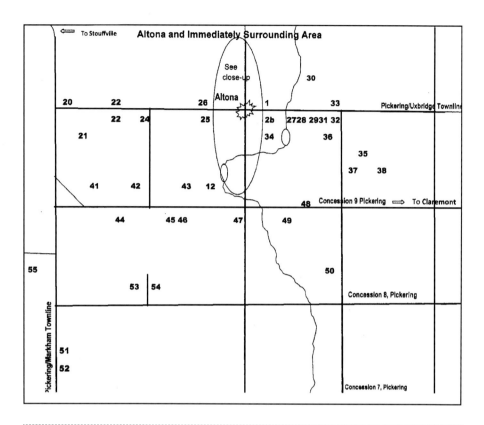

Altona and Immediately Surrounding Area

20. Eckhardts
21. Bertha Hoover/Kerswill
22. Hodgsons
23. Fred McNair
24. Slacks
25. Will/Millard Reesor
26. Mary Jones
27. Isaac Lehman
28. Ramers
29. Tindalls
30. Bert Lewis
31 Fred Lewis
32. Pallister (later G. Wideman)
33. Stan Lewis
34. Carter
35. Barkey
36. Kerr
37. Ken Reesor
38. Stan Reesor

39. McKay
40. Art Wideman
41. Davis
42. Yake/Fretz
43. Beilby/J. Nighswander
44. Aubrey Spang
45. F. Bielby
46. Norman Neals (later P.Meyer)
47. Allan Meyer
48. Sam Fretz
49. John Spang
50. Norman Lehman
51. Em Nighswander
52. Henry Reesors
53. Abr. Lehman farm
54. Eli Lehman
55. Allan Wideman

Proximity of Altona to Toronto and Lake Ontario

# The Setting

The intersection of the Pickering-Uxbridge town line and Altona Road was the hub of the little hamlet of Altona where I grew up. There were no other streets in the village.

In the early days, long before my time, the little community with its hotel was a popular stopping place after a good day's journey for many who travelled up the Altona Road from Lake Ontario to points farther north. On the northeast corner of the intersection stood the establishment where travellers could find accommodation. The main part was a light-brick building with a white frame addition to the east that held the rooms for rent. A porch ran the full length of both parts on the south side and around the corner to the west. The latter part led to the stables for the horses; that building sat to the north, behind the main building.

By the time I arrived, the hotel had been turned into a thriving general store, an egg-grading station and living quarters for the storekeeper, Ollie Madill and his family. Ollie was a diminutive man who often wore a brown fedora, even in the store. His quiet, friendly helpfulness more than made up for any lack of magnitude. His wife, Flo, was quite a talker—friendly too— but was not one to tolerate much nonsense. Had Flo known the liberties Ollie took in pressing the change into the ladies' hands with a suggestive wink, I'm sure he would have heard, in certain terms, her displeasure.

North of the corner, on the east side behind the hotel, there were five houses on small lots. The first one housed the Elsons—Elwood and Isola and their eight children. Every one of those children was popular in our little one-room schoolhouse. Although they may have had scraps among themselves, everyone knew better than to say or do anything of a negative nature to the Elsons for they stuck together and stood up for one another.

North of the Elsons, Billy Clarkson, a sheep shearer, lived.

The Bunkers lived in the next small house. Norman, a quiet construction worker, counter-balanced his more vocal wife, Maggie. Most of their children were married by the time I remember. Their oldest daughter had been in my father's class. However, they had one son quite a bit younger than the rest and Mervyn was in one of the older grades when I started school. I gather there may have been some difference of opinion between Norm and Maggie on how to raise their latest blessing.

Fred and Elsie Pilkey lived at the north end of the little row of houses, on a slightly larger acreage. They had two daughters and two sons. Irene was no longer at home. Alma was just finishing school when I started. Carl, a real class clown, was in my older sister's class, and his brother Ken was in the class after mine.

On the farm on the west side, Vince and Eva Baker lived with their family of one son and three daughters. They were well known as Clydesdale breeders. Each fall before Toronto's Royal Winter Fair, Vince or Clarence paraded their huge Clydesdales up and down the roads getting them ready, tails all braided and beribboned, practising their high-stepping gait to impress the judges.

Across from the hotel, on the southeast corner, a little brick Mennonite meeting house sat, surrounded by a cemetery. Horse sheds, standing to the north, were reminders of former days, but those buildings were now largely unused, though sometimes people backed their cars in to avoid snow or sun. The outhouse in one corner was also occasionally used by young boys of the community trying their first cigarette.

Directly south of the church on the east side, stood the big building that used to house the renowned Monkhouse General Store. The ghosts of the past seemed almost as real as the current inhabitants, Fletcher and Ina Goudie and their son, Don. My grandparents told me many stories of the plethora of goods one could purchase there in the glory days of the store when the first floor was full of general store merchandise and the upstairs was devoted to fine dishes and kitchenware. Even the basement held a goldmine of supplies. I wished I could have seen it, for it seemed to me that it must have been a mini-Eaton's department store like the one in downtown Toronto. In my time, the entire first floor stood empty while the second story had been made into living area, and the third story, an apartment.

Both Fletcher and Ina drove big black Cadillacs. Much of the time, Fletcher was away working in the Elliot Lake mining business. His work was definitely not in the innards of the mine shafts, since he usually dressed in pin-striped black suits and white shirts, his fedora set at a natty angle. Ina impressed me as being a head taller than her dapper husband. She appeared to have her world by the tail and completely in her charge. Seemingly, when the whim struck her, she would pack her Cadillac and take off for the north to check up on her husband. Back in the forties that was rather unusual—a woman taking off on a trip like that—all on her own.

One member of their family that I did not appreciate was their little bulldog that found its main joy in waiting for bicyclists to come by so it could rush out and nip at the moving wheels. I still have a scar on my knee to prove what that dog did to me.

On the west side of the Altona Road, just south of the Goudies, at the bottom of a small dip in the road, the tall red-brick school, SS#17 Pickering, stood on an acre of lawn. The gate in the chain-link fence led to a wide sidewalk that arched to the right and left to steps and entrance for the boys on the right and the girls on the left. In the centre of that semicircle was a flowerbed and a few shrubs with the large window from the teacher's room just above it.

Inside that room a long rope hung from the ceiling. At nine o'clock and at the end of recess, the teacher or a trusted older student would pull the rope to ring the bell three times to signal time for classes.

Another one-acre lot and house followed the house of learning. In that little brick house lived Ab Davis and his daughter Esther. Esther served for many years as the janitor of the school.

Across from the school and a little to the south stood an impressive, large square dark brick house. The house had been built by the Monkhouses, but in my day, Mr. and Mrs. Crozier lived there—he, a handsomely-dressed drover, and she, a very tidy, community-minded housewife, involved in Women's Institute and leading 4-H clubs for young girls. Most of the adults in Altona were referred to, even by children, by their given names, but the Croziers were always Mr. and Mrs. to the children!

A small garden separated their house from a lane that led back to the mill on the left; behind which was a large pond that powered the mill. Across from the mill was a small story-and-a-half mill house where the miller, Earl Howsam, and his wife lived with their three older children.

The lane continued, further east, across the bridge that spanned the creek. At the top of a gentle rise just southeast of the large pond, stood Will and Lil McNair's white-plastered brick house surrounded by towering maples that spread their branches over most of the lawn. More peaceful surroundings would be hard to imagine. Although jolly and kind, Will was somewhat reserved. Lil had the tenderest eyes. Her warm smile always accompanied her gentle words and had a way of making everyone feel special.

Just south of the McNair/Howsam lane and much nearer to the road, was the one-and-a-half story dark-brown brick house with a wraparound verandah, where Hugh and Lillian McIntosh lived. They were retired storekeepers. He was a tall stern Scotsman with a twinkle in his eye that softened that strict demeanour—she, a short, rather rotund woman with merry eyes, a broad smile and white, white hair gathered into a small bun at the base of her neck. They still spoke

Gaelic and he taught us greetings—as I remember them, they sounded more like "Cimarachi" and "Hakama." For a long time, I didn't know how to spell them but found them to be *Cimar a thathu and Tha gu mat.* We practised the familiar words when he came each morning, walking stick in one hand and a little tin pail in the other, to get his fresh milk for the day. If, perchance, he was ill, Mrs. McIntosh would call over and one of us children would be sent to collect the pail. That was a distinct privilege, for on our return, we would be given a shiny nickel and a candy as payment for the favour.

There was another gift we got from the McIntoshes several times a winter. He had an outdoor pit made with a large cement tile submerged in the earth at the end of the garden. This was lined with straw, then filled with vegetables—savoy cabbage, Chinese cabbage, carrots, beets and other vegetables. They were covered with straw and last of all, a lid. When the pit was opened in the winter or early spring, the vegetables were crisp and fresh as if straight from the garden. What a treat!

Right across from the McIntoshes, well back on the west side, facing the Altona Road, stood the orangish-red brick house that was my home. The lane entered between two stone pillars. On the south side of the lane an apple orchard whispered of bountiful fruit. On the north side a vegetable garden flaunted its bounty in neat rows that marched from the road allowance to the front lawn. The row closest to the lane and the first six feet of each row was reserved for a variety of cut flowers.

The lane rose slightly as it neared the house on the north side. A spruce tree stood sentinel at the southeastern corner of that lawn. Two maple trees took up guard duty in front of the house. A decorative wire fence separated the lawn from the lane. Between the spruce and the first maple, a gate provided entrance to the cement sidewalk, which led to the steps close to the east end of the verandah. At the top of the steps, a door led directly into the living room. The seldom-used front door faced the road. It would have allowed guests to enter the hallway at the bottom of the stairs, but the side doors—one into the living room and one to the summer kitchen— were more accessible and handier, so the front door remained closed and locked except for twice-yearly house cleaning.

At the northeast corner of the house at the end of the verandah, an insulbrick addition contained the *Doddy-haus* (Grandfather house) where my grandparents lived after my parents married. My Aunt Mary, who was 24 when I was born, and my Uncle Joe, 16, also lived there. A covered verandah sporting white posts, with green trim, wrapped around the east and south sides of the house and continued around the west corner to the summer kitchen door. Still west of the flat-roofed summer kitchen stood a two-storey woodshed and perhaps twenty feet west of that a carriage-house that had been turned into a garage.

If you continued up the lane from the woodshed and garage, you came to the barn hill leading to the upper story of the big hip-roofed barn. From the barn, the land sloped gently down before it rose again to the west line fence. The land on which these buildings were located, plus the Davis house and school, took up the north half of the 200–acre parcel purchased by Martin Nighswander Senior in 1838. During his ownership, the house was built in 1850. The builder also had the foresight to plant trees along the north and east sides of the farm. He planted maple trees that years later spread their branches over the road along which his great-great-grandchildren would skip their way to the school.

South of the Nighswander lane, the road descended through a cedar swamp and across a cement-sided bridge over Duffins Creek. That stretch always was a bit scary—especially if it was almost dark. Thankfully, there usually was a sibling along, but when I was alone, I preferred to run. If I saw lights coming from either direction, I ducked into the ditch and hid behind a small tree or shrub.

Just south of that stretch a house stood on the west side, on a small lot off the south one hundred acre parcel. Stan and Flossie Thompson with children Kathleen, John, Earl and Lorne lived there. Flossie, the McNair's daughter, had dark brown eyes that always sparkled with friendliness. Stan was a joker and often called out to my sister and me, "Hello boys!" No amount of correction worked—he'd just laugh all the more. Finally we decided to join the fun. Next time we answered. "Hello Mrs. Thompson!" That brought a hearty laugh and an end to the salutation which had bothered us.

Further south, past another pond on Duffin's Creek, a lane crossed over a wooden bridge that spanned the churning waters that spilled over the dam. Across the bridge, the lane forked, one road going to the left and the other slightly to the right. The left fork passed the big old cider mill and went on to the mill house. During my public school days, one of my best friends, Norma, lived there with her parents, Jim and Jean White, and her brothers, Frank and Ken. The right fork rose to cross another bridge over the mill race and on to a large house set high on the hill to the right, with a huge barn to the left of the lane. This farm was an important part of my roots as well. My grandfather David, great-grand-father Enos and great-great-grandfather Martin Junior were born in this house. In my time, my grandfather's brother, Peter, and his wife, Amelia Nighswander, lived there with their two children, Harvey and Edith.

These were the last buildings in this block even though there was another half mile or so through more cedar bush before you got down to the Ninth Line of Pickering. Duffin's Creek crossed the road again under an iron bridge just north of that corner. This section of the Altona Road may have seemed rather remote and lonely to a stranger, but to the children who lived along that stretch, it held many opportunities to explore, and explore we did.

From the main intersection—east from the Madill General Store—the road dropped down a steep hill towards Duffins Creek that fed the ponds. The Missionary Church stood beyond the bridge that passed over the creek. Continuing east, there were five houses on small lots. Isaac and Emma Lehman, my grandmother's brother and his wife, inhabited the first of those houses. Isaac and Emma were always special to me because Isaac and my grandmother were very close to each other. He always had a kind word for even the children.

Fred and Susie Ramer lived next to the Lehman's. I never got to know them very well. The main thing that stands out, the few times I was in their house, was the darkened windows. I wonder now, why they were always kept that way. When you entered that shadowy abode, your nostrils were assaulted by stale air.

A widow, Mabel Tindall, lived in the next house with her youngest few still at home, when I first remember. They seemed to be a jolly, active and, at times, mischievous bunch. One by one, Roy, Ruby, Elsie, Murray and Harry got married, and except for Harry, they moved away. Harry and his wife lived there with Mabel until her passing.

The next house is where Harold Lewis and my former teacher, Luella Harper, lived. Harold was a shy, handsome man, and I thought the perfect match for my beloved teacher with black hair and shining eyes.

Fred and Ruth Lewis lived in the next house. Fred was the same age as my Uncle Joe, but Fred and Ruth were married when they were very young and had quite a brood before Uncle Joe took that step. Fred started a feed business in the barn behind their house, so we often went over there to pick up supplies as well as being invited over by their children to play.

At the corner lived Johnny Pallister. I knew his name but have no recollection of ever seeing him.

On the north side were two Lewis farms— Stanley and Ada right across from the Pallisters, and Bert to the west. The latter farm buildings were at the end of a very long laneway.

Those twenty dwellings and four public buildings comprised the hamlet of Altona, unless you wanted to include the two sets of farm buildings at the top of the rise west of the main corners—Will and Ethel Reesor on the south (or left), and Mary Jones on the north or right. Will was a former reeve of the township, well respected in the eyes of the community. Mary Jones, on the other hand, was the remaining one of three unmarried siblings; her house was as gray as any barn boards in the neighbourhood. It was said that the door to the room in which her sister breathed her last had been shut and everything left just as it was when she died. One never saw Mary in public. The Reesors got her groceries and any other needs. That grey house felt almost haunted to us.

The one hundred or so neighbours within its boundaries helped make up the fabric of who I am. The ones well known and those less familiar still etched themselves into my memory and became a part of me.

# INTRODUCTION

**M**emories are often meandering and circuitous. Ask five different people about the same event after a number of years, although they all were present when something happened, there will be quite a disparity in their stories.

My memories are my perceptions of the way things were. My siblings and friends may remember the same things quite differently. I hereby acknowledge that I honour your truth. I also assure you that I am truthful about my perceptions.

I present them as my truth—the way I experienced it.

CHAPTER 1

# The Beginning of My Time

> "Childhood memories are inner luggage we carry throughout our lives. How blessed we are if that space is filled with warm, fuzzy belongings that delight us with each opening."
>
> —**Author Unknown**

There was an ever-present tension in what was supposed to be my ordinary life. The sameness and the difference; the things we could do the same way our neighbours did and the things that were *verboten* (forbidden). As a child, some things made sense and some I didn't understand at all. We lived in a typical small community, most of us having much in common; it seems it should have been an almost idyllic existence. It was in many ways, but our family was a bit different. We were Mennonites. As the Holy Book said, and we were frequently reminded, we were to be "in this world, but not of it." Too young to differentiate, I thought even those who went to other churches and the way they lived were part of the world that was forbidden to me.

In my early years, home was the middle of my universe. But even there, I was aware I was different. My most vivid memories are small incidents, yet important for the feelings they evoked. Although not associated with the fact that we were Mennonites, those feelings nevertheless increased the confusion and disparity in my struggle to accept myself.

Sometimes I still hesitate to share one part of my life, for the difference between most people's experience and mine sounds almost preposterous. My memories start so much younger than almost anyone I know—in the first three to six months while I was still in the cradle.

Lying in my cradle, I felt very new to the world. Although I couldn't put it into words, because I had none at that age, I was sure I had recently arrived from God's presence to experience life in this new place.

The first months of my life, I slept in Mom and Dad's bedroom where my sister Eva also slept. Her large crib was beside the north window. My cradle, for the first six months, extended from the foot of her crib along the east wall. When we got ready for bed, Mom tucked us in, and went back to her work as she sang for us from the kitchen.

In the first spring of my life, after a November birth, I recall being held in someone's arms at the south window. Across the lane, the apple orchard and the dandelions were in full bloom. I thought it was part of God's welcome for me into this world. They were just across the lane, but it seemed to be a far country–somewhere I had never been. The beauty was reminiscent of where I had previously been.

There were only my sister and I in our family at that time, but at the other end of the double house, my unmarried aunt and uncle still lived with my grandparents.

When I was 16 months old, my uncle, seventeen-year-old Joe, played with me by swinging me by my arms between his legs, and then high up over his shoulders. He'd let go and catch me in his arms. On one of those swings, my shoulder slipped from its socket. I loved my Joe, but it hurt so much I had to cry. Mom and Dad took me to Dr. Freel's for an x-ray. In the process of holding me down on the table, the shoulder popped back in place. Years later, as a teenager, I asked my mother about the time that I was laid on a shiny, cold table in the back of Dr. Freel's office. Mother looked at me incredulously, "Why Ruth, you couldn't remember that!" I most certainly did. I also remember Dad carrying me into the house and Uncle Joe and Grandma and Grandad being there too. *Should I have kept that to myself? Am I an oddity to be able to remember these things?* The unbelief in my mother's voice deepened the anxiety I felt about myself.

My sister Eva, four years older than me, was born a meticulous little lady, keeping all her possessions well organized and cared for. I came into the world a climber and explorer, more often interested in discovery than orderliness. I often ruined her neatness and sometimes her toys. I soon perceived this difference between us was a nuisance and frustration, especially in her eyes.

Once, Mom found me up on the aluminum-lined dry sink. The sink wasn't much more than an inch deep and used mainly to drain the dishes after being washed in an enamel dishpan. There was a cold water tap about a foot above the sink. I had turned the tap on and was joyfully splashing in the water. Luckily one of Dad's inventions was a drain at the end of the sink, so there was some escape for the deluge that would otherwise have caused a flood. Momentarily, it had been so much fun, but I soon perceived that it was naughty pleasure and not to be repeated.

Had I been able to figure out a way to get there, I would have climbed to the top shelf of the glass cupboard where another of Eva's treasures was stored. It was a wind-up merry-go-round outfitted with bells and bangles and that played music as it turned. I loved the times Mom got it down and Eva was allowed to wind it up. Each time I eagerly reached for it, Mom held my hands and cautioned me, "Ah-ah! Just look, don't touch!"

Our toys were kept in a closet off of Mom and Dad's room. A string hung from the light so that we could reach to turn it on when we wanted to play there. One Christmas, Eva and I each received a doll. Eva's came with the name 'Bubbles,' mine came as 'Toddles.'

Eva had received a doll carriage before my arrival on the scene. Occasionally, she would share it, but usually I used a cardboard box as a cradle for Toddles, while Bubbles would have the more luxurious sleeping accommodation. I was learning that in this world one needed to accommodate and respect the belongings and space of others and that, not always, did things appear or feel equal.

When I outgrew the cradle, Eva was moved upstairs to an adult double bed and I took over the larger crib. When I was about twenty months old, it was my turn to move upstairs to Eva's bedroom. How exciting! I would be sharing a room with Eva once more. Aunt Mary, who lived with Grandma and Grandpa, at the other end of our house, often helped Mom, and it was she who helped me make the move. We made several trips taking bedding upstairs, but I wanted to carry my own pillow. I looked at that long flight of stairs that appeared to me almost the equivalent of the height of our high barn roof. I tried to figure out how to get up with my little pillow in hand. *I'll heave the pillow up to the first step, and then I'll climb up there myself. Now for the second step. Oh-hh!* I nearly fell, but Aunt Mary's hands caught me.

"Let me carry you and your pillow, Ruth."

"No, I want to do it by myself!"

She set me down and I viewed the next level of the great expedition. Aunt Mary held the back of my dress as I heaved the pillow to the next step. The effort made me lose my balance again.

"That was a good try!" Aunt Mary's voice encouraged me as she picked up both me and the pillow. I didn't object this time, and we both went to the top of the steps. She set me down and I smiled with satisfaction as she handed me the pillow to carry to our room at the far end of the hall.

Fascinated by the stairs, I decided on my return, to lay down on the second one from top. I didn't quite get settled on the smooth, painted surface, when I tumbled to the bottom. Darkness broken by firework-like stars was all I could see. The wind was knocked out of me. Gasping for breath as I lay at the bottom, I heard footsteps fast approaching. Aunt Mary came running down the stairs, Mom raced from our part of the house, and Grandma from her part.

As my breath came back, I gasped and cried. There were hugs, kisses and sounds of sympathy from all sides. There was great comfort in the concerned examination from the most loved adults in my life. I wasn't seriously injured, but I vowed to never lie down on stairs again.

Mom often boasted that I never needed a bottle. I went straight from being breast-fed to drinking from a cup. Before bedtime and going upstairs, Eva got a glass of chocolate milk, and Mom gave me plain milk. However, I saw mom mixing the chocolate into Eva's cup.

"Mama, brown milk too!" I pointed to Eva's cup.

"You're too young for chocolate, but just a minute I'll fix something special for you. She dissolved a bit of brown sugar with warm water, and then filled it with milk. The colours didn't match, but I was satisfied with the extra attention and my own special tint.

Besides the big move upstairs, that year held something very special and quite intriguing.

One day while we were out in the garden close to the vines that had nice big pumpkins growing on them, Aunt Mary said, "I'll make you a Jack-o-lantern out of one of these."

"What is a Jack-o-lantern?" I asked.

"I'll make a face on the pumpkin. I'll make eyes and a mouth and it will shine in the dark," she said.

I imagined what it would be like, and pictured it at the bottom of the stairs, where it was dark and a bit scary. The idea of shining eyes and mouth in a dark place frightened and excited me at the same time.

"Good morning, girls! It's time to get up," Aunt Mary called us from the bedroom door on the morning of the twenty-fifth of September. "Let's get dressed quick, because there's a surprise waiting for you downstairs."

*The Jack-o-lantern, of course!* Excitement filled me at the thought of seeing this thing Aunt Mary had told us about. We hurried to get down the stairs. *Be careful so you don't fall, though,* I told myself. *The Jack-o-lantern must be somewhere else, for it isn't at the bottom of the stairs. Maybe it's in the cellar!* That, too, was a scary place for me.

When we got to the kitchen, Aunt Tilly Dunkeld, the neighbourhood midwife, stood beaming! Aunt Mary, instead of mother was busy at the kitchen cupboard. She, too, was smiling with excitement.

"Come see your surprise," she said, leading the way to the bedroom. *The Jack-o-lantern must be in Mom and Dad's walk-in closet. It's dark in there!*

*No, that's not it either! Mom's still in bed!* I spied the cradle in which I had slept at one time. In the cradle was a tiny baby.

"Come see your new brother." Mom grinned.

It was a little disappointing when I had been expecting this mysterious thing called a jack-o-lantern with eyes and mouth that shone in the dark! My disappointment soon disappeared when I had a chance to look closer at my little brother. When Mom let me hold him in my arms, I was absolutely overcome with love for him.

When Enos—named after my great-grandfather—was just a wee bit older, mother often set a stool in front of our small child's rocker, which had been hers as a little girl. I sat in it with my feet up on the stool of just about the same height and then Mom placed Enos in my arms. What delightful and motherly feelings arose in my little breast! He was the apple of my eye.

Hearing Mom refer to him, in our German dialect, as *Suis Hertz* (Sweet Heart), I too wanted to call him by a pet name. I had misunderstood though, and so my pet name for him became 'Suis Cashe' (which means Sweet Cherry) or sometimes, 'Oh du kleine Hammely' (O my little calf) —instead of 'Lammely' or 'Lamb' as mother called him. No matter the name, he couldn't have been sweeter to me. I just loved holding him and singing to him and telling him all the sweet things I could think of. I felt like a big girl, being able to help take care of him. If he went to sleep I sang, "Er schlafed now!" ("He's sleeping now") so I wouldn't wake him with my sudden talking. Mother came, lifted him from my arms and laid him in the crib, and I went back to my play with a warm, satisfied heart.

With Enos' arrival, as much as I loved him, I felt a little rejected. I had been named after my father's much-loved cousin, thus I enjoyed a special spot in my Dad's heart. Now I probably didn't lose that spot, but a son was special too, and as he grew older, it was Enos who got to sit on Dad's lap. After meals, he hung onto Dad's suspenders as he swung from side to side. It looked like great fun.

"Dad," I asked, pulling at his shirt sleeve, "Can I have a turn?"

Dad abruptly rose, setting Enos on the floor. "It's time for me to get back to the barn."

Such rejection, as I experienced it, came other times too. Often he took Enos along when he went to town, or even let him ride along on the farm implements. I longed to do these things with my papa too, but feared asking lest I suffer that let-down feeling again.

When we were older, Dad decided he would show Enos how to turn wood on the lathe. That was a creative thing that I would have dearly loved to do. When I asked if I could learn too, he told me, "This is men's work. You go into the house and help Mom."

As an adult, I'm quite sure he was trying to reinforce Enos' self-image, since he was the only son stuck in the middle of a family of five girls. However, at that age, I felt rejected and I thought life was unfair.

From that time on, I struggled to find a special relationship and approval from Dad and set out to prove that a girl could do anything a boy could do. It seemed that Enos was allowed to accompany him and do things that he had less interest in than I did. But I was different—I had a handicap—I was a girl! Why couldn't I have been born a boy so I could work in the shop and fields and barns and with the animals? And why, if I was a girl, did I enjoy that kind of work more than housework? What was the matter with me?

I had other questions about myself. In the middle drawer of the big glass cupboard, where the good silverware lay wrapped in flannelette holders, tucked right at the front, lay a picture that was taken at a sewing circle. The women stood behind in several rows, and we children sat on the grass in front of them. In those days, we did not have a camera at our house. Dad was at a stage that he didn't really approve of taking many pictures. It was the only picture of me that we had, as far as I knew. Occasionally I shoved a chair over to the cupboard, climbed up on it, and opened the drawer just enough to get the picture. I looked and looked at it, wondering, *How I can I be both in the picture and standing on the chair. Could there be two of me?* It really was quite a mystery! The whole experience made me wonder who I really was—rather like taking a look at me through someone else's eyes. I wondered if that other *me* could do the things that she wanted to do, even if she was a girl.

## CHAPTER 2

# The Fun and Foibles of Growing Up

> "Be glad of life
> because it gives you the chance
> to love and to work and to play
> and to look up at the stars."
> —Henry Van Dyke

When my mom spent time with us, I felt truly accepted and the closest I ever did to being really treasured. Always busy with housework, Mom didn't have much time to be at ease, so the times she played with us were precious indeed—because they didn't come often.

One of my warmest memories is when she pretended she was baking bread, but at these times, Eva and I were the bread dough. We knew the process from watching Mom bake bread. She 'kneaded' our bodies all over, which tickled and made us giggle. She then curled her daughters together in an imaginary bowl and covered us with a cloth, so we could 'rise.' Mom returned to her work, and we kept still under the cloth knowing she would faithfully check to see if we were rising. Finally, it was time to punch the bread down, and knead it again. Her knuckles on my stomach and legs and arms and even my face, felt full of love. Again she covered us with the cloth for the next rising.

When we had sufficiently risen, she pretended to shape the 'bread' into loaves, talking about the process all the while. Again she covered us with the cloth, but this time we were side by side, in individual loaf pans.

Finally, she put us in the 'oven' which was always in the little corner between the cupboard and the cellar door. We quietly waited as we baked, for her to say, "I think the bread must soon be done! It's starting to smell delicious!" After a while she came to look. Sometimes she pronounced us not quite brown enough. We would lie still again. When we were 'done,' she dragged us by our feet out of the oven and lined her loaves up in another part of the kitchen to cool.

I loved the times when she exclaimed, "Oh, oh! I smell the bread. I think it's getting too brown, I have to hurry!"

That, of course, signaled a rapid exit from the oven. The last and best part came when she smelled us and declared us mouth-watering good. She pretended to take a bite of our neck. Of course that, too, tickled, but it was a wonderful feeling of love and fun and togetherness.

## CLASSROOM BEFORE SCHOOL LEARNING

> "The whole of life, from the moment you are born to the moment you die, is a process of learning."
> —Jiddu Krishnamurti

Very early in my life, I became a pupil of my older sister who must have been born to be a teacher. Eva started school in 1942, so I was only three years old. Her favourite after-school activity was to set up a school room, with me and the dolls as her pupils. As she learned more and more at school, she had more material to pass on. Once when Mother overheard Eva giving me an assignment, she told her, "Eva, Ruth is too little for that kind of work. Find something easier for her to do." Eva had a quick solution for that!

"Let's play upstairs," she said.

She knew that Mom wouldn't be there to run interference! I soon learned to try my best to do as she told, for she warned me, "You'll be sorry if you don't!" I had no idea what she had in mind, but I was sure it must be torture of the worst kind!

However, the day she gave me a list of titles from which to choose a topic for my first composition, I floundered. *What is a composition?* I searched my mind to see if I could remember what I missed. Finally I got the courage to tell Miss Nighswander, "I don't know what a composition is."

"A composition is just a story. See what title you want to write about and then write about it," she said. The title that stood out as easiest was 'My Dog.' I longed with all my heart to have a dog, but I didn't. *How can I write about my dog if I don't have one?* But that seemed the simplest topic. Now remember, I was still not in school. In spite of the fact I had worked my way through the second grade speller, my vocabulary wasn't big enough to write what I thought I would like to. I thought and thought, while occasionally *Miss Nighswander,* as Eva had told me to call her, would ask why I hadn't begun. I really felt quite inadequate. Finally as the teacher's remonstrance grew more severe, I began to cry. I thought perhaps I was getting close to 'being sorry' and I was frightened at the thought. Miss Nighswander chided me for crying, "Ruth, when you're at school, you are a big girl and big girls don't cry in school."

After a while, Mom's voice came from the lower hall. "What is the matter up there?"

"Eva says I have to write a composition about 'My Dog' and I don't know how!" I sobbed.

"Oh, Eva, maybe you could find something easier for Ruth to do. She can't write well enough for compositions yet!"

"All right," Eva said, but when the door was safely shut and Mom was back to work, she said, "All right now, we'll choose another topic, but you write that story, and don't you dare let Mom hear you crying or you'll be sorry!"

Well, what alternative did I have, faced with that threat? I wrote a story! Probably not very long, and probably not so good, but I learned that if you go ahead and try, you can do more than you thought possible! That was a good lesson to learn and I still profit from that awareness.

One of our favourite pastimes was singing. Eva couldn't read music yet, but she knew quite a few songs. We often sat up on the living room windowsill that had a hot water radiator right in front of it. There we could look out at the traffic along the road, or the lane, watch the birds fly past or sit on the clothesline between the posts of the verandah. One day as we sat there singing, Aunt Mary and Mom came from the kitchen where they were washing dishes.

"What were you doing, Ruth?" they asked in surprise. *What did I do wrong,* I wondered.

"Just singing," I told them.

"But you were singing alto," Aunt Mary said.

I didn't know what alto was, and if it was a good or bad thing to do, but I soon gathered that Aunt Mary, especially, was extremely pleased. She proceeded to teach us "Once in Royal David's City," since it was coming close to Christmas. I soon wished she hadn't heard me harmonize, because that was a rather difficult song to master.

By Christmas, however, we were able to sing it quite well without coaching. Eva and I sang it for Grandma, Grandad, Uncle Joe and our parents. When we had the larger family gathering with Uncle Peter, Aunt Amelia, Harvey and Edith and Aunt Bertha, Mabel and Louie, Aunt Mary asked us to sing. That was just too much! With a lot of coaxing, we did sing it from our hallway with Grandma's living room between us and the crowd of people. Everyone marvelled at me singing harmony and, again, I felt odd. I couldn't figure out what the big deal was anyway! After all I was just singing with Eva. Even though it pleased Aunt Mary, my being different had put added pressure on me.

It was around the same time that I learned something more about music. When we visited at Norman Lehman's, we saw his phonograph player. It was an RCA Victor with the image of a little dog listening to a big horn on the front of the player. After supper, Norman wondered if we would like to hear a little music. He lifted the lid, placed the record in it, wound it up, then he shut the lid. Behold, a man began to sing! The phonograph was a large floor model, with cloth behind the cut-outs in the front of it where the sound came out, but still, I thought it must be an exceptionally small man with a big voice to fit in that box and yet sing so beautifully! I stared and stared, hoping to catch a movement behind the cloth. When the music was finished, Norman just opened the lid and moved the needle back to its resting place, but left the man in there! I wondered if he would let him out when we went home.

When I was going on to five years old, and tucked into bed one night, I went off to sleep. Suddenly I awoke, and saw a light at the foot end of our bed. I was sure it was an angel. I half sat up, feeling a little scared. The angel didn't speak audibly, but gave me the message, "I just came to bring your little sister." The angel faded away and I lay back on my bed and slept again feeling warm and excited.

Once more, we awoke the next morning to hear Aunt Tilly's voice downstairs. She often came to visit Grandma, but the last time she had been at our house, Enos joined the family. Sure enough, there was another baby in the cradle that morning. And yes, it was a sister. Esther had raised the number of children in our family to four. For a long time I didn't tell Mom about that visitor, or why I wasn't surprised by the arrival of my little sister. It felt like a very nice, but private, happening. However, the reality of it never went away, and when I did tell my mother, she was touched, and didn't doubt, even though she suggested it could have been a dream. I, though, was sure I had been fully awake. Mom never let us children in on the upcoming event, but looking back now, I realize that was the reason Mom had stayed home for several Sundays prior to Esther's arrival. Those were special times too, for Mom would sit down and colour with us.

Growing up is such a nebulous thing—the different stages are not always clear. I faced one of those times the summer Esther was born. I became aware that I was a big sister now and I needed to act like it, but there were some parts of juvenile behaviour that were tough to relinquish. I had a small quilt that became a favourite. I was allowed to take it upstairs with me, when I moved to the bedroom with my sister, and always had it on top of the other quilts on our double bed. Sometimes I carried my quilt with me. I held it in my hand as my tongue made a sucking action and, occasionally, I would move my hand to a colder part of the quilt. For some reason that cold sensation was more satisfying, and made the saliva flow more freely. Through the night when I would wake up and feel thirsty, I would just find a cold spot on my little quilt and get my tongue sucking and sleep would come again.

That summer, Eva Reesor, later Mrs. Paul Burkholder, came to work for mother. Mom had already been trying to persuade me to give up my blanket. Big Eva, the hired girl, added to my guilt about hanging on to my infant habits. She teased me a bit about it, asking me if I was a baby. Now that embarrassed me horribly, for there was nothing I wanted more than to be a big girl—and a good girl. Somehow I felt that it was not good to be so attached to my quilt, yet I couldn't imagine how I could get to sleep without it!

Finally, I came to a compromise. The quilt was quite tattered by then, so it was easy to tear off a corner of it, and stow it away on the slat under my bed. Hugging the quilt close to me one last time, I carried it downstairs and out to the summer kitchen. I crawled under the table and gave it one last-minute caress. I felt all the cold spots and said goodbye in my heart.

When Big Eva came into the kitchen from outside, I emerged from under the table and making sure she saw me, I approached Mom.

"Mama, I'm ready to be a big girl now. You can have my quilt."

"Are you sure you won't want it again?"

I glanced at Big Eva and in my desire to please her, renewed my determination. "No, I'm a big girl now."

Mom gave me a big hug. "Good for you!"

Big Eva grinned as she bent to give me a hug too. "Good for you," she whispered in my ear.

That affirmation made me feel guilty. I knew I wasn't quite as big as I was leading them to believe. That little piece on the slat of my bed weighed quite heavy on my conscience, but it didn't stop me from retrieving it every night after I had knelt in that specific spot to say my evening prayer. Each night I went to sleep holding that little piece which eventually got smaller and smaller. In the morning, I stored it safely again for the day on the slat.

By and by, it was time to go to school. I felt quite safe in leaving my treasure, for I was the only one who knew about it. One day I came home from school to find Mom and Aunt Mary had been busy spring house cleaning. I recognized our quilts airing out on the clothesline. I raced upstairs to find the mattress against the wall and the slats all washed and clean. What a dilemma! I cried, but I didn't dare let them know why I was upset. They thought I had become a big girl a long time ago—two years, in fact. The remaining little tatter was probably not big enough to be recognizable to them. Eventually I settled down, but I couldn't eat much supper thinking of the night approaching and knowing I wouldn't have my little bit of comfort to hold while sleep took over.

The first night was the worst, but for a long time I missed that little bit of security. I searched for a quilt with the same kind of feel to have as the top cover of our bed. When I found it, subconsciously, my tongue would make that sucking action just as I was falling to sleep, and that happened for many years. In fact my sisters teased me that if I got married, my husband would wonder what I was doing when I fell asleep. I became paranoid when I slept over with friends and tried to stay awake until they fell asleep in case I would involuntarily begin that noise, which by that time was so much ingrained that I did it automatically in my first moments of sleep. That little habit was another thing that to this little girl who so wanted to fit in, set me apart and made me feel odd.

## CHAPTER 3

# War Time Looms

> "Here is the world.
> Beautiful and terrible things will happen.
> Don't be afraid."
> —Frederick Buechner

The Second World War began the year I was born. Although my life was quite trouble-free, I was painfully aware there was a war going on. It had a lasting effect on my thought processes throughout my life. It instilled in my mind quite early that life wasn't a thing to take for granted, that even the young could die. There was a lot of hushed talk about the war and the atrocities of battle scenes, the sinking of ships, and of children and parents crying out to God to save them as the ships sank, as happened to one such ship load of children sent to Canada to send them out of harm's way. My child's mind tried to imagine a situation where not even my parents could save me, and thinking of sinking in the water, under the big waves of the ocean, had long-lasting effects on me. I never did like the feeling of being on the water in a boat. Later I learned to swim, and dearly loved being in the water of a creek or lake; but on the water in a boat still is not my favourite place to be, even though one would think that an adult mind could overcome those childish fears.

During the war, Lucille, the daughter of our neighbours, the Howsams, was being courted by Lloyd Weldon. They were a dashingly handsome couple. I wasn't very old, but I was thrilled by their courtship. When Lloyd had to leave for the war, I was extremely afraid for him and would join my grandmother on the front porch when the mail came, to find out from the pages of the Globe and Mail how the war was progressing. She always kept in touch with Mrs. Howsam, and Mrs. McNair whose son was also overseas, to know where their boys were stationed. She would read how the battle was going in those places. Sometimes when I asked if she thought Lloyd and Bud McNair were alright, she would avoid my question. At those times I feared for their safety. When she said she thought they were all right, I would feel better.

Probably the underlying concerns about the war began to spawn nightmares. There were usually animals involved. Bears, lions and tigers stalked me in my dreams. I ran and ran until I couldn't run any more. Often it was Aunt Mary who would come to my rescue in my night-time terror. Usually I would begin to sob, and that would awake me, or else my sobbing would wake Eva. She roused me by asking what was wrong, and sometimes Eva ended up calling mother. Often it was before mom went to bed. Once when she came up in her nightgown, I was startled. I had no idea that adults needed to sleep! I had always been a good sleeper and slept through the night from very early. I was also always put to bed long before my parents retired, and I guess up until that night, if I did wake up, it was before they went to bed. I just assumed that sleeping was something only children did.

One night I dreamt that I went down to the cellar by myself. I was on my way over to the potato bin, when a chicken with bloody feathers and missing its head began to chase me. I thought perhaps I could run upstairs, but each time I got near the steps, the chicken was too close for me to slow down enough to climb the steps. That dream was very scary, and I never did like chickens much after that, nor did I like to go to the cellar alone. I had seen the adults kill the chickens at the top of the barn hill. After their heads were chopped off, the chickens would flip flop down the barn hill and dance around for a while. Afterwards Dad or Grandad would gather them up and take them into the barn to scald and pluck them. It was not a sight that I enjoyed, so that scene worked itself into my nightmares.

In another recurring dream, as I walked down the road from the store, a big black bear came out from the flowering shrubs around the school and began chasing me. Aunt Mary came running with a pitch fork, scaring the bear away, and allowing me time to escape into our house. It left me frightened for both Aunt Mary's safety and my own.

Another dream I remember from that era came after hearing war-time stories, and also having several barn fires in our neighbourhood. I dreamed that we were in the old Eaton store in downtown Toronto. Hitler's soldiers came into the store, gathered up all the men, and marched around on a lower floor, where we could see them. The enemy put something on their heads and set them on fire. I saw Dad, with flames shooting from his head, and I cried from the bottom of my heart.

Not long before, I had heard an adult say something about someone crying as though their heart would break. When I awoke, I was crying with such pain that I thought surely my heart would break. When Mom came, and I finally was able to tell her of my dream, I begged her to hold me tight so my heart wouldn't break. Several times I said, "Harder, please!"

Mom hugged me, "I don't want to break your ribs."

"Just hug hard, Mom, don't worry about my ribs!" I thought I'd rather have a broken rib than a broken heart!

In those years, rationing was in effect. Everyone had their own ration books, and somehow that made me feel a little more grown-up. Each week, Mother took some of the coupons from my book to buy the week's groceries and supplies. It felt as though I was helping to provide for the family. When rationing was lifted, Mom gave us a few of the books with unused coupons in them. For a long time I kept them, but once in my effort to overcome my pack rat tendencies, which Eva in her efficiency certainly was not, I threw them away. Now I rather wish I had kept them.

Anyone who had a sweet tooth or looked forward to Christmas goodies or birthday cakes found it difficult during the war to find substitutes for that sweet substance. My father grew sorghum and took the corn-like stalks to Ezra Grove, who had made a press to extract the juice which was boiled down to a thick syrup or molasses. Mom didn't appreciate it very much, but I liked it on fresh tea biscuits. An enterprising fellow in Stouffville began to sell Baker's Sweetener by the gallon. I believe that it was liquid saccharin. It, too, had a bit of an after-taste and I doubt it was really healthy, but it did fill the gap in those years when sugar was restricted. Those seeming hardships were little compared to the holocaust that many in Europe faced. We didn't know the half of it until after the war was over, but even during the war we heard enough and, young as I was, I felt grateful to be in Canada instead of in the midst of the war-torn countries.

I was only five and a half when the Second World War ended, but the memories of that day are very clear. Eva and I went to town with Grandad on some errands. He parked behind the drugstore and told us he would be back in few minutes. All of a sudden, the town fire siren sounded, car horns began to honk, and people thrust flags out of upstairs windows. People came running out on the sidewalks and streets, hugging each other and shouting. We wondered what in the world had happened. It was awhile before Grandad, too, came running. "The war is over!" he told us, his voice full of jubilation. I had known nothing but war years, but I, too, was happy.

Lloyd Weldon came back, and he and Lucille got married. We watched as the decorated car came back to their house across the road, and my heart was full of romance. As we got bits of news about their honeymoon and about them setting up house in Stouffville, I was even more thrilled. I thought they must be the nicest looking couple there ever was. Already, I dreamt of having a wedding like theirs.

CHAPTER 4

# *Beginning School*

> "Education is a personalized process,
> a reciprocal dance, and a
> cumulative experience."
> —**Author Unknown**

**M**y Dad wanted to keep his children at home as long as possible. However, the spring after my sixth birthday, I was finally allowed to go to school beginning right after Easter, for what was called Primary Class. Charlotte McNair had just turned six in April, and she, too, was to begin. Steve Wideman was to be the third person in our grade. We were invited to Fred and Evelyn McNair's for supper one evening so that Charlotte Ann and I could get acquainted. My English was not perfected yet, so it added one more hurdle besides shyness for me to overcome.

Alas, just the time I was to begin my educational career, I got a very bad ear infection with a high fever. I still remember the pain. Mother often poured a bit of warm water into my ear for temporary relief. Next, she put a dab of Raleigh's Medicated Ointment on small piece of wool which she inserted into my ear canal. Last but not least, she put a little blue flannelette bonnet on me. She filled the hot water bottle so I could lay on it. The living room couch became my bed for the next while. It seemed like weeks to me, but it was probably no more than one. I know now that mom did not get much sleep during that time. Every night I waited as long as I could, but when the pain got too bad, I called her. At first I called softly, for it hurt my ear to speak too loudly. If she didn't hear, I called louder. What a comfort it was for her to share those lonely pain-filled night hours. Every once in a while she even rocked me. That was very special.

By the time my health had returned, there were only six weeks of school left. There was some discussion about whether to bother sending me, or to wait until fall. However, I was anxious to get started, so I was allowed to go.

Teachers of Altona Public School boarded in the attic of the Crozier house across the road from our place. When I was about to begin school, I had the advantage of knowing the teacher, Gloria Harding, already, for she had been to our place for supper several times—and, of course, she was one of Eva's heroes!

Nevertheless, that first day of school was a big day. Charlotte and Steve had already had time to get used to it. The first day, Miss Harding asked me to come up to her desk. She handed me a box of coloured sticks and took the lid off.

"Count the sticks, putting them in the lid as you count," she instructed me.

"One, two, three," I began, when one of the older children raised their hand to ask a question. This needed Miss Harding's attention. "Just keep counting," she told me.

The problem with the other child took longer than expected. When she returned, I was counting 181, 182, 183, and the lid was almost full.

"Oh dear, you can stop now," Miss Harding's eyes twinkled, "You can count a long way!"

Not all was such smooth sailing though. One day, she gave us each a catalogue and a piece of paper. We were to cut out pictures and paste them on the paper.

"When you're all done, I'll come back and you can tell me the story about your pictures," she told us.

When she questioned me, I explained what I had on the page, a mother and father, a sister and brother and a baby, and a bed with a 'kissie' on it. With that, the whole classroom erupted in laughter. I couldn't for the life of me figure out what was so funny about a pillow on a bed! The problem was that I didn't know that *kissie* was the German word for pillow, but the other children thought it was a pet name for my pillow, probably thinking I kissed my pillow! How embarrassing—not only for me, but also for my poor older sister! Another difference had reared its head.

On the whole, I thoroughly enjoyed school. Miss Harding soon decided that Grade One would bore me since I had already read the whole First Grade reader, as well as the Second Grade reader, memorized quite a few poems and had done Grade Two spelling and much of the math. Miss Harding left the school, after those brief weeks, to get married. In the fall I went directly to Grade Two.

A NEW TEACHER

The fall after Miss Harding left, we had a new teacher. Miss Luella Harper was the niece of one of Dad's teachers. Dad assured us if she was anything like her aunt, she would be a good teacher and demand our attention.

"Miss Irene Harper had sharp black eyes that could look right through you," he said. "Sometimes when she was writing on the blackboard and someone misbehaved, she seemed to know who had done it. We sometimes wondered if she had eyes in the back of her head!"

I had thoroughly enjoyed my brief experience at school and was longing to get back. However, the thought of a teacher who could look right through you, and may even have eyes in the back of her head, was rather daunting. On the first day of school, I made sure I had clean underwear and that everything was tucked in right underneath my dress, for if she could look right through me, she would surely be able to see if my under things were not neat,

When she met us at the door after the bell rang, I saw that sure enough, she did have sharp black eyes. She must be like her aunt! When she turned to write her name on the board, I looked carefully to see if she had eyes peeping out from underneath a generous head of dark hair. For months, I watched carefully every time the back of her head was turned my way, determined I would get a glimpse of those eyes.

Our Miss Harper was not the disciplinarian that Dad's Miss Harper had been. She had a delightful smile and a cheery laugh, and she loved us. Sometimes the older boys took advantage of her and raised her ire. She was not able to hide her anger, for a bright red blush would begin on her neck and rise up until her face would be quite flushed. Those black eyes would sparkle with anger and frustration, but it seemed only to goad those boys on. They enjoyed watching her blush.

I felt sorry for her. I loved her and didn't want to see her angry or frustrated. When I saw the boys begin to annoy her, I hoped she would be able to keep her cool and fool the boys by not blushing.

## A RASH OF BARN FIRES

One night in that following year, we were awakened in the night to watch the happenings across the road. The Howsam mill down beside McNair's pond was burning! It was a horrible sight, and knowing that Dad and Grandad and Uncle Joe were down there helping to fight the fire, to keep it from spreading to the house, filled me with fear. A few times, one of the men would come back for something and give us a report on how things were progressing. Faces were blackened and the smell of smoke was very strong. To this day, I wonder why they woke us to watch. We would probably have slept through the whole thing.

That was just the beginning of a long string of fires. One by one, many barns in the area burned. It became an all too usual occurrence to come down for breakfast in the morning to see the men just come home from fighting a barn fire. The strong, acrid smell of smoke and sweat is still as vivid a memory as the fear it invoked. After that Dad and Grandad became nervous, watching and listening for any unusual sights or sounds. Finally, a man from Uxbridge Township was arrested for setting fires. He had left one too many clues.

Soon after all those barn fires, we heard a car coming in the lane one night, horn blowing all the way, and someone shouting "Fire, fire!" Fletcher Goudie was building a big trailer for a truck right beside their house, just south of the little Mennonite church at the corner. Someone set it on fire and their telephone line had been cut. Eleanor and Helen, the Goudie daughters, jumped in the car and drove down to our place, shouting all the way. They wanted our tractor to pull the burning trailer away from the house. Dad rushed out of the house, got the tractor, and raced up to the scene. I, of course, was afraid that Dad would get in trouble while trying to help, but it was accomplished and the trailer finished burning at a safe distance.

With all these fires going on, I started to be afraid of what might happen if our house burned. I dwelt on all the implications, and realized how much would be gone if that were to happen. I wondered how much time one would have to get things out. Finally I came to the conclusion that it would be a good idea to have the basic necessities ready to grab in a hurry. I stacked a full change of clothes, my Bible, my doll, and a few other treasures in one corner of my drawer, so that in the event of a fire, I could grab those. I figured if I couldn't get down the stairs, and out the door at the bottom of the stairs, I could open the window and get out on the porch roof. From there, I hoped someone could reach me with a ladder.

One day at school, as I thought about the fires that were happening in the community, the horrible thought crossed my mind, *What if a fire at our house happened while I was at school*? I couldn't get the thought out of my mind, and my fear became so great that I began to cry. The teacher asked why I was crying. I couldn't tell her I was afraid our house would burn and no one would know to get my stack of treasures and necessities—so I said my stomach ached. This wasn't altogether untrue, for I had a knot in my stomach so big, it really didn't feel good at all.

Miss Harper concluded perhaps I had better walk home, since it wasn't very far away. I raced toward our house. All checked out ok at home. *Whew! What a relief!* I was ready to return to school. However, Mom thought it better to stay at home if my stomach was bad enough to leave school. That set up a difficult dilemma. I hated to miss school, but when the fear got strong enough, I couldn't stand it any longer. So for a while, I was sent home fairly frequently with a 'stomach ache.'

After two years, Miss Harper left to be married to the handsome but shy Harold Lewis. When their first born daughter, Patsy, came along, mother let me go over to their place to take a gift for her. She too, by the way, had dark eyes and a head full of black curls.

The year I was in Grade Three, Miriam Heise took Miss Harper's place. She was the daughter of Orla Heise, a member of the Brethren in Christ Church at Gormley. Miriam wore a prayer covering as did the women in our church, and to me it was a great joy to have her as teacher, for sometimes we got teased for being Mennonite, and I figured it would put the brakes on that kind of joshing. I just adored that smile of hers and the fun way she had. She taught us a lot of music, and drilled us on our scales, so that we could reach any note easily from any other note on the scale. That ability made sight reading easy and would serve me well for the rest of my life. The Christmas concerts she put on were quite elaborate productions for our time. Mothers were asked to make costumes and some of our class time was spent making back-drops. Music and drama were carefully orchestrated.

Each year, the first day of school in September lasted only for a few hours. We were given a list of books and supplies that were needed for the coming year, and sent home. It was up to our parents to take us to town, to the local drug store where all these supplies were available. This included text books, work books, scribblers or binders, pens, pencils, ink, erasers, pencil boxes, crayons or watercolours, pencil crayons, rulers and art books. No such supplies were provided by the school board. In fact the board supplied little else than the building and basic furniture.

Our 'library' consisted of five shelves that were perhaps six or eight feet wide. The top shelf was filled with a set of the Book of Knowledge Encyclopedia; another shelf was mostly filled with Audubon Books that had full page illustrations of birds and plants. The bottom shelf held books with old, old bindings. Some of the old classics with small print and rather difficult reading had probably been there since my grandfather's day. The music books took up the remaining footage at the bottom. The remainder of the space contained a variety of reading geared to different grade levels and some resource books. The only new books that were ever added during my time there were a new atlas and two different sets of music books. Although we did keep the old ones, they were quite ragged and fragile. I read most of the books in that library at least once and many of them numerous times, but it was no wonder that any avid readers had to rely on outside resources to satisfy their desire for literature.

Charlotte and I were avid readers, and shared any books that came into our possession. Thanks to Charlotte and her dad, I had access to the Stouffville Library. She would take out six to ten books and give half to me. We would exchange them as we read them, and have them all ready to return in two weeks' time. In our Grade Five year, toward the end of October, our teacher suggested that we try to read twenty books by the end of the year. Charlotte and I had already surpassed that number since the beginning of school, and had reached forty-eight by Christmas.

Her Dad, Fred, whose brother had been a class-mate of my dad's, was a kindly soul with a real love for children. The McNairs went to the Missionary Church around the corner where I loved to go too, whenever I could. He opened many doors for me, taking me along with Charlotte to concerts, music programs and other places my parents would not have gone. Perhaps the most memorable moment he gave me was to take me along to see Princess Elizabeth and Prince Phillip when they came to Toronto. I shall forever be grateful for his kindness.

Since Steve, the other student in our grade, transferred to the Stouffville School after primary class, Charlotte was my only classmate until Grade Four when Norma Jean White moved into the area and also became a very good friend to me. One of those years Walter Barkey, who had skipped a grade, also joined our class. Norma Jean was delayed after the Grade Five year, but she remained one of my closest pals.

CHAPTER 5

# Skipping Through the Seasons

> "When the seasons shift, even the subtle beginning,
> the scent of a promised change, I feel something stir
> inside me. Hopefulness? Gratitude? Openness?
> Whatever it is, it's welcome."
>
> —Kristin Armstrong

Each season of the year brought its own activities, its own work and play, its own excitement. As a child, one season stretches out for a long time. When one season begins to show signs of letting go for the incoming one, there was always within me, a sense of anticipation.

## SPRING DAYS

Awake, thou wintry earth
Fling off thy sadness!
Fair vernal flowers, laugh forth
Your ancient gladness!
—Thomas Blackburn, "An Easter Hymn"

With the first spring-like weather one year, Eva and Shirley Bielby, with me in tow, decided to explore the spring run-off. Wearing rubber boots, to handle the melting snow, we walked in the low spot in the field west of the barn where the spring run-off created a temporary waterway. We took branches along to feel the bottom of the creek the melting snow created and walked the half mile or so down to the culvert that took the water under the back lane and on to the creek that fed Uncle Peter's pond. Occasionally, when the water was quite deep, even though the jeopardy added excitement, a little water would get in our boots as well. I remember once when the mud was soft enough to hold my boot firmly in its suction, I couldn't step ahead. Shirley and Eva came and held my arms as I stepped out of my boot, then they pulled it out, so I could get it back on my foot. Knowing the dangers of run-off and the coldness of the water, I wonder if Mom and Dad knew what we were doing. Although we had a lot of fun, if we had encountered a deep washout, we could have been in trouble.

Shirley Bielby lived in the house on 'the other farm,' kitty-corner to ours. Grandad had purchased it for Uncle Joe to farm someday. Shirley's father, Frank, was a jolly man who worked for Grandad. When the weather was good, Shirley often returned from school by taking the short-cut down our back lane and through the woods on the corner of their farm. She, however, didn't like going through the bush by herself, so Eva and I would walk with her to the other side, and then come home.

For Eva and I, that was a much longer walk than Shirley would have had going around by the roads. Eva and I did not complain, even though Mom occasionally was a little resentful of the time it took, for those walks were leisurely adventures into nature. There were delightful fencerows where we saw birds and little animals as we walked, and in the early spring we spent many hours looking for and picking wildflowers on the way. We knew just which areas of the fencerows and bush to find each flower in the progression of the season. The spring beauties were the first to arrive, followed closely by dog-tooth violets, yellow violets, trilliums (first red, then white), and what we called ladies slippers but were really dutchman's breeches and, of course, the blue violets. The latter we could sell at market.

We knew where the earliest ones flowered, and there were four or five patches that followed each other's season. We, therefore, had probably about six weeks of picking on Thursday and Friday nights. Each bunch consisted of enough flowers to make an inch-radius of stems, then we added leaves to surround the bunch. These we fastened with elastics, and submerged the stems in water while we picked more. Friday night, after supper, we would take them down to Sam Fretz who went to the St. Lawrence Market in Toronto each week. I believe we were paid 10 cents a bunch for them, which seemed like good money.

Besides the flowers, we also found wild strawberries that were sweet nectar in our mouths in comparison to the chokecherries that puckered our mouths. There were a few wild apple trees that yielded tart bites of refreshment as well. In the fall, the beechnuts provided a tasty treat.

We always looked forward to being able to discard our stockings for the summer. Others wore socks, but for some reason those were too worldly for us, so we would just put our bare feet into our shoes. However, there was one big problem! No matter how warm May weather was, we weren't allowed to take our stockings off until Dad saw that the killdeers had returned from the south. We sometimes unhooked our garters when we got to school and rolled our stockings down to our ankles. I thought they at least looked a bit like socks. Of course, we had to roll them up again to go home for lunch so Dad wouldn't know we'd had bare legs before the killdeer returned.

## SUMMER DAYS

"Then followed that beautiful season … Summer…
Filled was the air with a dreamy and magical light; and the landscape
Lay as if new created in all the freshness of childhood."
—Henry Wadsworth Longfellow

Summers in my childhood stretched infinitely longer than the years seem to be now. There were mornings of sleeping in and late breakfasts. When we appeared from our bedrooms, mom would brown a bit of butter in an enamel cup over the wood stove— or later, the gas stove— then she would cut a piece of bread in long strips. We would dip the end in the browned butter before eating it. It was a treat to eat alone without the usual bustle of a big family. Another hurry-up breakfast was a few crackers with hot water poured on, a dab of butter melted by the hot cracker, then topped with a bit of milk. Although it doesn't sound too appetizing now, I used to like it. If Mom had more time, she might make a poached egg that we could 'mash' and add some bread crumbs.

By the time of our late breakfast, Mom had probably been out to the garden to pick vegetables, or had the wash already done. I can still almost smell her warm scent on a hot summer day. What a wonderful secure feeling it gives me.

Many activities filled those leisurely days. Through the muggier days of summer, we sought relief in the cool canopy of leaves in the wooded acres at the corner of the farm. We explored just about every corner of that sanctuary. After we read the *Anne of Green Gables* books, we named all the special places—Violet Vale, and Lady Slipper Glen, Beechwood Bounty, for instance. One spot that was more utility than fancy was May Apple Dale. The broad leaves of that plant made an acceptable substitution for the Eaton's catalogue when nature called!

Eva, ever the teacher, often turned these forays into a learning experience, teaching us the name of plants, trees and birds. A few times, she made a mistake in her identification. For years, I avoided touching bindweed because she had pointed that out as poison ivy. But most of the time, she was right. I often marvel at the ingenuity and motivation she had to find out information and then to pass it on to us.

One summer we went on several extended Nature Trips which she carefully plotted and planned. She put considerable research into these. On our shorter expeditions, our first stop would be a shallow part of a creek or stream where we could put our drink to stay cool and stow our lunch. She gave a short lecture about what we were to learn from this outing, what to be careful of, and how to gather specimens.

One longer jaunt took us down through Uncle Peter's bush, alongside the pond that was fed by Duffin's Creek, then through the cedar swamp along that same creek that crossed first the Altona road, then the Ninth Line, before going through Spang's bush. Along the way, she pointed out the different kinds of soil, and the lay of the land, where the different trees chose to grow: for instance, the maples, ash, and others in the older areas of the woods, the beech where the cows had pastured more recently, the cedars in the swampier areas. We took along writing pads to make notes of what we observed, and pails to gather samples of leaves, moss, rocks or interesting plants, feathers or whatever we came across. Backpacks would have been a welcome convenience to carry the lunches, drinks we had packed and all our paraphernalia, but they were unheard of at the time. Instead we used baskets or pails.

Another time we went through our bush and Millard Reesor's, right next to ours, then across the road to where Ray Yake, a bachelor lived (where Orville Fretz lived later). I remember being a little afraid that Mr. Yake might not really approve of us being on his property, even though I think we had asked permission. On that trip, we ended up the other side of Davis' bush on the farm behind the Yake property. [I'm not sure how comfortable I would have been to let my children go from nine or ten in the morning until four or five o'clock in the afternoon, and not know for sure how many creeks they were crossing, how many trees they were climbing or how high, much less the possibility of people who might see them or take advantage of them.] But we learned a lot and the days were pleasant. The following days we sorted through our treasures and often wrote reports on our findings. I know my life is the richer for those nature hikes. I still like the woods—the coolness the umbrella of foliage provides, the quiet calm and the earthy smells, the vast variety of plants that grow there. Just walking through the woods lets the calm and quiet seep into my soul and brings me into intimacy with my Maker. That, in turn, helps me to be more truly what I'm meant to be.

A play house amongst the trees was a fantasy of mine that never came to fruition. We did set up sort of a play house in the woodshed upstairs, with makeshift furniture and dishes that served quite well with a liberal dose of imagination. When the weather was warm and the woodshed upstairs too hot, we found a substitute in the triple row spruce hedge that ran along the north side of the house to the back lane. By the time I was 10 years old, the bottom branches of the middle row had begun to die out, so we trimmed those out to form rooms. Along with binder twine strung up for a bit more definition, and chunks of wood for tables and chairs, we lived out our imaginary family life on many lazy afternoons.

Dad built a swing for us, attaching it to a big, sturdy beam that ran through the woodshed at the peak of the roof at second story level. It extended probably twelve feet to the north outside. On this he fixed a long rope which gave us hours of pleasure. We used to swing high enough that the rope would buckle, and then we'd free fall until the rope was once more taut. While swinging there, I often recited "The Swing" by Robert Louis Stevenson.

How do you like to go up in a swing,
Up in the air so blue?
Oh, I do think it the pleasantest thing
Ever a child can do!
Up in the air and over the wall,
Till I can see so wide,
River and trees and cattle and all
Over the countryside—
Till I look down on the garden green,
Down on the roof so brown—
Up in the air I go flying again,
Up in the air and down!

That swing was a place for dreaming, for feeling the air whispering against your face, and the sunshine blessing your head with its warmth. There was freedom and satisfaction in the accomplishment and a sense of physical fitness to be able to pump oneself to that height, finishing with the glory in the ride as it slowed once more.

With a creek and ponds nearby, there was another whole world of fun to be explored. While we were still quite young, Mom let us go swimming in the creek, just above Uncle Peter's pond. At the beginning, we were only allowed to go when Kathleen Thompson was there to watch us. We went with a change of clothing—no bathing suits, just an older dress and pair of panties. There was a big stone up on the bank on our side of the creek. There we changed clothes and left our dry ones, our shoes and towels for later. From there we walked down the bank to the water's edge. There was always a yard or two of rather mucky stuff to wade through, after which came a deeper area where we carried the little ones to get to the nicer beach and sandy creek bottom on the other side. We settled the little ones there with an inner tube and a few water toys. Those who were just learning to swim waded over to a fallen tree that lay at the north edge of the creek just as it turned toward the pond. There we could hang on and learn to splash our feet, and get the feel of floating. When we were brave enough, the older ones took us for a swim, holding their arms under our tummies for assurance. I remember the day I was finally brave enough to try on my own without Kay or Eva's arms underneath. Only then did I learn to go under the water. I never really liked the feel of the water in my ears though. I preferred to keep my head out of the water as far as possible when swimming. I do remember the bravery I felt when I walked on the sandy bottom from one side to the other of the 'deep hole.' It was over my head for probably two feet!

Occasionally we were joined by other children of the neighbourhood as well as Kay, John and Earl Thompson. Norma Jean, Ken and Frank White were often there and sometimes Paul Meyer joined us. I wanted so much for my mother to come and watch me swim on my own. I believe she did come once and stayed just a little bit.

We did have a near mishap once. We had situated Enos on the inner tube at the edge of the creek and went about our own pleasure. All of a sudden I saw Eva rushing through the water, and realized that Enos was nowhere to be seen. The tube was floating alone. She found him, and he came up sputtering and coughing. After a few slaps on the back, he was able to breathe normally once more. We agreed not to tell mom in case we would not be allowed to go swimming any more.

## HOLIDAYS WITH COUSINS

The summer break from school also brought holidays with our cousins. We took turns going one or two nights to Uncle Willis', Uncle Fred's and our place. Often when we were at Uncle Willis' place, we walked or biked down to Uncle Wilbur and Aunt Mary's place for a meal since it was less than a mile away. From Uncle Fred's, we sometimes went to Grandma and Grandpa Reesor's for a meal and an afternoon of play. Sometimes we helped shell peas or snap beans at the different homes. We often went swimming when they all were at our place, and at Uncle Fred Drudge's because there were swimming holes near those places. Most of the time, we just played different games, jumped rope, went on walks, wandered over the farms or on really hot days, sat and played games like I spy.

Come evening, though, without fail, we played Spook. This was a game we concocted. We formed two groups, each containing a span of all the ages. One group was given ten minutes to find a hiding place before the other group went to find them. The rule was that no outside lights be turned on or used. It had to be dark, and only eyes and hands used to find the other hiders. Of course, the spooky part of the game was bumping into live bodies or feeling flesh all of a sudden. Screams emanated from the seekers when the hiders were found. If it was not too late, we switched, and let the other group hide. Some were easier and more fun to scare than others. Once after our game of spook at our place, Margaret and I thought we should take advantage of Naomi's edginess. We quick washed and went upstairs to hide under the bed where we girls were to sleep. The light was directly over the bed, and one had to stand near the bed to reach the string to pull the chain and turn on the light. We waited in quietness until Naomi, the tallest of the girls, came to put the light on. Spontaneously, we reached out and grabbed her ankles. The resulting scream was all we had anticipated and more!

When bedtime was called, everyone washed hands and arms and feet, then as many as possible fit into a bed, often cross-wise, girls in one room and boys in another. More fun and storytelling was enjoyed before a bit of sleep and another long day. Sometimes, our scary night activities were not for the best. Once at Uncle Fred's, Ethel woke us several times in the night with a nightmare. It took the older girls quite a while to get her fully awake before we could get her settled down again. That's the way it was when we all got together. We helped each other out. The older ones looked after the younger ones.

One night at Uncle Willis' place, one of the first years that John Drudge was old enough to come along, he got his pajama string tied in a knot. The older boys couldn't get it undone, so they called the girls for help. Some were working on the knot, and the rest of us were surrounding John for moral support. Suddenly John looked up with his big eyes and surveyed the circle of people around him. "I must be dearly beloved!" he said. And so he was!

What wonderful memories of extended family. (Even though we were related, I distinctly remember the different smells of the different households. I don't know if the source for that was the laundry soap used or what, but that is a distinct part of those memories.)

One summer, Mother and Dad gave Eva and me permission to ride our bikes down to Uncle Willis and Aunt Annie's, a distance of ten miles almost due south. I had my big CCM man-size bicycle and was still not tall enough to straddle the bar, so with bags of clothes tied to the handle bars, we set off. We had planned for a stop for a drink at Grandma Reesor's. I can tell you exactly where the dogs along the route lived, and which ones made us fear for our safety. There were only two that were nasty and bit at the wheels, but we were able to make it past. Eva was able to peddle fast, and then put her feet up on the handle bars to avoid the dogs nipping at her feet, but I didn't have that alternative. There again, she generously offered to ride closest to the house to take the most of the dog's attention, while I peddled as fast I could to get past them to safety.

That holiday time when we were down at Uncle Wilbur's, I had a mishap. Uncle Wilbur was always a lot of fun. We had decided to throw water at him when he stopped at the pump to get a drink. Of course, he chased us, just as we had hoped. Unfortunately, I tripped and my knee came down hard on a root of the cedar hedge that grew around the perimeter of their lawn. It made quite a hole in my leg. I'm sure that today, it would have required a few stitches. Uncle Wilbur carried me into the house, and Aunt Mary and Ida worked at getting it clean. I remember Ida going to get antiseptic powder to treat it before they bandaged it up. My leg was quite stiff and sore the next morning when we were to leave for home. I wanted Eva to phone Mom and Dad and have them come for us, but she wanted to finish what we had begun, so we started toward home once again. When we neared Grandpa Reesor's, I begged her to call our parents from there, but she was adamant that we go all the way. We did make it home and my knee eventually healed with only the scar to remind me.

When we were a bit older, we were called a little earlier in the morning when the peas were ready for picking. Mom and the hired girl, whoever she was, picked the peas early while the dew was still on them. (Later still, of course, we helped pick too.) As the peas were picked, the younger children carried them in and dumped them into rinse tubs filled with cold well water. When the picking was done, we set chairs around a bushel basket, filled a bowl with peas and, resting our feet on the basket, shelled and shelled and shelled! It was not out of the ordinary to have five or six bushels of peas to do.

While we shelled, we often played, "I spy with my little eye. . ." It was a real triumph if you picked something so obscure that the rest finally had to say, "We give up!" and you would have another turn. Another favourite was "I packed my suitcase for a trip and in it I put. . ." starting with an item that started with *a*. The next person repeated that item and added something that began with *b* and on through the alphabet. It was a nice relaxing chore as long as you didn't think about the hot cook house where those peas needed to be blanched afterward.

When they were all done, we packed the peas in berry boxes lined with waxed paper, covered them and put elastics around them or tied the coverings with string. All the podding seemed to produce only a very small amount of finished product. When all was done, they still needed to be taken out to the cold storage lockers at the Stouffville Creamery. I never liked going in there. Now I know that it was claustrophobia I felt as we opened those big, heavy, insulated doors and shut them behind us to put something in or take something out of the locker. There was a long narrow aisle with floor to ceiling lockers on each side. The cool air was welcome, but I always had to fight panic while I was in there.

## CHAPTER 6

# The Seasons Continue

AUTUMNS
To step out on a fall morning
To smell pungent leaves and the sod.
To crunch through the leaves in autumn
See purple-lined clouds in the sky,
Dew-kissed flowers and webs,
And catch them with camera's eye …
These, just a few that bring delight,
That in this life I'd hate to miss,
In truth, as I pondered it o'er,
Certainly they're what I would call bliss.
—Ruth Smith Meyer

Probably like most children, at least in the country, we had big piles of leaves to rake together in the fall. There were three big maples in our yard, so the pile was quite high. It was great sport to bury someone in the leaves then go in and ask Mom, "Where is Enos (or Esther or Anna Mary)?" She'd come to help us look. She made a great show, looking under the steps or verandah, behind the trees, in the woodshed and on and on, announcing as she went, "He's not behind the tree" or "She's not in this pail." Finally she started walking right through the pile of leaves. "Oh, oh, there's something is this pile of leaves. Why that feels like an arm—I think this is a leg!" Finally she brushed the leaves aside, lifted the buried treasure and exclaimed, "Why here he is!"

Fall was apple-picking time, too. We had many varieties. Some were earlier than others. The Transparents or Harvest Apples always came first. Three large Snow Apple trees closest to the lane were earlier than some of the winter apples, and I loved to stop and pick one off the tree on my way home from school. Their shiny red skins and pinkish flesh were sweet and crisp and juicy. I liked them best a little before they were ripe and still a little tart, even if Mom cautioned me not to eat green apples. The bounty of those trees was followed by St. Lawrence, Tolman Sweets, Bananas, McIntosh, Cortland, Delicious, and last of all, the five varieties of Spy apples.

Mom always enjoyed setting up a display on our front lawn. Bushels of apples, pumpkins, squash, the last of the tomatoes, beets and any other fruit or vegetables formed a cornucopia of bounty from our gardens. The more perishable items had to be taken to the cellar and properly stored, if the weather was too warm, but she left things out for a while just to enjoy the sight and the goodness of our Maker.

Just north of the hedge, caraway grew wild. In the fall, when the seeds were brown, we would harvest the seeds by shaking them into a brown paper bag. When mother had enough for her use, we were allowed to take the rest of those, too, to Sam Fretz so he could take them to market. We were allowed to keep the money from the violets, the asparagus—if we cut it and bunched it up for Mom—and the caraway. Of course, the money went into our savings banks. We would not have thought of spending it. I liked the feeling of saving, making my bank heavier with each deposit.

My first bank was a replica of a till that only held dimes. There was a slot in the bank where you could set the dime, and a lever to press down, which made a satisfying ding as the dime dropped into the till. One Sunday we had company from Pennsylvania. I got out my bank and quietly sat in the living room with the men while Mom was getting the dinner ready. I pressed the lever repeatedly until one of the men took notice and asked how it worked. The gentleman got a dime or two out his pocket to see for himself how it operated. Dad was too busy visiting to notice. The next time we had company, I tried it again. It didn't always work, but quite often I was successful in adding considerably to my saved stash of dimes. Once there were several men who were fascinated by the unique workings of the bank, and I must have netted at least fifty cents before Dad saw what was happening.

"Ruth, you'd better put that away." He didn't approve of handling money on Sundays, and here I was taking advantage of the curiosity and goodness of these men. Dad had promised us that when we had saved twenty dollars, he would open a bank account and add another twenty. Those Sunday afternoons got me much closer to the goal.

When there was nothing to do outside, we could always play in the barn. Fall was a good time to do that, when the hay and straw mows were full. Eva, Shirley and I often played in the hay in the tallest part of the barn. The first beams were up probably 15 feet high, with another beam 15 feet above that. The hay was piled even higher than beyond the beams almost to the roof.

We forked it around to make little rooms up there and played all kinds of imaginary games in those hollows. However, another thrill lured us. We talked about it, first with misgiving, then with possibility, and finally with intention. We forked down what we thought a considerable amount of hay onto the barn floor. We climbed to the first beam, hovered on its edge, stomachs in knots and ears tingling with excitement, until we built up sufficient nerve. Finally we jumped through fifteen feet of space to land on the soft hay we'd thrown from the mow. After the first jump, we could hardly wait to climb the ladder and jump again and again until the thrill was diminished by the familiarity of it all.

By and by, we eyed the second beam. We climbed up to that greater height. Standing on the beam we shivered with a mixture of delight and terror as we gazed far down at the little pile of hay on the distant barn floor.

"I dare you!" said Shirley to Eva.

"Do you think I can't do it?" Eva said. "If I do it, you have to do it too!"

"I dare you!" Shirley said again.

With a prolonged look and a deep breath, Eva made a huge lunge and leaped from the precarious perch, sailing through the air to the relative safety of that pile of hay.

"That was fun!" Eva declared, "Come on, you try it, Shirley."

What was Shirley to do? She moved to the edge, took a deep breath, and she, too, flew through the air to join Eva on the floor of the barn.

"Now it's your turn, Ruth," they called.

I stood petrified at the thought of that long leap into space. I thought of the stories I had heard about pilots parachuting out of planes when they were hit in the war.

"Come on! Jump!" Eva and Shirley said.

I closed my eyes, bent my knees and pushed at the beam with my feet. My heart almost leapt into my throat as I held up my arms in freedom as the air whizzed past me. I opened my eyes to aim for the pile and fell into the soft hay. Wow! That was fun, just as they had said. We did it over and over again.

On one of my trips, just as I took off, Uncle Joe came up the stairway from the lower part of the barn. "Oh girls!" he said in alarm, "You can't jump from that far up with only that little pile of hay. What if you missed?"

"We've been doing it all afternoon," we assured him.

"Let me at least make a bigger pile." He did that for us, but we were a little astounded that Uncle Joe would be such a fuddy-duddy. He was only 11 years older than Eva, so we had expected him to be more understanding of our fun.

I often thought of that scary feeling before my first leap when I faced other fearful situations in life.

## WINTERS

November comes—the world waits in hushed and contemplative silence
like a lady stripped of her clothes, standing in front of her closet mirror,
picturing herself in the gown she will wear for the upcoming gala.
Anticipating her beauty—clad in snow-laden, silvery branches—
pristine whiteness highlighted by blue skies
or the full moon, at night.

—Ruth Smith Meyer

"Girls, wake up and look out your window!" Mom called on a late fall morning. What excitement to wake up to a world made white while we slept.

Snow pants, winter coats and hats, scarves wrapped around our foreheads and necks, galoshes on our feet—it took a long time to get ready to go out, but, oh, what fun to wade through the snow, make snow angels and dig in the drifts.

When we finally tired of the snow games, we'd tramp indoors to have Mom help us get our gear peeled off. As a reward, she always claimed a fresh kiss from our cold cheeks.

One year when snow came early, we begged for small shovels that would be easier for us to manage. Finally, Christmas came and with it our shovels. Alas, the snow had disappeared a few days before December 25. What a let-down! Later in January, we had ample opportunity for using those shovels. The drifts caused by the snow fence on the north side of the garden were perfect places for digging holes or tunnels and for building an igloo.

For a long time, we had only a small sled or wooden skis to slide down the barn hill. We didn't use the skis as intended, but placed them close together and sat on them as you would a toboggan. Another Christmas, we received a real toboggan. After that we went further afield on the slopes south of the house and later on to the hills on the Fretz farm just north of the Ninth Line.

Once we were in school and in the older grades, Norma sometimes came in to our place. I would deposit my books, gather up my skates and hike to her house. There, her mother helped us lace up our skates and made sure the boys cleaned the snow off the ice on the pond. That was John and Frank's job with their large shovels or scrapers. John and Earl, Frank and Ken, Paul Meyer and sometimes other neighbourhood children joined us in skating on the pond.

Norma's mother made sure everything was alright. After warning us to stay away from the dam, she went back to the house to get hot chocolate ready for when we tired of skating or it started to get dark, whichever came first. Into the house we tracked with snow on our boots, but she welcomed us just as heartily as she did in the summer time when we came in wet from swimming to change to our dry clothes in her bedroom. I don't remember her once yelling at us or even chiding us for the mess. She just seemed to be glad to have a small part in our pleasure and happiness. I thought she was such a neat mother—not in the sense of tidy, but loving and accepting and fun. If Jean was fun, so was Jim, Norma's dad. He loved joking and teasing us. It always seemed such a jolly household.

Walking home from school or to my friends' homes through the snow was almost magical under those big maple trees, sometimes covered with snow and flakes falling gently around me. At those times, I often felt as though I was a tiny character in a snow globe. On moonlight nights the enchanted atmosphere was even more unmistakable.

Of course, winter brings Christmas. Especially in a child's eyes, that is a definite highlight of the year. My mother delighted in Christmas. Her excitement started six or seven weeks before Christmas in the making of the Christmas cake.

Mom always let us help as much as we could. She got the big baking board from its nail in the cellar-way and placed it on the table. She helped us cut up dates, raisins, fruit and all sorts of goodies on that big board. She instructed us on measuring the flour and dry ingredients and to mix them together in her big bowl. The next step was to add the fruit and stir until it was well coated.

"Coating the fruit with flour keeps the fruit from sinking to the bottom of the cake when it bakes," she said. "Next we need to line the pans with brown paper. You can grease it when I get it fitted in."

"Now everything is ready so I can pour the batter into the prepared pans."

By that time Mom had the oven in the wood stove heated to just the right temperature. "The cake needs to bake in a slow oven for several hours," she said. "If it's too hot, the cake would burn before it's done in the middle.

The delicious smells permeated the kitchen all the while. When the cakes were finally done and cooled, they were taken out of the pans and wrapped in clean cloths and set in the cellar-way to ripen for the big day.

The weeks following that, we spent many days making other Christmas cookies and candy. Mom always left the shortbreads until the last week. We had a cookie press to form those shortbreads into flower or Christmas tree shapes. After they were baked, she dipped them in melted chocolate. Mm-mm! Those treats were delectable bits that melted in your mouth.

The fall of 1946, it was different. Mom did some baking and preparation early, but as the end of December approached, she seemed to be tired and not interested or as animated as she usually was. I began to get worried. Finally, it was the day before Christmas. Something was definitely wrong. We children were sent over to Grandma's for supper. When I wanted to go back to check on Mom, I wasn't allowed to go. Aunt Mary took us upstairs from Grandma's end of the house. It was hard to go to sleep without Mom's goodnight hug and kiss, but Aunt Mary wouldn't let me call her.

Christmas morning came, and Aunt Mary was the one to wake us.

"Come see what came to you for Christmas."

We quickly got dressed and rushed downstairs. Yes, there were gifts at our plates on the table, but Aunt Mary rushed us past the table and into my parents' bedroom. There in the cradle was a new baby sister. Mom smiled at us from her bed.

"Can you guess what her name is?" Mom asked. "Her name is Anna Mary. Don't you think that is suitable for a Christmas baby? Anna welcomed baby Jesus to the temple and Mary was Jesus' mother. So now we have our own little Anna Mary to remind us of Christmas all year."

Anna Mary—a sweet little baby with dark hair, ready to be loved. She certainly was the most important gift we could have been given that year. I loved rocking her, too, and helping to care for her as I did with all my younger siblings.

In 1947, the summer after Anna Mary was born, I got to care for her quite a bit. My stomachache was no hoax that year, nor caused by anxiety. I had severe pains in my abdomen. Sometimes I settled down in Grandma's hammock, trying to focus on the sounds of summer to drown out the pain I had. Mom sometimes chided me, because I believe she felt I was just trying to get out of the chores she assigned me. Occasionally she said, "If you can't do anything else, I'll put a blanket out on the lawn and you can lay there and watch the baby. Make sure she doesn't crawl off the blanket or put something in her mouth that she shouldn't!"

Mom must have consulted the doctor about it, but I don't recall any special visits with him.

Sometimes when it was very bad, I moved in to Grandma's couch under her clock shelf. She covered me with her blue and gray afghan. I didn't talk, because to do so just increased the pain. I listened to the tick-tock of the mantle clock and Grandma's soft singing and prayed that I would go to sleep so I wouldn't feel the pain. It was one of the longest summers of my life with the recurring pain that troubled me much of the time.

CHAPTER 7

# Grandparents

> "Grandparents are a delightful blend of
> laughter, caring deeds and wonderful stories
> and love."
>
> —**Author Unknown**

## GRANDMA

Grandmas! How special they can be. Throughout my childhood, many, many happy hours were spent listening to Grandma Nighswander read to us. Because of her close proximity at the other end of the house, we could freely visit her often. The "Song of the Lazy Farmer" from the *Farmer's Advocate* was fun when Grandma read it. It was written in rhyme and included a great deal of humour. She often chose books and stories on our level too. A drawer in the desk held toys with we could play with. Many were bought with coupons from Kellogg's Cornflakes. There was a Marble Game and small plastic pan flute, a stringed tiger that would wiggle his tail, sit on his haunches or kneel before you, depending on how you pressed the bottom. Many more items waited to be chosen.

Sometimes Grandma went to the closet off of their living room and got her guitar-zither to play hymns on it. If we looked longingly enough, she would give us the pick, and help us play a song. This is one that I remember:

There was a little pussy,
Her name was "Silver Gray,"
She lived in a meadow,
Not very far away,
She'll always be a pussy,
She'll never be a cat,
For she's a pussy willow,
Now what do you think of that?

The first line of the song started on middle C, and each line, thereafter, moved up a note, so it was a simple song to play. That gave us self-confidence. When we mastered that, she taught us "Jesus, Lover of my Soul." That was also the first song she showed me how to play when I got my first mouth organ, probably at the age of eight or nine.

Grandma told some wonderful stories, too. Her family was a close-knit one. She was the third youngest of a family of ten and the youngest surviving daughter. We heard many stories of her brothers and sisters and could readily see the love between them when Aunts Tilly or Bertha or Uncles Isaac or Eli visited. Unfortunately, there were also stories of death: her mother died when Grandma was a young woman of only twenty. Two years later, her sixteen-year-old sister died. Brothers Henry and Joseph and her sister Mary all died in their thirties, and several nieces and nephews died young of tuberculosis. As she shared about them, though, there were also such good memories that we felt we knew them, too.

One of the most special times with Grandma came when the spearmint in the herb garden was growing nice. Grandma sent us to get a few leaves. She washed the leaves, then put them in boiling water in a small brown one-cup teapot that had an iridescent glow, and let the tea steep a bit. When the tea was just right, she poured the fragrant brew into a few small china cups from her cupboard. Often we took our tea out on the verandah in the shade of the Dutchman's pipe vine to drink together. Now I didn't care all that much for spearmint in the beginning, but out of that little teapot it tasted like some sweet nectar! What a wonderful little Grandma she was. I am so thankful to have that same little teapot in my own cupboard now.

Grandma didn't usually roast her own beef. Mom fixed a big roast for our two families. When it was ready at noon, Grandma came over to our part of the house to get enough meat and gravy for her and Grandpa. I can still see her standing in the kitchen with her little granite gravy pitcher held against her stomach, rubbing it while she waited for the gravy to be thickened and ready. It was perhaps done that way to save heat, especially in the summer when it was better to heat just one house rather than two, or maybe because meat is really better when cooked in a larger roast.

Grandma didn't tolerate heat very well, so another picture I have in my mind is her sitting out on her canvas lawn chair underneath the large spruce tree beside the lane, podding peas, snapping beans or just reading a book—the damp tendrils of her hair blowing in her face that she'd push back occasionally. She never seemed to mind if one of us came to lie on the grass beside her. She would either lay her book down and visit a bit, or read little bits and pieces she thought we may find interesting. She loved to sing, too, and often in the winter in a lull between meals, she sat in her rocking chair beside the stove and sang through the hymnbook. One of her favorites was "Jesus, Thy Boundless Love to Me." She liked when we sang along with those we knew.

Sitting in that rocking chair, she always rubbed her thumb on the arm. Gradually a little dent was formed from all that rubbing. The present owner of that rocking chair has a visible reminder of this little habit of Grandmother's. That trait also inspired me to write the following poem.

## GRANDMA'S PEARLS

She sat rocking,
my "little grandma,"
her thumb rubbing the smooth hollow
it had already worn in the arm of her rocking chair,
telling oft-repeated stories of her childhood—
siblings' work and play,
and the loss of four of ten
at different ages
by dreaded T.B.

wisdom of her parents and grandparents
joys experienced,
hurts encountered
growth and understanding,
each telling another pearl,
the cadence of her voice matches,
the movement of her thumb,
wearing out a little hollow in our world
—smoothing out a place for us,
giving us roots.

Sometimes she'd sit,
a leg curled behind the other
cradling the guitar-zither she bought
when she was seventeen
taking it from the upper closet shelf
plucking and singing,
"There was a little pussy, her name was Silver Gray,"
"Jesus, lover of my soul, let me to thy bosom fly,"
a melodious score
for the lyric of our lives
and giving us wings to fly.

## GRANDPA NIGHSWANDER

My first memories of Grandpa were from the time he was still very much involved in running the farm and occupied with activities in the community. He was an achiever and mover, and did not have much patience for waiting. In fact, his nickname was *Push* and we could well understand the reason for that. We soon learned that when he came in at mealtime, we had better vamoose, because he wanted his meal promptly so he could get back out to work. Grandpa sometimes teased us about missing the best part of the day by sleeping in so long.

As the years passed, Grandpa became more mellow and patient. In 1946, Grandpa, Grandma, her brother Uncle Isaac and Aunt Emma decided to take a trip out west. He left the farm in the care of his sons and a hired man, Stan Elson. I think it was sort of a trial run to see if he could indeed trust them enough to retire. My grandparents were away at least six weeks, and on their return, the decision was made to allow my father to take over. It took some years yet for him to learn to trust someone else's judgment and, at times, there was considerable tension between him and Dad when they disagreed on any procedure or the timing of the seeding, harvest or ploughing.

One time I felt that kind of tension, I was in the middle of it. Eva had been riding Uncle Joe's old bike and I wanted to learn too. This caused some friction, because there were two of us vying for the same bike, and neither of us owned it. Grandad, I'm sure, meant well when he went to town and purchased a new CCM bicycle for me. I should have felt nothing but thanks, but it was a man's bike, and a full grown man at that. It was so heavy I could scarcely lift it up, and I had to ride *under-bar*. I think that Mom and Dad resented that he didn't even ask their permission, and perhaps thought it was showing favouritism. Anyhow, I felt torn between thankfulness and guilt. I wished that Grandpa would have measured me and chosen something a little more my size. By the time I was the right height for it, I was driving the car!

In the years before I can remember, different men from the township had the responsibility to care for certain sections of the road. Grandad was one of those, and he took great pride in grading the roads just right. That carried over in tending our laneway. He could often be seen grading it carefully. My first memories were of him doing it with the horses and later with the tractor. In the spring, when the snow was melting, he would make little tracks with a hoe or shovel so the rain and melting snow would run off into the ditch rather than down the tracks where the tires went. He thought less gravel would be displaced that way.

## GRANDPA AND GRANDMA REESOR

My early memories of my maternal Reesor grandparents were not as plentiful. Occasionally they stopped in for a short visit on their way home from their weekly shopping trip to Stouffville. It took a lot to persuade them to stay for a meal, though. We found the best bet was to have a winter cherry pie on hand.

Grandpa was a quiet man with such a gentle spirit, yet he exuded strength and security. He understood my shyness and often patted my head without looking at me or whispered something without making any fuss. Perhaps my appreciation of him stemmed from my mother's deep love and respect for her Dad.

Grandma had a pleasant personality and a good sense of humour. When we visited at her house, she let us play with her dolls. One had a china head, feet and hands, the other was tin. The dolls looked more like grown ladies than babies. They rested in a little cradle made for my Mom when she was only two years old.

## CHAPTER 8

# *Life in the Community*

"We need to haunt the house of history
and listen anew to the ancestors' wisdom."
—Maya Angelou

Growing up on the same land that three generations of your family has inhabited makes even a small child aware of family history and the values that ruled their lives. Witness of this was the little meeting house that stood on the corner and the school house that claimed part of our farm. We could see that it was of significant value to our ancestors to have a place to gather to worship God and a place to educate their children. We knew our ancestors made some hard choices to follow God, and even when many other tasks or pleasures demanded their attention, they found time to erect these buildings and faithfully use them. We grew up instinctively knowing we needed to sort out the voices and activities that vied for our attention

The farm south of ours was intricately tied to us and was an important part of my roots. Uncle Peter and Amelia Nighswander lived in that place with their two children, Harvey and Edith. Our two families often worked together on bigger jobs such as harvest, haying and butchering. It was a tradition to have an ice cream night at the end of harvest. Earlier on, we made it by hand in an ice cream maker. Uncle Joe and Harvey often took turns to crank the handle until the sweet treat became thick and ready to eat.

Harvey always was special to me. He was full of fun and yet somehow gentle in his teasing. When he became engaged to Elva Martin from Ohio, I was enthralled! My parents were invited to the wedding in Ohio, but I had to make do with pictures and the little swatches of fabric from her wedding dress and going away outfit. In those days, it was the thing to do—hand out to the guests those little 1 ½– inch squares as keepsakes of the wedding along with the napkins embossed with the name of the couple and the date of the wedding.

When Harvey and Elva were married about six months, Elva returned to Ohio with guests from there to visit with her family. A week later, Harvey went to get her. Frank and Ida Barkey went along, and he also invited Norma Jean and me to go with him. What an honour and what an adventure for a pair of ten-year-olds! We were warmly welcomed and had a lot of fun with Elva's two much-younger brothers.

At that time, Smarties were only available in the U.S., so one day when they took us to town, I bought some to take home. We bought them in bulk at a Dollar Store and watched as the clerk weighed out ten cents worth. I was proud to think I'd be taking home a treat for the family. While walking around looking at what else was available, the one corner of the bag slipped out of my hands and all except two or three rolled all across the dirty floor. What disappointment. I was embarrassed that they had to call someone to come clean it all up. That was bad enough, but I had no money left to get more Smarties.

Sadly I ate the last few and tried to swallow the disappointment of not giving my family a surprise. Before we left, Elva's mother let Norma and me choose a piece of fabric to take home. Their feed bags were made of cotton with all kinds of designs so that they could be used for clothing or other purposes. She had quite a stack. I chose a red and white check with tiny blue flowers. That dress brought back warm memories as long as I wore it.

When Norma Jean and I walked home from school, we had a rather lonely stretch on the road for two little girls to walk through. I could have turned in our lane, but I often walked down the hill with her and sometimes almost to the bridge just before Thompson's, to give her company. At the bottom of the hill south of our lane, there was a cedar bush on one side with a brush-filled ditch, and pine tree plantings were on the right side of the road. We had great talks and shared dreams and fantasies, and little girl desires and heartaches. On my return I was alone, so I would run back up the hill and into our lane.

I was glad I wasn't on that stretch yet, when once I was walking home from school alone. About half way between the school and our lane, a car coming from the north slowed down. There were two people in the car. The passenger was very heavily made up and wore a large hat and white gloves. Right away, I wondered if it was a man in woman's clothing. "She" asked if they could give me a ride. I replied, "No thanks, I just live at the next farm." She said they'd be glad to give me a ride in the lane. Again I refused. She offered me candy and still I refused. She opened the door and made a grab for me. With my heart beating rapidly, I ran down through the ditch, up the other side, climbed the fence between the road and garden and ran for the house. The car door banged shut and the gravel flew as they took off at high speed down the road. After that, I hid behind trees when I saw or heard a car approaching in that lonely stretch—especially in the dark.

Jean and Shirley Lewis were good friends of mine too, although they were a bit younger than I was. They came from a large family, and I enjoyed being in the midst of that joyful confusion that was a part of their home. Jean and Shirley alternated in living part-time with their paternal grandparents just to ease the situation for their parents. I found that rather odd, but they seemed to enjoy the special attention they got when living apart from their family. They usually spent some time after school at home, but went back to the grandparents by suppertime. When I went home from school with them for supper, while they lived with their grandfather and grandmother, it was an entirely different feeling, for the attention was focused on us children. When they were home with their parents, Fred and Ruth, you just sort of mixed in with the gang and fended for yourself along with everyone else, yet there was real love and care there too.

The Elson's were another large family. Isola (Mrs. Elson) was a Nighswander, so we always felt vaguely akin, which we were, although not closely related. However, their way of life was quite different from ours. Their oldest son, Mansell, had married and they had a son six months older than Mansell's youngest brother, Earl. Arnold and Lionel had graduated from elementary school by the time I was in Grade One. Stan was in the seventh grade when I started school. Nelda was a class above Eva, and Alan was a year younger than me. Shirley was the same age as my brother Enos, their youngest son, Earl, a year and a half younger. They, too, went home for lunch as we did, but they were usually back to the school by 12:15.

"How do you do it?" we asked. "How do you go home, eat and get back to school so soon?"

"We go in the house, grab our food, chew and swallow it on the way back!"

Isola must have had sandwiches or some simple food ready the minute they came in the door, so they could grab, eat and run. We usually went home to a hot, full-course meal, and often had to wait for Dad to appear and get washed up before we could ask the blessing and eat. If we got back to school by 12:45, we were lucky. Of course, if they were playing move-up baseball, we never made it to batter position— day after day after day. It was a little discouraging, because those who stayed for lunch would race out when dismissed and positions were taken on a first-come basis. I would rather have had sandwiches at lunch!

Madill's General Store, at the main corner in Altona, was a very important part of the community. We were given our allowance of five cents a week. Oh, what a delight it was, to go to the store and stand before the candy counter to choose what to buy with those five cents. It took three cents to buy a piece of sea-foam candy about 5"x3"x1", or you could get three jaw-breakers for one cent, licorice pipes for one cent, or spend the whole five cents on an ice cream cone. Once in a while, I got the little heart candies with a message on them, but I gave most of those away, for to me, they were way too sweet. There were candies the shape of a small banana, which also were quite sweet, but every once in a while, I bought one. There were other kinds of candy too, but I don't recall all of them. I usually stuck with the first four I mentioned. The licorice I really liked, and the jaw-breakers, besides having the outer licorice coating, had a lovely array of colours as the layers were sucked away down to the anise seed in the middle.

Occasionally, I saved my allowance two weeks in a row, so that I could buy my own can of sardines for seven cents. I could still get a little candy with the other three cents. When I got the sardines, I'd eat them on bread with a little mustard at supper while my siblings looked on in envy.

"Can we have a little taste?" my siblings asked.

"Maybe, but if you wanted sardines so bad, you can save your allowance for a week too!" I said.

Once I remember getting five cents worth of brown sugar so that I could make a batch of brown sugar candy. I guess Mom let me use the butter it took to make them. We had to melt the butter and sugar together until the mixture became slightly browned, then drop them in little bits on waxed paper. The sardines were more to my liking than the extreme sweetness of that candy.

Some of the fun of buying candy was to compare it with what other children got. Sometimes we shared, but often we just talked about our choices.

CHAPTER 9

*Sharing the Sickness*

> "Staying in bed while a fever ran its course
> had advantages and disadvantages.
> If you were sick enough, it was a good place to be.
> When you were recovering, the time crawled by,
> incredibly slow. If there were a few siblings sharing
> the time, it gave rise to some ingenious
> ways to break the boredom."
>
> —Ruth Smith Meyer

With school and close contact with other children, we were exposed to any illness that went its rounds. In the days of my childhood, when we had a fever, we went to bed for the duration. Mom kept us there until our temperature stayed normal a full day. Meals were brought to us on a tray and pillows propped behind so we could sit to eat. We weren't even allowed to sit on the edge of the bed. While the fever raged, soups and liquids were the only food permissible, with perhaps a cracker or two. Of course that meant cracker crumbs and it was inevitable that some of those wound up in the sheets. It still disgusts me when I think of the discomfort those crumbs inflicted! Breakfast in bed never felt like a luxury to me.

Lying in bed all day got boring—especially when you no longer felt sick. Mom gave us a bell to ring or a cane we could use to thump the floor if we needed something. Poor woman! Even though we had been told not to call unless necessary, we found all kinds of legitimate reasons to ring or thump, just to relieve the boredom. She got very creative in finding quiet activities to amuse us. Reading could have used up all my time, but when I had a fever, mom was cautious about how much reading I did in case it would unduly strain my eyes. Paper dolls were one activity for such a time and simple jigsaw puzzles another, but the pieces were apt to get lost in the covers. Those days were a lesson in endurance.

The first solid meal always consisted of mashed potatoes and a poached egg. Not that exciting unless you had nothing but fluids for three or four days or more. The wait made the choice taste like a meal for royalty.

To me, the best part of being sick was the evening of the day my temperature stayed normal all day. Just before supper, Dad would come and carry me downstairs. Swathed in blankets, set in the rocking chair close to the table, I got to eat with the rest of the family. What made it really special, though? It was the only time I was touched by my father or held in his arms. I liked the feel of his strength and care.

The childhood communicable diseases in my time didn't have any immunization possibilities, so our family of six ran the gamut. One June, Enos contracted chickenpox. One by one, the rest of the family got them. It took all summer, and being one of the last to get them, I was anxious to get back to school. We weren't allowed to go until the last scab came off. I had one stubborn pox scab on my chest that didn't want to let go, so I secretly picked at it until it came off. I still have the scar to remind me of my impatience!

Another June, Enos again, started off with red measles. Those who hadn't had measles were quarantined twenty-one days after the outbreak. One by one, just as the time of quarantine was coming to an end, another of us would come down with them. A few of us overlapped a bit, but it was a long summer for the ones who were last to get them. When I got them, my fever went up to well over 104 degrees and stayed there several days until the rash finally broke out. The room was kept dark to save my eyes, but it did nothing to stop periods of delirium. I kept feeling that I was sitting on a planet trying to reach out to someone on another planet, but my arms, though they stretched out what seemed to be zillions of miles, could never quite reach. Mom kept washing my face with a cool cloth in attempt to bring the fever down. I think it was as much of a relief to her, as to me, when the rash appeared and the fever began to subside. But I was covered with the rash on all parts of my body—then the itching began! Mom made a paste of baking soda and water to try to relieve it. In September Dad got measles too, and he was really sick as well. In fact he developed viral pneumonia after that and was sickly over a year.

The mumps came next. Mine were so bad, on both sides, that it looked as though I had no neck. Mom tied a wide piece of cloth under my chin to the top of my head to relieve the pain and the sense that I was going to burst. During that time, Uncle Willis Reesor stopped in and Mom brought him up to see me. He laughed, which I could understand, but it did feel rather humiliating.

Just before Christmas, Eva was the last one to get the mumps, but she started with whooping cough at the same time. Thankfully her mumps weren't quite as bad, but still quite painful when she had to cough. This time, several of us had whooping cough at once. Of course that, by the very nature of the illness, lasted much longer, giving time for the next victims to catch it before the first were over it. What a desperate feeling—that whoop, when the cough got bad. It made me feel as though I was going to suffocate. Mom used all the home-remedies including mustard plasters and then also kept a mixture of honey, lemon and ginger beside each 'whooper' for the times when the coughing was severe.

It was a year we wouldn't soon forget. Although the teacher regularly sent work home for us, missing so much class time, we did get behind. I especially liked the notes Charlotte Ann sent along with the school work. They were an absolute delight to me and I kept them for many years. During that time our class began to learn more complex fractions. Because no one fully explained it to me, I began to struggle with Math like I hadn't done previous to that. Math was probably never my strongest subject, but I don't recall having any real problems before that time. I think it created a mental block that still makes me feel I don't do well with numbers.

That time was so hard on Mom. After the measles and mumps, Dad was left with viral pneumonia which lasted months. With Dad sick, he worried over the smallest details and was always sending Mom out to the barn, night and day, to check on something that entered his mind. Of course he slept a lot during the day and so probably didn't sleep so well at night. Awake in the dark of night, he began to worry that the water wasn't shut off somewhere, or that there may be a fire or the gas pump hadn't been locked. Mom not only had to keep doing the house work, but had to oversee the farm work as well and make those middle of the night trips to the barn to assure Dad. We had a hired man for part of that time, and the church men came to do the seeding, help with the harvest, and cut firewood and such things, but Mom had quite a lot of responsibility on her shoulders.

CHAPTER 10

# Another Sibling and Reaching Out

> "No matter where you go in life
> or how old you get;
> there's always something new to learn about.
> After all, life is full of surprises."
>
> —**Wazim Shaw**

In 1950, unbeknownst to me, my mother was pregnant again. On Labour Day that year, Eva woke me up in the morning to tell me Mom had gone to the hospital.

"What?" I asked in unbelief. "What's the matter with her?"

"There's nothing the matter with her, she just went to have the baby." She sounded a little disgusted that I'd have to ask.

I had no idea that Mom was about to give birth. Why, I can't understand, because I knew when Aunt Elsie was expecting my cousin David in June of 1949, and when Elva was expecting Rosalie later that year, but I suppose Mom just gradually got bigger, and I hadn't suspected anything, and she didn't even hint about the fact to me. In fact just a month or so prior to that morning, my older cousin had snidely reported that my mother was going have *another* baby. I hadn't believed her, because I thought mom would have told me before she told other people. It was Eva's first year out of public school and she would be expected to help. That's probably why my sister got the inside news. Why didn't she tell me? When I got over my initial surprise, another burning question arose. "Why would she go to the hospital to have a baby? She always had them at home."

"She thought with five children, she needed a quieter place to have the baby, and she's going to stay ten days so she can have a rest," my older sister told me. I was shocked, but soon looked forward to another baby in the family.

It was later that afternoon when the telephone rang and we got the news that we had another sister. The next ten days seemed to take forever! I was anxious to meet my new sister. Finally the day came and I was aching to hold her, but Mother made us wait and take turns when the baby woke up. She was determined that we wouldn't spoil her because there were so many of us to take care of her needs.

Mom had been hoping to name the baby David Benjamin, but since it was a girl, she said her name would be Martha, named after her dear Aunt Mattie. She and Dad let us children choose a second name, but informed us that it needed to be a name from the Bible. We hunted and hunted and finally decided Lois was the most modern name we could find and it went well with Martha.

Just as with my other younger siblings, I loved singing Martha Lois to sleep. I was overjoyed to hold her when it was my turn. I read books to her as soon as she was old enough and tried to help her with saying words. I loved her dearly. When she was perhaps five years old, I did the washing in the old woodshed, with Martha playing around beside me. I taught her the Bible verse, "Thine ear/ shall hear /a word behind thee/ saying,/ 'This is the way,/ walk ye in it.'" We'd chime it out together, phrase by phrase, until it was thoroughly imbedded in our minds.

When we went to the end of the lane to get the mail, I'd hold both her hands in mine and swing her ahead as far as I could. Of course once I had done it, she wanted it repeated over and over again.

As the family grew, I sometimes felt lost in the demands for Mom's attention. I liked writing the thoughts that I needed to share. When I noticed a pen-pal column in the *Farmer's Advocate*, I began to look for a girl whose birthday was the same as mine. I never did find one the same day, but I found two whose birth years were the same and only days apart from my birthday. Ruth Ruggles was from Bear Creek, Nova Scotia, and Jean McKinnon from Bergland in northwestern Ontario.

*Words of Cheer,* a children's magazine from Herald Press also carried a pen-pal column. There I found Wilma Martin from Ohio and Anna Good from Pennsylvania. Those four girls began a love of writing letters which grew over the years until I had thirty-five pen pals. Each of those got at least one letter per month. That meant writing a letter every day and sometimes more. We shared a lot of our growing up in those letters. Putting it down on paper was a valuable experience and one reason why I find journalling so helpful and writing such a joy.

It was soon after Martha was born that we got a new hired man. Alydus Sieben, who had just emigrated from Holland, came to work at our place. The handsome, gentle giant with a delightful accent soon endeared himself to us. He told us of his family and we got to feel as though they were an extension of our own. Sometime after he arrived, his girlfriend, Christine, also came to Canada. She worked first at Harvey and Elva Nighswander's home, then moved to another family's place outside of Whitevale, eight miles south of Altona.

Eva and I had a great time with Christine when Alydus took his turn to do the milking every other week. While she was learning to be more proficient in English, we often helped her find the right words. We developed quite a friendship and learned a lot about a different culture. When they got married, they moved to Dixie, close to where the Toronto Airport now is located. Martha Lois, not realizing that he wasn't an older brother couldn't accept the fact that her beloved *Ledelee* was leaving forever. When they drove out the lane with all his possessions, she stood at the front window protesting, "Don't go, Ledelee, don't go!"

I'll always be grateful to Alydus and Christine for taking us places Dad and Mom didn't go—the most notable, a day at the Canadian

National Exhibition in Toronto. It happened to be the year that Marilyn Bell swam across Lake Ontario, and we were there to watch her come ashore after her amazing feat! We even stayed to take in the grandstand show which culminated in a great fire-works presentation.

After Alydus left, Roelf (Ralph) Schuringa, another Dutch young man came to work at our place. He was another tall, fun-loving young man we enjoyed and he, too, expanded our worlds. He took Enos and me to Schomberg to buy us each a pair of red wooden shoes which we wore for a long time after that. I even bought several new pairs to do the milking and barn work. Cows stepping on my toes were no longer a threat! Our whole family was invited to the wedding when he married his beloved Margaret who had followed him to Canada a year later. Most of the entertainment at the wedding reception was in Dutch and they served a typical Dutch meal which we found quite interesting and enjoyed. (Ralph and Margaret's first daughter was a month older than our first son, their second a month older than our first daughter. They had one more before we both had babies again when our second daughter was born. So we had a lot in common and stayed in touch for many years.)

## CHAPTER 11

# Fun and Frolic in School Days

"Children need the freedom
and time to play.
Play is not a luxury.
Play is a necessity."

—Kay Redfield Jamison

O n days when it wasn't raining, we played an amazing assortment of games on that one-acre of school ground. The wide front sidewalk was ideal for skipping and hop-scotch, although our janitor was distressed at the chalk drawings for that game. The smaller children played Anti-i-over on the small back basement entrance, and the same game, over the tall school by the bigger boys—unless a ball inadvertently smashed a window, after which that game would be ruled out for a time. We played Prisoner's Base outside too at times, but that was usually reserved for basement play when the weather was too cold or wet to be outside. Occasionally when things got too boring, the boys would take to wrestling down on the basement floor. I couldn't stand to watch that! I always felt sorry for the one on the bottom and found it hard to understand how anyone could get pleasure from pinning another person to the floor, when at times it was evidently painful.

It was more fun to play Brush Tag upstairs. Everyone sat in their seats. One person was chosen to be 'it' and another to chase. Each of these put a clean blackboard brush on top of their heads. Carefully running up and down the aisles, they tried to tag each other without letting the brush fall. If the brush fell, the one seated closest to the brush had to quickly pick up the brush, place it on his or her head and take up the chase or try to keep from being tagged, as the case may be. Once the brush was placed on your head, you were not allowed to touch it. If you did, you were out.

Simon Says was another game we often played inside. Sometimes we were allowed to just visit, draw on the board, or choose our own activity with a group of friends.

In the winter, some of the bigger boys often cleared a spot on the lawn, piling the snow around the perimeter, and then flooded it with water from the pump. This made a nice little skating rink that was mostly used by the boys to play hockey. However, when the weather got cold enough for the pond to freeze, we were allowed to take our skates across the road at noon and through Goudie's property to McNair's pond to skate there. The teacher rang the bell at ten to one. At the sound, we scrambled to get skates off, and boots on, for the run back to school. It was there along the pond that the senior boys usually went to find a Christmas tree to put in the school as well. It was a bit of a competition to out-do the previous year in size. We often had trees that must have been at least twelve feet high. I remember the teacher insisting one year that some of the trunk be cut off.

MY ACTING CAREER

Christmas, in my first years of school, brought about a real source of conflict in my young heart and again pointed out the difference in my family. When my older sister, Eva, started school, Mom and Dad did not allow her to attend the Christmas Concerts until she was in Grade Four. Probably because of Dad's position as a minister in a conservative Mennonite church, my parents did not choose to attend such entertainment. They thought she was too young to go by herself until that age. I suppose, having established that rule, they naturally felt it should be maintained. I, however, could not see how they could justify denying me the right to attend, because I didn't need to go alone— the reason for keeping Eva at home that long.

I loved taking part in the Red Cross and Audubon Society meetings that were held Friday afternoons. The formality of those sessions intrigued me. Business was duly taken care of, and then entertainment in some form—such things as a recitation, monologue, short skit or music in some form. I felt right at home "on stage," and it delighted me to be someone else for those few moments when we could act out a part. The first recitation I did in front of the school was the following rhyme:

> Christmas is coming, the geese are growing fat,
> Won't you put a penny in the old man's hat?
> If you haven't got a penny, a half penny will do.
> If you haven't got a half penny, God bless you!

The year I was in Grade Three, the teacher offered me main part in the junior play for Christmas. I was thrilled, and sure that since it was just one year sooner than the rule, Mom and Dad would be just as delighted at the honour and would agree to bend a bit. Much to my chagrin, the rule held firm. I thought I had to find some way to change their mind! I wheedled and coaxed and finally began to sob, trying to explain why I had to go.

Finally, Mom said, "That's enough now, Ruth. We're **not** changing our mind no matter how much you cry, so stop right now, or I'll have to spank you."

I swallowed hard and tried to stop. But the thought of telling the teacher I couldn't do the part came washing over me, and I felt as though I was about to burst! I knew that I could not hold it in, so I went out into the cold summer kitchen, thinking Mom wouldn't hear me there. However, by the time the door shut, the racking sobs were too much to let go quietly. I heard Mom coming to the door, and thought, *Oh no! Here comes the spanking, but it will just have to be.*

She held out a coat to me, with an understanding smile, "Maybe it was too much to ask you to quit all of a sudden. Put your coat on and when you are finished crying, you can come in."

My Christmas concert experiences waited another year.

The remaining concerts of my school years became a real highlight. I couldn't wait for the parts to be handed out, and I practised faithfully, imagining myself into the part and trying to feel what those people would be feeling. If the play happened to be a comedy, I added actions and expressions that would make full use of the opportunity.

One play, *The Census Taker,* in which I had the lead role, was to be a dialogue with only Grant as the Census Taker and me as a harried housewife with eight children. Grant fell ill with rheumatic fever that year and missed a lot of school. He returned about a week before the Christmas concert, and only for part days. The teacher decided that since he needed a big ledger book for all the census information, he could read much of his part.

I decided to make up for what he was not able to do, and rendered my part with aplomb. When he asked for my name, with great exaggeration and expression, I told him all the nick-names people had ever called me, and what my husband called me when he was pleased with me and, what he called me when he wasn't, the different names my children had for me, and that the pastor called me Mrs. Jones, but the neighbours called me. . .

Finally he interrupted, "Could you just show me a letter addressed to you?"

Well, that insulted my sense of privacy. "You want to look at my personal mail? What is the matter with you? Most people in these parts are too polite to ask to read other peoples' personal mail!" When he, in an aside said, "Is she ever dense!" I replied indignantly, "If you had smallpox when you were young, you'd have dents too. It's not very nice of you to bring that to my attention when I'm painfully aware of what the dents do to my looks!"

Each census question, in turn, was an opportunity for that harried housewife to tell a long tale the census taker didn't want or need to hear. He was almost driven to distraction. Needless to say, Grant and I got a lot of laughs, and I was hooked! I did several monologues in my acting career, landed the lead part in several plays, even sang a solo and enjoyed every minute of it.

One year the play was about a family at a train station on their way to spend Christmas with the grandparents. I was the mother and Frank the father of a rather large, boisterous and rowdy family, one of which was played by my brother Enos. After I had called him down for a misdemeanor, I heard a voice from the audience commenting, "What an opportunity for an older sister!" At one point I had to faint in Frank's arms, and thus began a time of teasing by our fellow classmates, and an ongoing thing between Frank and me that lasted through the rest of our school years.

I dreamt at times of being an actress, but couldn't quite figure out how that could come to pass for a little Mennonite girl, the daughter of a minister!

Only one issue was a thorn in those acting opportunities. My parents never came to see my performances at Christmas concerts, Valentine or Hallowe'en parties. I grieved their absence. However, after a while, I noticed that Ruth Lewis, a cheerful young mother of a large family, never missed one of these occasions, so I extended my imagination past my acting and pretended that she was my mother also. Her dark brown shining eyes reflected love and pride in all the children, so it wasn't too hard to imagine I was special to her too.

## ARBOUR DAY

When spring came, we looked forward to Arbour Day. Everyone brought rakes and shovels, wheelbarrows and pails. We raked the whole lawn, dug the flower beds and burned the winter's trash. By noon, the task was completed. Children in the first three grades were allowed to return home and everyone else busied themselves filling jute bags with bits of torn-up newspaper. When six bags had been filled, four or five of the older boys were given a fifteen-minute head start, while the rest of us waited inside. We were not allowed to look out the window. It seemed like much longer, but eventually the clock ticked away all fifteen minutes and then the teacher accompanied the rest of us outside. There we saw the beginning of a paper-trail which we eagerly followed. Up or down the road, over fences, fields and lawns. Usually it wasn't too long until we got to the creek. We had to find our way across and figure out where the paper trail took off from there. It was surprising how far six bags of paper could be stretched. Most often, I'm sure, the trail went on for at least a mile and a half, sometimes more. The end of the trail was indicated by a pile of paper bits signifying that the 'foxes' were near. It usually didn't take too long to find the trail makers, then we all headed towards home. As I recall, there usually was no problem with excess energy those nights. A good supper and early bed time was quite acceptable and to be anticipated.

There weren't many field trips in those days, but when Miriam Heise was our teacher, probably when I was in fourth or fifth grade, she and the Glasgow School teacher planned a train ride from Stouffville to Toronto. Early in the morning, parents transported us to the train station, complete with lunches and a few dollars of spending money. It was different seeing Stouffville and Markham and the other little towns from the backside as we travelled the rails.

On our arrival at Union Station, we hung on to a rope as we walked from there up to the Parliament Buildings. There a guide took us on a tour to see where our government took place and explained some of the procedures and pointed out the architecture. From there we walked to the Royal Ontario Museum and sat on the grass outside to eat our lunch before a tour of that marvelous place. To this day I can well remember some of the displays, of clothing of the past, the Egyptian mummies, and the dinosaur skeletons we saw there. Finally we grasped the rope again for the walk to Union Station and our ride back. At the Museum, Gloria, the Glasgow teacher was picked up by her fiancé, Doug Mansbridge, and the Glasgow children were left in the care of Phyllis Pugh, who had accompanied us. Unfortunately, Gloria had forgotten to turn over the return tickets to Phyllis, a fact that was not discovered until we reached the station. Some tense moments followed before they allowed the children to return to Stouffville. I am not sure what deal was made, but I do remember Phyllis, who had quite a lisp, saying over and over as she wrung her hands, "Oh, ithn't thith thympathetic!" She might have meant pathetic, but that's what she said.

When Miriam Heise became our teacher, we began to have music teachers come to our school. Our first was Mr. Buckley. He was a tall thin man and quite stern—a no-nonsense kind of fellow. I'm sure we learned some from him, but there wasn't a lot of fun. He did not stay long and was replaced by Mr. Martin who came once a week with an enthusiastic smile and a surety that we were not only going to sing well, but also that we'd have a good time. He said there was no such thing as a child who cannot sing, and gently set about to prove it. We learned fun songs, and although he never seemed to draw attention to anyone, somehow he gave a bit of extra encouragement to those who had difficulty carrying a tune by singing close to them, or placing them beside a stronger singer. When he announced that he would no longer be coming, we felt a great sense of loss. Even though Mr. Williams, who replaced him, was also a good teacher, it somehow just wasn't the same.

Several months after Mr. Martin quit, I happened to be at the McNairs when our dear former teacher called Fred, a school board member. When we realized who it was on the phone, we begged Fred, "Tell Mr. Martin we miss him and wish he could come back." When Fred got off the phone, we asked what he had said. "Bless their little hearts!" was his comment. From Mr. Martin, it felt like a real blessing!

Miss Heise's classroom was not as quiet as some parents would have preferred, and I remember one parent coming to the door for something and going away remarking "the classroom sounded as if you were downtown Toronto in Eaton's store!" However, we did learn and I think it was a happy learning as well. One of the most valuable lessons she taught me was not to expect perfection in myself—not that I completely learned it, but I still often think of her when I am getting frustrated with myself for not being able to reach the level of perfection I would like. One day she had asked us to look out the window and draw what we could see from our seat. All I could see were the bare branches of a maple tree. I tried and erased and tried and erased until I had almost worn the page through! She came along and asked what my problem was. I told her I couldn't get it right—it looked too flat and stiff and the trees limbs looked so much more interesting than I could make them. Furthermore there were so many little branches I couldn't get them all in the right places with the proper proportions. She patted my shoulder and said, "Ruth, you don't have to draw every branch, exactly like it is. Just draw the idea. It doesn't have to be perfect!"

Miss Heise left us part way through my Grade Six year to go and nurse her mother who was sick. That year wasn't the most productive year as we had chickenpox, and we had three more teachers between Christmas and the end of the year.

After her mother's death, Miriam went as a missionary to what was then Southern Rhodesia in Africa. I wrote her several times and she wrote back and even sent a few pictures along once.

With the arrival of Mrs. Woodcock the next fall, a whole new era began. Gone were the days of friendly chatting while we worked. We sat in our seats quietly as we worked diligently to become "worthwhile contributing citizens of Canada."

The strap was used occasionally, but much more to be feared was a tongue lashing that made you feel that you had not only disappointed Mrs. Woodcock, but also your parents, community, and the entire country of Canada!

We learned from our textbooks, of course, but even more from her interesting storytelling and commentary on the lessons. We used to feel we were getting away with something if we could get her started on a story instead of a lesson, but in fact, we just got our lesson in a more enjoyable form. She, I'm sure, was quite well aware of what she was doing. She did instill in us a responsibility for our own actions and a sense of responsibility to the community and the world. I don't think anyone who sat in her classes ever left without a distaste for anyone who would do such a lowly thing as litter or deface a public building.

Can you imagine children wanting to come to school early just to listen to their teacher? Mrs. Woodcock had us all wanting to get there early because she would regale us with all kinds of stories about her experiences, or her reflections on what was going on in the world. She would tell us about people she had heard speak—the most impressive to me was that she had heard Stephen Leacock recite his poetry. She always made the tales fascinating and we hated to miss anything. A few children opted to stay out on the playground until the bell rang, but most of us were in the classroom eagerly absorbing every word.

She was our teacher in the early fifties and she, at that time, felt the Government of Canada had betrayed the aboriginal people on the shores of Lake Huron. Their reserve with thriving farms had been taken over for military purposes, with the promise they would be returned after the Second World War. She couldn't believe that the promise was still unfulfilled four years later. Had she known how many years would pass before it was rectified, she would have been horrified.

The ability Mrs. Woodcock had to motivate pupils to learn is probably best exemplified by a certain young student who had been expelled from the Atha School— the next school district south of us— because of his bad behaviour. His parents pled with Mrs. Woodcock to give him a try. The first day, Bill, as I shall call him, began to shoot spit balls around the room. When Mrs. Woodcock saw what was happening, she addressed the young man.

"Oh, Bill, I'm so sorry that I didn't tell you that we don't do things like that in our school. We're all here to learn, but if everyone wants to do that, we can. Shall we put it up for a vote?" she paused. "How many students would like to throw spit balls, whenever we feel like it?"

She looked around the room. No hands went up.

"Are you sure?" she asked.

Still no hands went up.

"Well, Bill, I guess that's what the whole school wants, so I'm sure now that you know, you will honour that."

It wasn't long until she found his strengths and commended him for his quick mind. She assured him that she thought he was going to be a success in life. He buckled right down to it and finished the year with good marks. Bill went on to establish a successful Paint and Paper business in town and did well. He gave much credit to Mrs. Woodcock.

She, too, let us have our paper chases on Arbour Day, but she didn't always accompany us. She expected us to behave properly and safely on our own. I don't think we had school picnics at the end of the school term in earlier years, but at the end of her first year she rallied the parents around us to provide a potluck lunch and rides to Greenway Park for a picnic and a day of games and fun. These days again, we, as good citizens of Canada, were on the honour system, to behave well, clean up after ourselves and not destroy anything, and not complain about the heat.

"Everyone knows it's hot," she said. "It's not necessary to say it again and again. That is the last time I want to hear that today!" The day was just as enjoyable without the weather commentary.

## CHAPTER 12

# Insight about My Sight

> "If you're not like everyone else, you're going to be misunderstood. People are going to wonder why you're trying to be different; you don't know you're different because that's the way you've always been."
>
> —**Anonymous**

The year I was in Grade Eight, the school nurse sent a note home that I needed to have my eyes checked. It wasn't the first time. My mother noticed that, as a baby, my eyes sometimes wandered. She would draw her hand over both my eyes, and usually they would come into focus. Around the age of two, she wanted to check my eyes, as they still were doing the same thing. She took me to Dr. Iris MacDonald in Markham. She wanted to outfit me with glasses, but Dad's reaction was, "You're not going to put glasses on my two-year-old."

When, in Grade Three, the nurse notified my parents that my eyes needed attention, Dad took me to Dr. Forsythe in Claremont. He examined my eyes and finally told Dad, "I think she must just want glasses—she isn't consistent in her answers."

On the way home, Dad chided me. "You mustn't lie, just to get glasses. Glasses are meant for people who really need help to see. When you go to a doctor, you have to tell the truth."

"Dad, I did tell the truth," I objected. "I told him what I saw."

"Dr. Forsythe didn't think so."

Inwardly I grieved. I wanted so much to be a good girl and have my dad's approval. How could I change what I had done?

Two years later, the same concern was relayed in a note to my parents. This time Dad took me to Dr. Grubin in Stouffville. On the way, he instructed me to be truthful and say just what I saw when the doctor asked. I promised I would. I was determined to accurately assess what I saw and be absolutely truthful.

After some time of testing, Dr. Grubin cleared his throat and looked at Dad. "I can't quite figure out what's going on with Ruth. Her answers don't seem to be constant. She answers one way one time and a different answer the next time."

"This happened once before." Dad sighed. "The last time we had her eyes tested, the doctor concluded she just wants glasses."

"Well, I'm not sure about that, but I can't figure out what it is, so perhaps that's the problem."

Once more, I got a lecture on the way home. I felt offended and wronged. I did tell the truth, but I couldn't tell Dr. Grubin more than what I saw.

As a thirteen-year-old, I faced another eye test. For several years now, I had trouble seeing the blackboard, but I feared mentioning it because of the previous perception of my dishonesty. Another optometrist had come to town. Dr. Garnet Gray was just starting out in an office in Stouffville. Dad decided to give me one more try.

"Now you be truthful this time!" he warned me. "If Dr. Gray comes to the same conclusion, we're not going to go through this anymore."

Dr. Gray was a very young man and he greeted us warmly. Each question he asked, I carefully assessed what I was seeing and answered truthfully. On and on the test went. Over an hour later, he said, "There's something going on, but I can't figure out what it is."

My heart sank. *Oh, no! Here we go again.*

"Twice now, we've had Ruth's eyes tested by different optometrists and both of them concluded she just wants glasses. She's probably doing it again." My dad looked disgusted and I wanted to cry.

"Oh no! I don't think that's what it is at all," Dr. Gray assured Dad— but it was also sweet affirmation to me.

On and on the tests went until suddenly a light went on in Dr. Gray's eyes. "Here, we'll try this," he said, giving me an old-fashioned stereoscope with a postcard on the end—two images of the same mountain scene side-by-side. "Look through the eye piece and tell me what you see."

"I see a lake with mountains behind it and trees around the lake."

"What do you see in the middle of the lake?"

"Once when I look, I see a line slanted this way," I showed with my hands which way it leaned. "And when I blink, I see a line slanted this way," and I demonstrated with my hands.

"Do you never see an X?"

"No, just a line slanted either one way or the other."

Dr. Gray looked almost jubilant. He positioned a card with printing in front of the eye piece, held a pen a few inches in front of it and asked me to read what I saw. I did so, missing no words at all, in spite of the pen being a few inches in front of the card.

Dr. Gray almost crowed, "She can read right around the pen!" He grinned with his whole face alight.

"Now I think I know what the problem is with Ruth's sight. Sometimes babies have wandering eyes because they aren't a matched pair. Usually when that happens, the strong eye takes over and the other becomes lazy. One of two things happen—the person either sees a double image, or the lazy eye deteriorates and goes blind. Ruth has adapted so that she blocks out what she sees with the lazy eye, but she switches from using one eye to the other, so that both have been consistently used. The amazing fact is that she can use both eyes at once as well. That is very unusual. I think if we get the proper prescription for both eyes, they will work together most of the time. She will need to be very careful in getting regular tests in case one should deteriorate faster than the other. To keep both working, she will need to have up-to-date lenses."

What a relief to be believed and to know that there was help for me. When I got my new glasses, I was amazed at how clear everything looked. The other benefit—no longer did one of my eyes sometime wander off to the side leaving people looking at me wondering who I was looking at. Each time I went back to Dr. Gray, he played around with my eyes to see what all they could do. He got a kick out of the fact that I could read around his pen and see things ahead with greater field of vision than persons unable to look with one eye or the other. Of course, I got some ribbing about being an oddity, but I was glad to have the matter understood and settled

CHAPTER 13

# The Shattering of My Dreams

> "When it seems that someone
> has shattered your dreams …
> pick up even the smallest pieces
> and use them to build better dreams."
> —**Anonymous**

L ittle by little, dreams are born in the heart of a growing girl. Mrs. Woodcock had inspired possibilities in me. Her graphic and spirited stories about historical events or her meeting inspiring Canadian authors birthed dreams in my heart of motivating others in the same way. Words became a delight and I found great satisfaction in arranging them to express my thoughts and feelings. My pen pals were my first audience as I wrote long letters to them. My dreams of writing grew larger.

In my last year at Altona Public School, Queen Elizabeth was crowned. The death of King George offered the opportunity for prolonged lessons on English history through Mrs. Woodcock's impromptu speeches and informal sessions. The months before the coronation were spent researching what was involved in the traditional rite—who could be expected to be present, the steps throughout the day, the route of the carriage bearing the future queen to the cathedral, the parts of the ceremony and the ride back to the palace afterward.

The Grade Seven and Eight pupils were assigned to write a poem about the significant event—a welcome challenge to me. What a surge of delight filled me when the words began to come together with proper metre and deep meaning. My poem entitled "I Wonder What She Will Think" outlined verse by verse each of the routes and the rites that would take place on that historic day. Trying to imagine the thoughts in Queen Elizabeth's mind, I ended each verse with the line of the title, "I wonder what she will think."

We carefully copied our finished poems onto pages of foolscap and tacked them on the decorated bulletin board at the back of the classroom. The careful, neat printing in itself was quite a task—I was not the neatest printer and very self-conscious about it.    This time, my efforts turned out better than I expected and I felt good about my accomplishment—almost as good about the printing as the poetry itself.

It was fun to make big plans for June 2, 1953. That day, the world flocked to London to take part or observe the festivities. In little Altona, Ontario, students and community adults came dressed in our best for the occasion. A special afternoon program in the school began the celebration, and then everyone filed out to the edge of the school yard to plant a maple tree in honour of the coronation. My grandfather, as secretary of the board and 92-year-old Mrs. Barkis Reesor, the oldest member of the community, did the honours with a shovel spray-painted a shiny aluminum. We finished by singing "God Save the Queen" which still sounded so different after having sung "God Save the King" up until King George's passing.

In our grade eight year, Mrs. Woodcock started a campaign to get us ready for high school. She made sure we had completed our year's work by early spring, then she began teaching some of the preliminary High School Math and English. At the time, knowing the young people in our church didn't go on to secondary school, I thought, *I'd better enjoy this because it will be the only higher learning I'll get.*

I didn't bother telling Mrs. Woodcock, since I knew she already thought it a shame that my older sister Eva was acting as janitor for the school rather than going on to High School. Throughout the year, they had enough talks that I'm sure she knew Eva would have liked to further her education. I, too, liked learning, but was resigned to staying home with the secret hope that Dad would let me do some tractor driving and field work. So, when I said good-bye to my classmates, I had mixed feelings but expected never to see them in a classroom situation again, although I hoped I would continue learning.

As I brought the remnants of my school years home and put them away, I tacked my poem to the wall above the desk in my room. Gratification, satisfaction, amazement and hope were wrapped up in that sheet of foolscap. The writing of the poem stretched my horizons. The careful and meticulous printing proved to my heart that when I took time and worked hard at something, I could accomplish it. Hung on the wall where I could see it often, it shone a beacon of hope for future challenges and the possibility of fulfilled dreams. If I could write a poem, perhaps one day I could even write articles or a book to share with the world.

But the world would have to wait as I faced one of the more immediate challenges—to keep my room neat and tidy. I knew I disappointed my mother in this area. It was one of the reasons I wondered if there had been a mistake in my make-up. Unlike most of the other females in my family and community, it was painfully obvious that my abilities and inclinations were not in housekeeping.

One day on entering my room, I noticed my poem gone from the wall. I saw the foolscap page on my desk and went to look. Mother, who wrote poetry sometimes, had taken the page, turned it over, and with a pen that bled through to my careful printing, had written a poem of her own—"With dresses on her chairs, stockings on her floor, dust on her furniture, bobby pins and more.....I wonder what she will think." On and on it went, verse after verse, using my composition and metre to methodically describe the clutter in my room and verify my failure.

It's hard to convey the dismay, and the humiliation that I felt. The light of my accomplishment was snuffed out in a flash. The defilement of my poem left only a nasty taste in my mouth and an indescribable ache in my heart. Without even bothering to copy my version, I crumpled the paper, threw it in the waste-basket, laid on my bed and sobbed at the defectiveness of my flawed character and of the ability I so obviously lacked. It left me with a lingering sense of futility and despair. Was it worth trying to make something of myself? Would I ever measure up? Was it worth dreaming?

# CHAPTER 14
## Rough Introduction to High School

> "The gem cannot be polished without friction,
> nor man perfected without trials."
> —**Chinese Proverb**

A little after the beginning of school that fall, we received a call from Pickering High School, inquiring as to why I wasn't attending classes. Mom told them I was staying home to help on the farm. It was only days later that we had a visit from the Truant Officer to whom Dad explained that our church did not approve of higher education, and that I would not be going. Dad was informed that if I didn't start of my own volition, he would be issued a summons, which indeed happened. Dad had to attend court, where he was told he had no alternative. He then asked the court to at least excuse me from physical education. That also was not granted. They asked what his objection to Physical Education could be. Dad told them that I would not be allowed to wear the gym outfit, which consisted of bloomers and a very short-skirted dress. The principal eventually conceded that I could wear another dress instead.

By the time all the wrinkles were ironed out, and agreements made, it was October 13, when I entered High School. This little thirteen- year-old girl from a one- room school of about 28 pupils had not attended orientation day, because she thought she was not going to be going to high school. It was indeed a formidable experience to enter a school of over 400 students after a two-hour bus ride, not even knowing where the office was located.

Charlotte, my best friend from public school days, and the rest of my class as well as all the other Grade Nine students had already a month and a half to get their bearings, and it was already quite familiar to them. I perceived that Charlotte may have been embarrassed to be my friend. I can't say as I blame her. I'm sure the whole community must have been buzzing with the gossip about it all. Thankfully, Helen Wilson, whose mother had gone to school with my mother, and with whom I was somewhat acquainted, took mercy on me and invited me to sit with her on the bus. She promised to take me to the office, which were the instructions I had been given.

The principal, Mr. Briggs, I surmised, was thoroughly disgusted with Dad and the measures he had taken, and was not inclined to be lenient with me, even though I had nothing to do with the decision. He was very abrupt with me and informed me that I had better catch up quick with the month and a half's work I had missed. He told me that I would be in class 9C, as that was the only class that had vocal music only—another request of my father.

He escorted me first to my locker, then to my homeroom, and introduced me to the teacher, Mr. Rogers, who thankfully knew how to smile and welcome me. He gave me a seat in front of a girl named Frances and asked her to make sure I got from room to room. He also asked her to share her notes with me. She gave me the pages that I needed to cover in order to catch up. Thankfully, Mrs. Woodcock's preparation had covered most of the work the rest of the class had taken in the first month and a half, so that was the easiest class to adapt to.

The next hour was English, and there I did not meet with such kindness. When asked what school I was transferring from, I had to admit in front of the whole class that I had not been attending anywhere.

With that information, I was told that in that case I had better have all notes caught up in a week. When one of the students was asked to share their notes, I was dismayed at the stack of writing that meant. How would I ever get it done when I had to be at the bus stop, a quarter mile away, by 6:45 a.m.? I wouldn't get back home until five o'clock.

The next class was even worse. Mr. Foyer, who taught French, announced the page for that day's vocabulary. I had no text book, as Mr. Briggs had not even suggested that I visit the school book store before classes, or even given me a book list. Mr. Foyer asked derisively, "Why are you sitting there without your book, Bright Light!" I told him I had just started today and did not have a book yet.

"Well, what book were you using in your former school?" he asked. Again, I had to explain in front of the whole class. Mr. Foyer stomped down the aisle and shoved my desk forcefully next to the boy across the aisle and shouted, "Well, share a book with someone, Genius!" I bit my lip to keep from crying. I'm afraid I didn't take too much in during that class. At the end of the class, Mr. Foyer stopped me as I passed his desk and said, "You'd better get your book by tomorrow's class, and I want your notes caught up to date by the end of the week!"

From there, we were to go for lunch. I had memorized my locker number, and I walked up and down the hall trying to find it. Alas the numbers did not go that high. Several trips up and down, and I still had not found it! Finally I thought, *I'll have to go to the office, down the leg of the T, to ask where my locker is.* Suddenly I remembered that there was another wing on down from the office. I ran to get my lunch and walked into the cafeteria just in time to see the others going off to the washrooms in preparation for returning to the classroom. Bless Frances' heart, she offered to wait to let me eat a bit of my lunch before the bell rang. Next class was gym. I had brought another set of clothes, as I was instructed. The girls, of course, questioned me why I wasn't wearing a uniform—didn't I have one yet? More embarrassed explanations. We entered the gym and Miss Emerson eyed me up and down with those black eyes of hers and asked, "What are you doing here without a gym outfit?" When I explained that Dad didn't want me to wear a gym outfit and had made arrangements for me to just bring a change of clothes, she snapped, "Well, where are your jeans?"

"I'm sorry, Miss Emerson, I don't have any jeans."

"Well you'd better sit out today and be sure to bring some tomorrow."

"I'm sorry, Miss Emerson, but I don't have any!"

"Well, get some!"

"I'm sorry, Miss Emerson, my dad doesn't want me to wear jeans any more than a gym outfit."

She glared at me and said, "Sit up in the balcony today until I can take care of this!"

In Science class, then History class, I was given more notes that I was to have done by the next week, or sooner if possible. By the time I got through the day, I felt about knee high to a grasshopper with a load a camel couldn't be expected to carry. When I finally got home, I wanted to go to bed, cry myself to sleep, and never enter that school again. There were notes that had to be copied, and Eva volunteered to do some for me. We worked together until I had to get to bed so I could be ready to get up at five-thirty to get my lunch made, hair combed, eat breakfast and be up to the corner by quarter to seven. It's an understatement to say that I was emotionally drained!

The next day and every day for several weeks, Miss Emerson kept nagging me, saying I had to take part in Phys. Ed, but I couldn't wear a dress. Finally she relegated me to the balcony, but woe-betide if I took my eyes off the action! If she suspected me to be doing any studying or doing homework, she hollered at me, "Just because you won't come dressed so you can take part, you mustn't think you don't have to pay attention!"

Do you think the other girls understood? I sure didn't, and it was hard explaining why I was sitting in the balcony day after day.

By the middle of November, I was quite enjoying my classes, and determined I was not going to be hounded all year for being behind. Christmas exams came, and I studied hard to do my best. As the exams were returned, I was gratified to get good marks in each of my subjects, including 100 percent on the written Phys. Ed exam. In fact I had third highest marks in my class. However, when we got our report cards, my average was way down. On examination, I quickly found the reason. My Phys. Ed. mark was 0! I marched down to the office and requested to see Mr. Briggs.

"Sorry, but he's busy."

"I'll wait until he can see me."

"But the bell will soon ring for the next class."

"I'll let them know why I was late. I'll have Mr. Briggs write me a note."

I explained I couldn't stay after school, because the bus would be gone and it was over twenty miles to my home.

Mr. Briggs became suddenly available after his secretary talked to him. I explained that I had got 100 percent on the test Miss Emerson gave, and even if that only counted for half of the marks, I would deserve a 50. I explained that he himself had given permission to wear regular clothing as long as I brought a change just for Phys. Ed, but Miss Emerson wouldn't allow it. He said I could go to my class, and he and Miss Emerson would work something out. My report was changed, and I can't recall how many marks I was awarded, but I determined to keep my other marks high to compensate.

That determination helped me in an unexpected way. When the next exams rolled around, I was most concerned about my Math marks. However, I studied hard and late the night before my last exams which were Math and French. When the alarm rang the next morning, I got up with a start, because I had wanted to study a bit more. At first I was very dizzy, but I got my balance back and hurried to get ready. I was very tired, but figured it was because I was up so late studying. In a bit of a daze, I hurried up to the bus stop, and got on the bus. I opened my book to study some more.

The next thing I knew, Helen was waking me to tell me the bus was arriving at the school.

"Wake up, Ruth!" she said, as she shook my shoulder. "Boy! You must really have been burning the midnight oil."

I struggled to wake up enough to exit the bus and get to my locker.

Exams were always administered in the homeroom. I put my books away and headed to Mr. Roger's room. The exam was handed out, and I looked it over. The trouble was, I couldn't remember from the beginning of the question to the end, what it was. So I just started. It seemed to be at least a mile from my face to the desk. Finally it was done, and we were dismissed for lunch.

I went to the cafeteria, but I wasn't hungry! Instead, I laid my head in my arms and slept soundly. I still don't know why one of my classmates or the cafeteria monitors didn't notice how sick I was. However, when it was time for the French exam, Frances woke me up and I proceeded to the classroom in a delirious state. I couldn't, to save my life, have told anyone what was on that exam or what I wrote on my paper. I stumbled from there to my locker and on to the bus and promptly fell asleep.

Instead of dropping me off at the corner, as usual, Jimmy Phillips, the bus driver, stopped at the end of the lane, and wondered if I was alright to walk in by myself. Dozy with fever, I wondered what he meant, and thanked him for dropping me off there. I started to the house feeling that it was the longest lane I had ever seen. Suddenly I saw Mom running out to meet me.

She called out in a worried voice, "What's the matter, Ruth?"

"I don't know. Why did you come to meet me?"

"I saw you from the window, and it looked as though you could barely walk."

When we got into the house, Mom promptly got out the thermometer after laying me on the couch. It registered 104.5! The next few days, I wasn't aware of much. The doctor came and went a few times.

As my temperature went down over the next week, I began to worry what kind of gibberish I had written on my exam. The doctor wrote a letter to explain and excuse me from being marked for those exams. I put it in my binder to hand to the teacher or principal on my return, but figured I would wait until I saw how I actually did on my tests.

Imagine my surprise when those two exams came back with the highest marks I had ever achieved in Math, French, or anything else besides spelling! I left the doctor's letter where it was and thanked God that my subconscious was working better that my conscious mind that day.

It was an enjoyable year, and by that time I was full of enthusiasm and ideas of what I could learn and the career opportunities I would have if only I could continue. I shyly mentioned it to Dad but knew, even before I said it, that it would embarrass him too much to allow me to go when he had gone to such lengths to keep me out. I promised myself that someday I would go back to school!

Two things gave me a great deal of satisfaction before my high school career ended. The first was in the spring, when Miss Emerson's class started baseball in Phys. Ed. Class. That was something that I had played in skirts all my life. It was boring sitting on the side lines, and although I understood why I couldn't do gymnastics in a skirt, and probably not jumping, I would have dearly loved to take part in volleyball and tennis. I thought I couldn't miss baseball, so I went to Miss Emerson's office and asked if I could please play baseball.

"Are you ready now to wear jeans?" she asked.

"No, Miss Emerson, I can't do that, but I have played baseball in my skirt all my life."

"What if you fall and your skirt flies up?"

It was still cool, so most of the girls were wearing their jackets over their gym outfits. Naturally, it looked as though most of them had nothing else on, because the jackets covered the gym outfits, which were very short.

"Pardon me, Miss Emerson," I said, "but I really don't think anyone would see as much of me as they see of the girls with their gym outfits on all the time. If it did happen, on me, they would only see it for a short while."

"Oh, all right," she said, "but you will take full responsibility for what happens." So I played baseball, and wished I had confronted her before volleyball and tennis.

The second bit of satisfaction came when I was awarded a silver cup for the girl with the highest marks in my class, and although it would have given me even more satisfaction to have Mr. Briggs hand it to me in person, my parents did not want me to attend the function.

One more contact with the school, as part of the Grade Nine Science course, we were to choose some kind of summer project which Mr. Ellis would come to inspect late August. It was to be some improvement or environmental project. When I showed Mom the list of possibilities, she was a little impatient, resenting the fact that someone else should make a demand on our busy summer. She wondered if home-canning couldn't be my project, since that was something we had to do anyway. Mr. Ellis happily agreed to it. When he visited us, I first showed him our large garden, then took him to the cellar to show our full shelves of canned goods, which I had carefully arranged to make as colourful and shining as possible. Of course the goodness of the garden produce that God had provided didn't need much help to look beautiful.

Mr. Ellis was duly impressed. I'm sure he had never seen so much home-preserved food—neither the amount nor variety—in his life. He wondered what we do with it all. I explained that there were eight in the family, plus whatever hired help we may have at various times. Furthermore, we often fed as high as 30 or more people on many Sundays. He was truly amazed and assured me I had top marks.

Except for two more visits from the truant officer that fall, that was the last of my association with Pickering District High. Dad considered sending me to Rockway Mennonite High School if the truant officers continued their calls, rather than send me back to Pickering High. I had very mixed emotions about that. I would have dearly loved to continue school, but Kitchener seemed a long way from home and my friends, yet it did intrigue me as an exciting adventure. I knew I could probably come home most weekends. However, because I had turned fourteen, and lived on a farm, I could now legally be kept out of school.

CHAPTER 15

# *Life after School*

> "Acceptance and tolerance and forgiveness,
> those are life-altering lessons."
> —Jessica Lange

O nce I became resigned to the fact that my school life was over,
I soon became immersed in other interests. Thank God for
books! I read all that I could get my hands on.

From my cradle days, I was conscious of God. As I grew, I heard
the Bible stories my mother read and continued to feel his presence in
the world around me. I was also conscious of the need to commit my
life to him and did so in my heart. However, as I grew older, I had the
desire to make that a public statement.

In the Markham-Waterloo Mennonite Church, that meant being
baptized and, for me, a woman, to wear cape dresses, black stockings,
a covering and bonnet. I perceived that as being formidable—I just
wanted to proclaim myself to be a follower of Jesus and walk with
him—to live the kind of caring, loving life that he lived on earth.
Therefore, I began to withhold my heart a bit. I struggled with that
until I came up with a solution. I thought fifteen was an age where

I could join the nearby Missionary church. I could walk over there each Sunday and come home afterward. I realized that I would spend much time alone, because the rest of the family would be visiting other homes, as was the usual custom. That was no small thing to me, since I valued my friends and would miss them, but it was a sacrifice I was ready to make. I hoped that the young people at the missionary church would become closer friends to me over time. Still I kept putting it off, knowing it would cause some friction between my parents and me.

Finally, one Wednesday morning, I could no longer wait. I knelt by my bed and told the Lord that I wanted to be his and asked him to take control of my life. I went downstairs happy in the thought of sharing my decision with Mom. Before I could say a word, she scolded me quite severely for taking so long to get ready for work. She said, as punishment, I would stay home that day instead of going to our monthly sewing circle. I thought, *I guess this isn't the time to tell her.*

Now I loved sewing circle, and I was sure if she knew why I was late, she would gladly let me go. She had already told me to make lunches to take along, so I began making enough sandwiches for us all. I tried to think of how to tell her, so as not to make her feel bad for scolding me when I was doing the most important thing I could do in life. When she saw that I had included myself in the sandwich provisions, she scolded me again for being self-willed. I didn't go with the rest but ate my lunch at home experiencing what I felt must have been a direct blow from the evil one. I really struggled with anger and resentment that day. The next morning, or perhaps it was that evening yet, I told Mom and Dad what I had done, and asked forgiveness for going ahead and making my lunch. However, I decided to wait a bit before I broke the news that I would not be joining the Markham-Waterloo Church. Dad didn't ask, so I thought I would wait either until he asked me or until I had spoken to Reverend Houston.

The following Sunday, Anna Mary was sick and someone needed to stay at home with her. I always tried to squirm out of my turn, because I loved being with my friends. With Wednesday on my mind and my new attitude, I offered to stay at home.

The following Tuesday on my way home from cleaning the school in the evening, one of the young men from the church stopped as he caught up to me. He rolled down the car window and said, "I'm so happy to hear you are joining the church."

"Pardon?" I asked.

"Your dad announced it on Sunday."

"He did?"

"Didn't you know?"

"No, I didn't. I told him I had asked the Lord into my life, but I didn't know he was going to announce that I was joining the church."

My heart sank! What was I going to do? I had so carefully planned and now I felt trapped. I knew it would be hard on Dad to know his daughter wasn't going to be part of the church where he ministered, but to ask him to tell the congregation that he had made a mistake— that was more than I could ask of him.

That started a time of conflict in my life. I had begun a new inner life, but now I was expected to exemplify that life in ways I couldn't see would enhance or reflect what that change or decision meant. Mom set about making cape dresses and coverings for me. My aunt, to alleviate the demand, offered a few of her dresses that no longer fit her. Much as I loved my aunt, I dreaded wearing those caped and collarless dresses.

I begged Dad to give me something to read that would prove what the church taught had some bearing on the Christian life. I'm ashamed to say that for a period, I thought that if I tried to persuade others, it would help me to see it too. It all sounded in my heart like a "noisy gong or clanging cymbal," as 1Corinthians 13 says.

I wore thicker black stockings and made my coverings bigger and my dresses plainer. Each step brought Dad's glowing approval— something that I sought throughout my life. Although I yearned for the books and the learning I left behind, I read prolifically and studied the Bible a lot. The study of God's Word and the reading and reading again, underlining verses that stood out, was a good experience, and good training for the days ahead.

While searching the Scripture helped me grow in my understanding, I also found myself feeling boxed in by the life patterns the church dictated to me. A recurring image came to my mind—a butterfly hatching out in a box too small to let it fully extend its wings. I was distressed over the disagreements in the church over so many outer things and the fact that I had no opportunity for service and sharing the good news of the gospel with others.

I continued to attend other churches in the evenings—Altona, Stouffville, Dixon Hill and Markham Missionary, Wideman's Mennonite, Stouffville or Springvale Baptist, Heise Hill Brethren in Christ—wherever special meetings were being held, or if nothing special was going on, where I felt like going. Often someone else went with me, but if not, I went alone.

The Bible and other books enlightened me and enlarged my views. I longed to go to Ontario Bible School and Institute in Kitchener, but my parents didn't think they could spare me. That hurt a bit, because Dad had encouraged many young people in our church to do so.

## WORKING WITH THE COWS

While Eva was at home, we took turns helping with the milking. After she got married, I was usually in the barn each morning and evening. That was work I really enjoyed, too. I would have liked to study up on feeding programs and the genealogy of the Holsteins, but I didn't know where to start, and I doubt whether Dad would have encouraged that, either. Wasn't that more "man's" work?

Dad's understanding and interest in his dairy herd was not avid. He always thought if a cow had a big udder, she must be a good milker. Mom was quite aware that a smaller, well-fastened udder could milk just as much or more and presented a lot less possibility of having a teat stepped on. It always frustrated Mom when Dad sold off some of his best milk producers, thinking he was getting rid of the culls. This difference in understanding was driven home one day when the Kahn brothers, who were of Jewish heritage, came around to buy cows. This time they brought a prospective buyer along. They came into the barn speaking Yiddish which was much like our German dialect.

One of the brothers told his customer, "Just watch—this man doesn't know his cows very well. As long as his wife doesn't come to the barn, we can pick out his best cows and get them at a good price, because he'll think he is unloading his culls."

They proceeded through the barn and chose two with a good build and tight little udders. They discussed how much they really would be worth and how little they could offer for them. In English they presented the deal. But Dad had understood all they had said.

"Not this time," he said in our German dialect. "I think I need at least…" and he named the higher price they had discussed as their real worth." The men went away in shock. From that time on, Dad consulted Mom on which cows should be kept and which could be sold.

## THE GARDEN

I much preferred the summers when I could work outside, and occasionally help with the fieldwork. I enjoyed, especially, keeping the lawn trim and neat, and working at cleaning up some of the neglected and messy corners.

I liked to see flowers from the kitchen window, so I dug up an area across the lane east of the hot bed to make a new flower bed. I hauled topsoil with the wheelbarrow to build up the back to a greater height. For several years before my marriage, I enjoyed washing dishes much more, being able to see the blooms as I worked. I loved mowing lawn, and kept mowing a little bit further out the lane each year. Grandad didn't think that was necessary, but I liked the neat look it accomplished.

There was an area behind the garage where junk and garbage had been thrown over the years. Behind that, and a little to the north, stood the little building that housed the "facilities" before the day of the bathroom. It was no longer in use, so I asked Dad if I could remove it and the garbage to make lawn and flowerbed in that space. He didn't think it was necessary but, finally, he brought the big trailer and I heaved the trash on, load by load, until it was all gone. I raked up bits and pieces of glass and pottery and sticks, dismantled the little outhouse and filled the hole. At last I worked it all up with the garden tractor. While I did get a few flowerbeds planted, I passed the torch to Esther when I got married, and she did some further work on it.

## CHAPTER 16

# *Life Takes a Different Direction*

> Piglet: "How do you spell love?"
> Pooh: "You don't spell it, you *feel* it."
> —A. A. Milne

ecause of Dad's position as a minister, he was expected to visit other churches in our conferences in Waterloo County, Indiana, Ohio and Pennsylvania. They would often ask another couple to go along and would be gone for a week or ten days. The spring of 1954, along with Levi and Fanny Grove, they went on a three-week visit to Pennsylvania and Virginia. Eva had just turned eighteen, but they asked Ella Smith to come and help while they were gone. Ella's brother Norman was hired to do the milking and look after the farm. I was going to high school at the time, so I wasn't home during the day, but both Ella and Norman were a lot of fun. Enos, of course, was delighted to have another young male in the house, and it wasn't long until they put their heads together to play a trick on us.

One evening the phone rang just before supper. An unrecognizable voice with a funny accent asked, "Do you live on the Altona Road?"

"Yes, we do," I answered.

"You'd better get off! There's a car coming."

*Click.* The caller hung up.

We tried to think who it may be, and I thought perhaps it was my old pal, Frank. Eva and Ella came up with another trick question and urged me to call Frank. I did.

At supper time, we told Norman and Enos what had happened. They found it very funny and laughed so hard I became suspicious that I had blamed the wrong person. It turned out that they had gone to Grandma's house to make the call.

The next night when Norman and Enos came in the back door, I was standing behind it with a glass of water which I threw over their heads. Norman grabbed me and poured the last of it on my head. The fun just grew. One evening when I went to bed, I found at least a cup of salt spread on my sheet. I gathered up the four corners, opened the window and shook the sheet out the window. The next morning, Enos kept asking me how I slept, and I, with a straight face told him I had a good night's sleep. A few nights later, I rolled several marbles in under their sheets. The fun went on.

I believe that it was the first Sunday that my parents were away that Anna Mary had come down with one of her frequent bouts of tonsillitis. Eva had just started to date John Reesor so I offered to stay home from the Sunday night singing, because I knew that John probably wanted to bring Eva home afterward. However, she took her responsibility very seriously, insisting that she would stay, so I may as well go. Since I was only fourteen, I could not drive, so after chores, I left with Norman.

I had long admired Norman's handsome looks, his crooked smile and sparkling eyes, but he was my older sister's age, so I had no thoughts of anything between us. However, that night as we drove the ten miles to Uncle Levi's place, I thought, *Wouldn't it be nice if I was a little older? I think I could handle going out with such a handsome fellow!*

One night while my parents were still away, John did bring Eva home after a singing. Norman, Enos and I made up a bunch of confetti. Right above the couch on which they usually sat to visit, was an unused stove-pipe hole with a small register over it. We took the register off and were going to wait until they were seated then throw the confetti on them. One person watched out the window to see when they would leave the car and come to the house. The others lay on the floor above ready to fire the confetti. We waited and waited and waited. Finally, Ella said she was going to bed. Enos, Norman and I waited, lying on our stomachs beside the hole, our heads almost touching. We whispered and joked. Finally a bit before midnight, they came to the door, but John just said good-bye there and didn't even come in. The joke was on us.

Little did I know that the fun between us started a longing in Norman's heart. I thought he was a handsome guy, but he was Eva's age and I was four years younger. I had no idea that Norman felt he had discovered the girl he wanted to marry. He said afterward, that he realized that I was too young and he would have to wait for his "rosebud" to mature, but he thought it would be worth the wait.

There was good company in the church youth group. Every other week, we had a "singing" on Sunday evenings in the homes of different people. We sang hymns for at least an hour, from the Church Hymnal, visited a little while before going home. Sunday evenings were for courting. The boys who were dating would be first to go and get their car, stop at the sidewalk and walk to the lawn where the girls stood in a group in the summer, or to the door in the winter while the girls waited inside. There they would claim their girl. Sometimes it was a young fellow's first time. Any girls who were unclaimed would wait with bated breath until he sought out his desired and asked, "Could I see you home tonight?"

After that, the other boys would bring up their cars and wait until their sisters came out.

On alternate Tuesday nights, after there was no singing on Sunday night, we gathered again. Once more, there was an hour's worth of singing hymns, although those evenings we usually used a different hymnal –Life Songs # 1 or # 2, Favorite Hymns and others with more gospel and modern hymns. "Jesus Hold my Hand" and "Precious Memories" were just a few of those we sang. We didn't have a piano to sing along to, so we had leaders who had a tuning fork and would find the right key and start the hymn. Everyone joined in four-part harmony and there was true pleasure and inspiration as we sang. At the end of each hymn, anyone was welcome to call out the number of their favourite.

Occasionally we had an *Impromptu Night*. The organizers would make up a program, designating duets, trios or quartets to sing special numbers do a reading that was provided, or act out a scene for which the audience would guess what they were portraying. That was always fun. One night a foursome of young men were asked to sing a quartet. They, as often happened, retreated to another room to decide on their song. When they came back, they solemnly announced that they were going to sing "The Song of the Lost Sheep." They found the right pitch and each sounded the starting note for their part, and after a short pause, on four different notes they voiced "Baa-aaa-aaa!" They sat down, their faces solemn and straight—for awhile—until everyone burst out in laughter.

Afterward we played games of different kinds. The final game would be one that matched up partners, so that a girl and boy always sat together to eat refreshments. Quite often there were more girls than boys, so some boys were paired up with two girls!

Because we took turns to host those nights, there got to be quite a competition in what was served. Sandwiches, elaborate layer cakes, sponge or angel food cakes, pies, doughnuts—each girl tried to out-do the host before, and the young men were quite willing to taste-test each creation.

In the summer, at times, we played several innings of baseball before singing. One game we often played in the nice weather was *Walk a Mile*. Most of the group was paired up, boys on the left and girls on the right to walk together hand-in-hand, leaving several without partners. We'd begin walking down a country road or a back lane. Those without partners ran along-side the line, girls on the girl's side and boys on the boy's side. The runners decided who they'd like to walk with and tapped the shoulder of that person's partner and asked them to step aside. The displaced person had to let go of their partner and run ahead or fall behind until they found someone else they chose to walk with for a while. It was good exercise and also a way of getting to know each other better.

Winters brought skating parties. With the ice cleared either on Uncle Peter Nighswander's pond, or later at Uncle Willis Reesor's, or wherever we could find a good patch of ice, we all laced up our skates in the evening and headed for the outdoor rink. Boys and girls often skated together, although sometimes we skated alone or with our friends.

Each June, the young people from the Mahoning County area of Ohio, and those from the Markham, Ontario, area met at Niagara Falls. Usually the Ohio young people supplied a picnic lunch at noon, and the Markham young people provided the evening meal which we enjoyed in the picnic shelters which, at the time, were right across from the American Falls. We usually met by eleven a.m. then after lunch we took a short walk to an area where there was a ball diamond to enjoy a baseball game or two. After that we'd be free to visit some of the tourist spots before the evening meal. Again there would be free time, but usually by eight or so, some of the young men would ask a girl to walk with him for the evening.

I was utterly stunned when Norman asked me on my first outing year to walk with him. I was only fourteen and nervous as could be, but we strolled up and down the sidewalk bordering the chasm until the floodlights that illuminated the falls came on. About 10 p.m., we all gathered to head toward home.

My mother's comment, when told about it, "You're stepping out quite young. You'd better not make a habit of it yet."

I had expected a reprimand, because I knew I was younger than my parents would think suitable for dating.

It was two years before Norman asked me out on another date—shortly after my sixteenth birthday, after a singing at Grandpa

Nighswander's place. Since he couldn't ask to see me home, because I was already there, Norman came to our living room door afterward and asked if I would like to go for a drive with him. That began a time of very occasional dating.

## LOVE HITS A GLITCH

The spring just after I turned seventeen, Norman asked me if I would like to go steady. Again, I was scared, feeling that I was too young. In our group culture, going steady was a serious commitment. I had been quite happy with the occasional dates and knew I had to make a decision, but hardly knew what it should be. I tossed it about in my mind, and finally decided to write him a letter to tell him that I was not quite ready for steady dating. My main concern was that I not make it so strong that he wouldn't ask me on a date again. I did send the letter, but as soon as the mailman picked it up, I wished I could run after him and take it back.

The very next day, we got a call inviting us to a surprise birthday party at Alvin Baker's to celebrate Norman's twenty-first birthday. I hardly knew whether to go or not. I hoped he hadn't received my letter yet. I did go, and, lo and behold, when we played a game that chose partners for the evening snack like we usually did, Norman and I were teamed up! Everyone thought it was such a lovely coincidence — a real birthday gift for Norman. By that time I sensed that he had indeed received the letter. I wanted so much to tell him not to take it too seriously, but there was no private time at all, so I left without being able to say anything. Truth be told, I hardly knew what I would have said if I had the chance. It was a very uncomfortable evening. Much later, I found out that Norman was berating himself for having listened to his friend, urging him to ask me that question. He knew I was still too young and had planned to wait until I was at least eighteen, but he had let himself be influenced by another.

The next few weeks, I prayed that Norman would take me out one more time so we could at least talk about it—or maybe write me a letter to tell me how he felt about it. Had I known him better, I would have known that both were an utter impossibility. He hated writing letters and he did not talk about feelings!

Months passed, and I heard nothing. There was real tension when, many times we got each other for partners at our "singings." The more time that passed, the more I regretted having written the letter. During that period he took a visiting girl from Ohio home from a singing. A few months later after he had taken a trip to Ohio, I heard that he had accompanied a girl home again. I feared it was the same girl. I found out it wasn't the same one, but when I heard who it was, my heart sank, because I thought she was such a gracious and graceful girl with such an engaging smile and such inner beauty, I couldn't fathom him having any interest in me if there was a chance she would date him.

I agonized for days about that. Without being too forward, I tried to catch his eye at times to somehow get the message to him that I had repented of ever sending him the letter. I vividly remember the "outing" we had at Midland the next year. I ended up riding in a car beside his brother Menno, while Norman was driving the car ahead of us. How unjust it seemed. My heart was definitely a few car lengths ahead of me all the way up. All day, as we hiked around the trails, Norman seemed to deliberately avoid me. My heart ached for just one look of interest.

When Eva and John got married, I was bridesmaid. I rejoiced when I saw Norman at the church. The custom was for a receiving line to form at the back of the church. Everyone in attendance would shake the hand of everyone in the wedding party. I had it all planned that I would give Norman's hand an extra squeeze and not let go until he looked me in the eye, so I could signal to him my interest. Alas! He was recruited to help "Granny" Barkey out of the church, and of course he took the arm that was furthest away from me. The opportunity I had dreamt of for months walked right past my nose and on out of the church!

That winter, Gary came to work for Dad. He and Norman were good friends. One evening he began to grill me, plying me with questions as to why I had broken up with Norman. I didn't know if I should tell him or not, but finally I told him that when he asked me, I just felt too young at the time to go steady, but that I had been regretting for a long time the writing of that letter, and I would like Norman to know that I hadn't meant forever.

## LOVE GROWS AGAIN

It wasn't too long after my talk with Gary, following a Sunday evening singing at Uncle Levi's, we girls and women were waiting outside the door for the men to get the cars. Eva says that when Norman stopped the car and started up across the lawn, that I stepped out to meet him. I don't know if I did or not, but walking to the car with him and sitting beside him on the way out the lane felt like coming home—so right! My heart sang so loud I was afraid he could hear it.

The occasional dating started again, and this time, he seemed to be determined not to take it too fast! In fact, Gary warned me that if I ever wanted to hold hands or kiss, I would have to be the one to make the move, because Norman would be too scared to try it! I was determined that I would not take that initiative, but would wait for him.

One evening in our dating years, the youth group took one of those moonlight cruises on The *Cayuga,* a boat used to go from Toronto Harbour to Niagara-on-the-Lake and back. Occasionally at full moon, they started off at about eight o'clock and came back after midnight. By the time we got back to our place, it was almost two o'clock.

That's when the precious memory turned funny. Dad was always nervous about fires. I guess he was probably in a deep sleep when we drove in the lane, and somehow, our lights reflected on their bedroom wall. He woke with a start and hopped out of bed, sure the barn or garage was on fire. He came to the door just as Norman brought me there. Dad was still not fully awake, and began quizzing us about the fire. I assured him there was no fire, and urged him to return to the bedroom, because he was in his short little nightgown, not adequately covered for others to see.

"Huh? Huh?" he asked over and over, to all my reassurances. It took some persuasion and a bit of shoving. All of a sudden he was fully awake and aware, and may I say more than a little embarrassed because of the state of his attire. He turned and fled to the bedroom. I, too, was embarrassed, but joined Norman in laughter. Mom warned me, in the morning, never to mention it to Dad, because he was horrified at the thought of what he had done. Each remembrance of that incident never fails to bring laughter again. Poor Dad!

## CHAPTER 17

# A Mystery is Solved

> "Life is a succession of lessons
> which must be lived to be understood."
> —Ralph Waldo Emerson

During the winter of 1957, I began again to have pains in my upper abdomen that felt like the ones I had as a six- and seven-year-old. Any time I exerted myself in mowing lawn or tilling the garden, I'd have another spell. The doctor, when consulted, couldn't figure out what was wrong.

After a trip to Ohio with Gary and Myrna, Norman and I, and two others for a weekend, Gary complained on the way home that he wasn't feeling well. That night he ended up going to the hospital for an appendectomy. After a few days, Norman and I went to see him. While we were there, I began again to have pain. I chided myself for imagining things. I went home and to bed, but by two or three o'clock, I woke with such pain that I couldn't stand having even the cotton sheet over my stomach. At four, mom called the doctor who told me to take five aspirin and he would see me in the morning. I slept perhaps part of an hour and woke again in excruciating pain.

The doctor came at nine, as promised. By that time I couldn't bear to talk aloud, so when he felt my stomach, I could do no more than whisper, "Ow-ww!" He told us he didn't know what it was, since the tenderness was way too high for appendicitis, which he had suspected. In that day and age before ultrasound and modern diagnostic tools, the only option was exploratory surgery to find out what was bothering me. Dad was to take me to Scarborough General hospital.

Each undulation on the highway caused such extreme pain that I wanted to cry out, but couldn't because that caused even more pain. On arrival at the hospital, nurses began to prepare me for surgery, but before I got to the operating room, an accident case came in, and they came to give me a shot for pain and said they'd have to do my surgery later. Finally, by 9 p.m., my turn came. It was the next morning before I was very aware of my surroundings.

My dear Doctor Button talked to my mother after the surgery and apologized to her for not having taken me more seriously.

"We made the incision where her appendix should have been but couldn't find it. With exploration, we finally found it a good five inches above its normal place. There was so much scar tissue that we couldn't believe it was still intact. The little bit of normal tissue was so inflamed it burst on the way out." Dr. Button said. "Ruth must have been in a great deal of pain. I didn't consider her appendix as the source of her problem, because she didn't yell when I examined her abdomen, and the soreness didn't seem to be in the right place. The scar tissue indicated that she must have had many attacks in past years. I'm sorry we didn't discover sooner what was bothering her. She will probably be quite sore for a while, and we want to watch her carefully for any signs of infection."

Once again, I was an oddity. I did wonder why Dr. Button apologized to Mom instead of me! He did come to visit me frequently though. And the mysterious pain of my younger days was solved. It was the same kind of pain, and I became aware that I was fortunate that my appendix didn't burst way back then. I felt lucky to be alive.

While I was in the hospital, I learned that my roommate was an elderly woman from near Pickering. We developed quite a friendship. She was enamoured by Norman's good looks when he came to visit me. She almost swooned because she thought he was the spitting image of one of her favourite movie stars, James Garner. I was glad for Norman's every visit, but my roommate would have liked him to come every day.

One day, soon after surgery, when one of my favourite nurses was on duty, we had an incident that will always stay branded in my mind. She was a tiny bundle of energy and cheer. I was still quite sore, but she helped me turn over on my left side. She rolled the draw sheet right up to my back, tucked a fresh one under the mattress and rolled up the excess the same way. Gently, she helped me roll to my right side and went to the other side of the bed. There she discarded the used draw sheet and pulled the new one straight. She gripped it tight and pulled with all her might to get it taut—too tight—because the sheet tore and she flew to the wall behind her. She laughed and my roommate laughed. I smiled broadly and tried not to laugh because it hurt too much. I flattened my hands against my incision, fearing it would break.

"Laugh, laugh!" my nurse said in her distinct English accent, between her own outbreaks of hilarity. "Laugh until your stitches pop!"

I groaned in pain but couldn't help but laugh again.

I was in hospital ten days before coming home to further recuperate. It took a quite a while to get back to doing a normal day's work.

## CHAPTER 18

# Work Experience

"For in every adult there dwells the child that was,
and in every child there lies the adult
that will be."

—John Connolly,
*The Book of Lost Things*

For several years, Eva had been janitor at the public school at Altona. I soon inherited that job after quitting school. I now was making a grand salary of $20 a month regularly. Besides that income, I also had some day work. My first domestic job was at Bob and Marg Lewis' home. I felt very young and inexperienced at working out, but while Marg worked out in the field cutting cabbages and cauliflower, I stayed in the house with their two young boys, Keith and Jerry. They were probably four and two-and-a-half. Keith, especially, had a very active imagination and told me tales by the yard! Most of them were quite unbelievable, but lots of fun to listen to.

I was also responsible for cleaning the house, and sometimes beginning the meals, although Marg usually came in to help finish the preparations. I will always remember their vacuum cleaner. It was essentially a glorified dust pan. One had to sweep the floor with a broom, since the vacuum didn't have enough suction to pick up the dirt properly. After sweeping, one could usually suck up most of the pile with the vacuum cleaner. Working at the Lewis place turned out to be a good place to start, because they were very accepting and affirming and had a good sense of humour.

When I was fifteen, I worked for the first time at Albert and Annie Drudge's. It was my first time to actually be live-in help. I enjoyed living with a different family, and finding new ways to do familiar tasks. However, one day Annie presented me with one I felt was far beyond my capabilities. She brought me a piece of red broadcloth and one of Eileen's blouses, which was a favourite, and asked me to make an identical blouse.

At home, Eva liked to sew and was quite good at it. So although I had some experience, Eva usually did the more difficult parts. Sewing, at that point, was not one of my favourite activities. My employer, though, could not be told this, so I asked for the pattern. "Oh," she replied, "I don't have a pattern. You can just use the other blouse as a pattern."

That was a whole lot more than I thought I could handle, so I told her, "I don't think I can do that."

"Oh, sure you can," she replied. "I won't look and make you nervous. I'll go out to the kitchen to work."

"But I may need your help," I said.

"I'm not much of a sewer," she said, "You just go ahead."

"What if I make a mess of it and waste the material?"

"Oh, I'll forgive you," she said, "but I'm sure you won't!"

What was I supposed to do? I opened the fabric and held up the blouse. It was no simple pattern. It had long sleeves and wide buttoned cuffs. The bodice back extended to the front to make a yoke from which there were gathers in the blouse. The collar with a lace edging was elongated with a round part at the front and was fastened to a band with a button at the front.

I felt helpless! Again, I told Annie, "I just don't think I'm capable of it!"

She just told me to begin, and assured me again that I could do it.

Carefully I folded the fabric in half and laid the blouse on the material, trying to pin it so that the front would lay flat. Leaving extra for the seam allowance and the gathers, I began to cut. Piece by painful piece, I measured and measured and marked and cut. Finally I began to sew. Unbelievably, it came together. Annie often told me it was Eileen's favourite blouse and that she could hardly get it off her to wash it. To this day, I can't believe that I could do it. Even now, with much more experience behind me, I probably wouldn't try it again, but that experience taught me a lesson that I never forgot. Actually, I guess, it reinforced the lesson Eva taught me much earlier. You can accomplish much more than you think you are capable of, if you just try! Sometimes we are like eaglets; we need to be pushed out of our comfortable nests.

One of the most valuable experiences of working at Albert and Annie's place was the table conversation. Albert asked many questions concerning my faith and my opinions on different issues. He was genuinely interested in what I thought and encouraged me to think about things I would normally have pushed aside as too advanced for me to figure out. While living there, I had a bedroom to myself, so undisturbed, I could read some of the books he gave me to consider, and check it out with my Bible. It was a growing time.

Soon after I worked for the Drudges, for at least one year, I babysat Rod and Ruth Torrance's daughter, Julie, while Ruth taught guidance class at Markham High two afternoons a week. The work there wasn't difficult. Ruth usually had Julie fed and in bed for her afternoon nap by the time I came. All I needed to do was sit and read or write letters until she woke up perhaps a half hour before Ruth's return. I kept telling Ruth I could do cleaning or baking or mending for her while I waited, but she said my job was to look after Julie. Finally, she consented to let me lengthen some of Julie's dresses. Each day, when Ruth came home, she insisted that I stay to have a cup of tea and some goodies— and she also insisted on paying me for that extended time! I could scarcely believe it.

OUT OF THE ORDINARY

Part way through that year, Ruth's neighbour fractured her back. Ruth wondered if, once a week, I would go to their place and do some cleaning in the morning. The arrangement was that I'd work from 8-12, they would give me my lunch before I'd go over to the Torrance's in time for Ruth to leave by 12:45. I did a lot of cleaning in those four hours. I vacuumed, dusted and washed the floors throughout the whole house, and also house-cleaned one room each week. That meant taking down the curtains and washing them, vacuuming the papered walls, or washing the painted ones as well as ceilings and washing the woodwork and the windows. Their house was one of those tall ones with at least ten-foot ceilings, so it meant climbing up and down ladders. The afternoon of ease was welcome those days.

The first thing I did after beginning to earn money was join a Christian book club. The books that I bought through that club became well-loved friends which I read dozens of times. Some of them were life changing. Many of them were Christian fiction, but the biographies and autobiographies, and stories of missionaries impressed me deeply. They called me to deeper commitment. I especially remember Elisabeth Elliott's books, *Through Gates of Splendor, Shadow of the Almighty, The Dayuma Story* and Catherine Marshall's books, *A Man Called Peter, Beyond Ourselves, To Live Again* and *Something More* among them. There were also the stories of Paul Brandt's work in Africa and Doctor Ida Scudder's in India, whose selfless commitment I will never forget.

Many of those books changed my life as I read more contemporary biographies and autobiographies of people expending their lives for the good of others, and in service to God and their fellow human beings. Dreams beyond my everyday routine filled my mind with possibilities.

Later on, I worked at the Drudge's again, when I was probably around eighteen or nineteen. Theirs was a nice place to work. I enjoyed the children, and my own room at night was a luxury I didn't enjoy at home. Albert continued to discuss things at meal time and urge me to study further. That time, besides housecleaning and sewing, I did a lot of painting and papering which was a job I also enjoyed.

At the time, Ken had finished elementary school, and in spite of his father's wish that he continue with high school; he was at home, but hardly old enough to help all that much with the farming. One day, Albert and Annie went with Elmer and Stella Reesor to Kitchener for a meeting. They said they would be back by chore time which usually was around 4:30.

When that time came, they weren't back yet, so I suggested Ken could maybe go and start the milking. He wasn't much enthused about it, so I told him that as long as he knew which cows were milking, or if there were any being treated for mastitis or something, I would help him, and perhaps we could surprise his parents. That got him excited. Everyone got ready to go to the barn, Eileen and Donna included. The more we got done, the more we hurried to see if the chores could be done by the time Annie and Albert got back.

We had the milking machines on the last cows when we saw them drive in the lane after six o'clock. Albert rushed into the house, and in record time came almost running into the barn. We were not disappointed in the surprise he registered upon finding the milking and the feeding done.

"Did you know which cows were being treated for mastitis?" Albert asked, his voice full of apprehension.

"Of course," Ken answered, pointing. "That one and that one."

"I didn't know you were that observant," Albert said with new respect and pride in his son.

After that, I often helped with the milking as well as the house work. I didn't mind, except after some late nights, because I liked working in the barn.

Throughout the years, I helped Elva and Harvey Nighswander a lot. Their children were almost like a second family to me. I loved every one of them. I helped Elva with house work, and I enjoyed visiting with her. As a teen, I could often share issues with her that I couldn't with my own parents. Even those things that I did talk over with my parents, I still found helpful to get another adult opinion, other than from my parents. My relationship with Elva was a very helpful one, and one that I treasure.

Rosalie was a conscientious little child, taking her role, as eldest of the family, with all seriousness. She was just a bit older than my youngest sister, Martha. She and I had some good times together, and I often felt that as she grew older, I was able to be to her and Cynthia, too, what their mother had been to me. It was very satisfying to me, for I enjoyed them immensely. It helped me stay in touch with young people. Cynthia, as a little girl, was such a loving person, greeting each new sibling with a charming mixture of awe and delight and bushels of love. We developed a good relationship which grew with the years.

I remember Daniel, especially for his imaginative stories. One time when he was only three or four, he told me of an amazing adventure he had out in their orchard. He killed a bear! He went into great detail of how big the bear was, and that he moved carefully, closer and closer, and then caught him. According to Daniel, he chopped the bear's head off, then he chopped his feet off, then he took all the feathers off!

Elva suffered from Meniere's disease when Ruth Ann was little, so Ruth Ann and John lived for a time with Albert and Norma Smith, a young couple from our church, and we helped quite a bit with Rosalie, Daniel, Cynthia and Mary Lois.

Many times I gave up free evenings to do Elva's laundry. She had much more than she could manage, and I felt for her. Sometimes people were critical of her instead of helpful or kind in their ways of helping. I loved being with her, and doing what I could to give her a bit of relief.

At different times I worked for other women doing house work. For six or eight weeks in July/August of 1959, I worked for Kees and Ella Koster (Norman's sister) over the time that David was born. Keith was just nine months old at the time. They lived in an old house just south of Maple. There was no running water or inside bathroom facilities. The bedroom upstairs had no screens and got exceedingly hot. However, there were all kinds of starlings and sparrows around, some of which nested between the outer and inner walls, and I did not want to risk having them fly in, so my window was opened only a crack. Even then, the flies would get in and buzz around my face as soon as the sun came up. Finally, I brought a screen from home so that I could get my rest.

They had a big garden, and we canned all kinds of vegetables that summer, since they had no freezer either. I sometimes thought I would look like a green bean before the summer was over. There was one tap at the far end of the basement, to which we attached a hose. The steps down to the cellar were more like a ladder than steps. Each time we needed water to blanch the vegetables, I had to run down, open the tap, come up to check when the big pails and tubs were full and then rush down to shut the tap before they overflowed. The same procedure applied to wash day. After David arrived, there was a double set of diapers to wash two or three times a week.

The Sunday after David was born, I took Keith home with me so that Kees could go to see Ella in the hospital. Norman came in the afternoon and got both of us and took us back to Maple. After putting Keith to bed, we sat visiting in the kitchen. Kees came home and, after a few words, went to bed too.

The next morning Kees asked, "How do you get Norman to talk that much? I couldn't hear what you said, but I heard Norman's voice and I've never heard him so talkative."

I was surprised, because I thought I did much of the talking, but I was pleased that Norman said more to me than most people.

It was a long and busy summer, but I enjoyed Keith and David and the chance to get to know my future sister and brother-in-law. I had told them my time would be volunteer service, but the last day I was there, they presented me with a beautiful reversible blanket, green on one side and yellow on the other.

When I exclaimed, "I just can't get over it!" (meaning my surprise) Kees commented, "You aren't supposed to get **over** it, you are to get under it!"

## CHAPTER 19

# *Love Declared*

> "We fell in love, despite our differences,
> and once we did, something rare
> and beautiful was created."
> —Nicholas Sparks,
> *The Notebook*

Many evenings, Norman and I would go for moonlight walks, or sit on the couch in the living room just visiting. I, in my love of the outdoors, mowed the lawn underneath the willow tree and moved the old porch bench underneath, with us in mind. We did use that on occasion.

When I was working at John and sister Eva's at the time of Miriam's birth, Norman asked if we could see each other regularly, every two weeks. By that time, I would gladly have made it every week, but was happy for that much.

Every now and then Gary and Myrna and Norman and I would do things together. One night the young people in the Elmira area invited us to come up for a night of skating at Amos Martin's tile yard. The four of us travelled together in Norman's Dad's Ford car. We had a lovely time, except for the fact that a young fellow, helping to serve coffee, spilled a cup on my wool skirt. It was hot when it hit my skirt, but on the way home, the heater in the car quit working, and by the time we arrived home, my skirt was almost frozen stiff! We had fun anyway, and my heart was definitely warm, if my legs weren't. The following Sunday, Norman's sister Martha presented me with a hankie I had inadvertently left in the car —all freshly laundered and ironed.

Eventually the time did come when Norman and I saw each other every Sunday night. By that time, Norman was working at Alan Wideman's at Mongolia. They and we always drove to the singings together, so that meant when we had week-night doings, we also saw each other then. Bonus!

As the months and years passed, Enos began to think it was time we were engaged. He kept asking and prodding me to tell him if we were. In that time and setting, in our circles, it was kept a secret until very close to the wedding. So, of course, I didn't tell him one way or the other—although I might have if we were. One evening as Norman and I sat on the couch together, Enos came into the living room and asked, right then and there, if we were engaged. I was highly embarrassed, as Norman hadn't asked the question, and I was afraid he would feel put on the spot. (I should have known better. Norman didn't embarrass easily and for sure couldn't be pushed into much.) Enos told Norman that he had taken the hubcaps off of his car, and when we told him 'yes' or 'no,' he would give them back. He finally went off to bed. I don't recall what we talked about after that, but it didn't force Norman to propose.

The next day, I began a search for the hubcaps. I don't remember how long it took, but I did find them in the rafters above the 'boiler' house behind the garage, where we made maple syrup and home-made soap. I took them into my closet and hid them until the next week. I returned them to Norman and he put them back on his car. However, for weeks, Enos asked us the same question, and told Norman that he would get the hubcaps when he answered the question. Finally, Norman told him that the hubcaps had been back on the car for a long time. The laugh was on Enos, but Norman still didn't propose!

My twentieth birthday was coming up. I had been working hard, for Mom had been experiencing what I now believe was an emotional breakdown. I had been trying to take the pressure off of her. Eva came up two days before my birthday and asked if she could take me home with her for the night. Mom seemed to reluctantly agree and said I must come home first thing in the morning. I almost felt guilty in going, but it was a lovely treat. I remember settling into their spare bed in the evening, much earlier than usual. I didn't have my alarm clock, so when I awoke in the morning, it was definitely past mother's 'first thing in the morning!' It was 8:30. I rushed to get dressed, thinking I would just have to skip breakfast and get home on the double. Eva told me to relax, she had called Mom and got her permission for me to go with them to Weston's to get a load of feed. I couldn't believe my ears. Eva assured me it was all right. I still felt that Mom would be upset, but we went.

It turned out that John had a few more stops to make, and it was 4:30 or 5 before we got home. By that time, I was really tense. I thought Mom would be extremely upset. I didn't want her to have a set-back. Eva seemed to be putting me off even then. I couldn't understand that she didn't comprehend why I had to rush home—she knew how Mom could be. Finally I got away and raced home, dreading what I may find. I came in the door to find the house all clean, good smells coming from the kitchen, and the table set with our good dishes for four more than our usual setting. I asked who was coming and what was up. They said I had come home too early and that I would have to wait to see. I thought of several possibilities, but none seemed to fit the number. Soon after, Eva, John and Miriam came in the lane—but that was only three more. The mystery was solved when Norman drove in. I was extremely surprised.

Mom had made one of her rare birthday cakes for the occasion and it had 20 candles on it. I blew but missed two. She immediately informed me that meant it would be two years yet until I would be married. I felt like saying "Sh-hh" because I had sensed the last several Sunday nights that Norman might be working up his courage to ask an important question. I hoped her statement wouldn't scare him away.

After everyone else left, Norman gave me a birthday gift. I was quite pleased but a bit embarrassed to find that I had ordered my gift the week before when I had been telling him about trying to find the kind of slippers I wanted, and how difficult it was to find my size. Mom usually wanted us to find such items on sale, and by the time sales came around, my size was not available. I loved the slippers though and wore them for many years. The warmth they gave me was not all in the material, but in the knowledge of the giver who cared enough to find just what I wanted.

Quite a bit later in the evening, Norman asked if I thought Mom would insist on keeping me to the pronouncement of the candle incident. With that, he asked me to marry him. I answered with a joyous "yes!"

The next morning, in fact, the whole next day, I felt as though my feet never did quite touch the ground. When I told Mom, she said, "Well, he'll have to ask Dad if he can have you!"

I was astonished. "Oh, Mom! You can't really mean that. Norman's so shy. It would be very hard for him to have to do that."

"If he really wants you, he will do it," she insisted. "That's what will have to happen before we go ahead with any wedding plans."

I really dreaded having to tell Norman that, but no argument changed Mom's opinion. So I did tell him. I don't know if Norman's heart dropped to his shoes or not, but he did ask and, of course, they said, "Yes."

## CONTINUED WORKING EXPERIENCE

That December, I worked at Elmer and Stella Reesor's when Edward was born. The first morning I was there, I woke up at 6:30, and jumped out of bed, thinking I must have missed my call. I went to the bathroom, but all was dark—no sign of anyone! I hardly knew what to do, so I went back to my room and lay down a bit. By seven o'clock, I thought something must be wrong, I couldn't conceive that any household sleeping that late! Finally, at seven thirty, I heard that someone was up. I went downstairs.

Elmer looked up in shock. "What are you doing up so early?"

"I didn't think to ask last night, what time I should be up."

"I still have over an hour's work in the barn. We don't have breakfast until eight-thirty, so from now on, you don't have to get up until at least quarter to eight."

What a decadent lifestyle it seemed to me! But I must say I got to rather enjoy it! I could get up much later than usual, have a nice long time to spend in prayer and reading the Bible, and still get downstairs early, according to them. I treasured the time working with that family. Elmer was lots of fun, joking about things that happen, as was Stella, who found joy in just everyday living. I saw a great deal of love between them, and they seemed to enjoy me as much as I enjoyed them. They had three older children: Joanna, James and Eugene. The children, too, endeared themselves to me, and I was glad to include them in the cooking and baking that I did. They were always anxious to help out and I usually had a chair on each side of me while they took turns stirring or doing little jobs.

Norman brought me back there after the weekends. One cold winter night, we walked out to the end of their long lane in the bright moonlight. On the way, we talked about where we would like to go on our honeymoon. When we got back, we weren't quite finished, so we sat in the car a while yet before he saw me to the door. The next morning at the breakfast table, Elmer asked, "So did you and Norman decide last night where to go on your honeymoon?"

I looked up in surprise, wondering if he had heard our conversation. It was always a tradition to keep weddings a secret until three weeks before when the banns were read aloud in church. I wasn't that much in favour of the tradition, and thought although I wouldn't advertise it, neither would I keep from sharing the news, if it was appropriate. I made a decision to be honest.

"How did you know what we were talking about? In fact, we couldn't decide whether to go to the East or West coast. Which would you recommend?"

Elmer laughed, thinking I was leading him on.

"Seriously, which do you think would be best?"

He just laughed all the more, but finally said, "If you really want to know, I would recommend the West coast." I could tell he didn't believe that I really meant it.

In February of 1960, I worked at Cecil and Ruth Reesor's when Norma was born. There, too, I enjoyed playing with the children, Arthur and Joyce, when the work was done. I remember allowing them to walk up the front of me while I held their hands, then holding their feet as I let them down over my back and to the floor again. They wanted more and more. They also liked when I read to them.

I did all the cooking when Ruth was away and when she came home. Of course there was washing and cleaning to do too. I also did some sewing and mending. Ruth said that I worked so quickly that she hardly knew how to keep the jobs coming fast enough. I think that was the first time I had been told that. At home, I usually had the impression I never was quite fast enough.

That February and March, we had severe winter storms five weekends in a row. Norman's parents celebrated their 30th anniversary that year on March 11. My parents celebrated 25 years of marriage on the 12th. Both weekends we barely made it, but the night Enos came to pick me up from Cecil and Ruth's, we got stuck on the sideroad just west of Dickson's Hill. We had to walk to Stuart Watson's to get help. I stayed there until they pulled the little Volkswagen to their lane. Once we got to the highway, we made it home. After church had been cancelled three weeks in a row, and the storm lasting all weekend, the fourth Sunday afternoon, the storm calmed down mid-afternoon. I was hoping Norman would be able to make it that evening. About four-thirty, he came driving in the lane and I rejoiced. He had taken his sisters to the Uxbridge Hospital where they worked and asked if I'd come to his house for supper then he'd bring me home after. I was very happy to do so.

In late March, Norman, his sister Martha, Kathryn Reesor and I went to Maschouche, Quebec, where Harold and Pauline Reesor were situated. They were also expecting their third child and were moving from their rented apartment to a house they had bought. I stayed there two or three weeks to help them pack and paint their new dwelling. That was a wonderful experience. I helped them get some work accomplished, but I got much more in return. I got to know a wonderful, dedicated couple and their two little charmers, Marc and Rachel. Harold and Pauline also took time to show me around the countryside a bit and took me on Sundays to fellowship with the Martin family and a few others in Montreal. Mom and Dad and Anna Mary came to pick me up with Enos' VW. We stopped at Notre Dame Cathedral on the way back and I drove, desperately hoping we would get home in time for the singing that was being held that Tuesday night. By that time, I was extremely anxious to see Norman again.

I shall always be glad I had the opportunity of working for other women in their homes. I learned much about different ways of doing familiar tasks. In those homes I was affirmed for my abilities, which meant so much to me, since I always sensed that I fell short of my mother's expectations in the house-keeping department. Stella seemed to feel I kept up with the work and got a lot done in a day. She also appreciated the time I took to play with and talk with the older children, and I enjoyed the love I saw between Elmer and Stella and the joy they took in one another. Ruth was amazed at how few dishes there were to wash after meals because I washed as I cooked, or at least rinsed well. These were big boosts to my self-confidence as I looked forward to keeping house for Norman and me. And at Harold's, I found a woman who knew far less than I did about cooking and sewing—and her husband still loved her deeply. I adored them too, and dreamt of having such an equal and open relationship with Norman in the near future.

In between those jobs, I worked hard at home. Mom had gone through a rough time in the few years before, and even though I thought I was doing my best, I often felt guilty that I wasn't able to accomplish all she thought we needed to get done. I was determined to give her my best before I left home. That whole time, when I was home, my alarm clock was set for five a.m. Monday mornings, I tried to have the washing well on the way before she got up, and all done by breakfast. Often I was able to even have some of the ironing done too, if the weather co-operated with a nice warm breeze. We worked hard at getting all the quilts done that Mom thought a girl needed before she got married. We quilted three in the month of January alone. That summer, we decided to have Ada Diller come to do some sewing for the girls' dresses for the wedding. On those Monday mornings, I was up at four and had quite a bit of work done by the time I left at seven to pick up Ada.

Bedtime didn't come until 10:30 or 11 p.m., so they were long days. It was a tradition to have fancy aprons for the waitresses at wedding receptions. I wanted to sew them myself early that summer. As I sat sewing, my leg swelled, beginning at my ankle and on up to my knee. Usually the swelling was down in the morning, but there was pain in my ankles. By evening, the swelling appeared again. I went to the doctor, and he couldn't seem to locate or name the problem. He even injected cortisone, a painful procedure in itself, however, nothing seemed to help all that much. I started wondering if I was bringing defective goods to Norman as a bride. Sometimes the pain was bothersome enough that I tried to pick sit-down jobs, which frustrated Mom, I'm afraid.

After supper dishes were done, things cleaned up, and the air a little cooler, I often worked outside on the flower beds, cleaning up corners and trimming up the edges of the lawn, until after dark. I enjoyed the out-of-doors so much. We chose to have the reception on the front lawn, so I wanted everything to be in tip-top order, and this gave double pleasure to my work,

One of the things I baked for Elmer and Stella when I worked there was their Christmas cake. I really liked the recipe that Stella used. That summer when I was ready to make the fruit cake for our wedding, I went to ask Stella if I could borrow her recipe, telling her that I thought it was about time to get one made. She looked a little curious as to why I would need a Christmas cake recipe in July, then all of a sudden, the reason dawned on her. Her eyes began to sparkle and that jolly laugh came from deep inside.

"Really?" she asked. "I'd be honoured to share the recipe!"

"Do you remember how Elmer asked about Norman and me making honeymoon plans? Well, we really had been talking about our honeymoon that night, but you just wouldn't believe me when I told you so."

"We thought you wouldn't have said it if you really had been talking about it! I guess the moral of the story is that tradition can sometimes blind us to reality."

My poor mother was still not over her nervous breakdown, so the wedding preparation weighed heavily on her. In her zeal to be a model housekeeper, she wanted the whole house from top to bottom to be spick and span. She worried that she hadn't trained me well enough in housekeeping and openly expressed her fear that Norman would be disappointed in me. That didn't do much to bolster my self-esteem. Much as I tried to rationalize her thinking, I couldn't just forget it entirely.

In all the wedding preparations, I also wanted to prepare myself for the relationship that would bring joy and satisfaction to us. The physical side of marriage was a mystery to me. My parents did not talk about sex! As our wedding approached, I talked about it with Eva, asking if she had received any information from our parents. She said there was no chance that I would get any direction from that source. Myrna and Garry, who had been married that May, gave us a book recommended by a friend from Ohio. That gave me more facts than I knew what to do with, but I still wanted to give Mom and Dad the chance to provide me with something, so I asked Mom one morning, when we were alone, if she could tell me something about what to expect, or if she could get me a book to read. She told me that they, too, had wanted to start their marriage informed, so Dad had bought a book. She said she would ask him and he would get me something to read.

The last few weeks were extremely busy. The Wednesday before the wedding, Norman and I went to Barrie to book a motel for our wedding night. It was situated on the north shore of Lake Simcoe, and with full moon coming up, promised to have a nice view. On our return home, I had a nice surprise. Enos, who had spent the summer helping Northern Lights Gospel Mission at Pikangikum, had returned.

Since he came home after the family had retired for the night, he had removed our wedding gifts from the spare bed and slipped into it for the night. Before going to my own room, I went in to view the wedding gifts and was rather shocked to find him there. Even though his face was covered with infected mosquito bites, he looked pretty good to me.

The Friday before the big day was a long one. We went out to the Almira Church to have a so-called rehearsal that evening. Without the minister present, I'm not sure how effective it was, but at least we could run through how we envisioned it. It was late by the time Esther and I knelt beside the bed to say our prayers. I couldn't wait to fall into bed, but Esther wanted to prolong our last night together. She began to cry, thinking of the room without a sister to share it. I, trying to coax her out of her sadness, began to make light of it by joking and getting her laughing. We ended up almost rolling on the floor. Comic relief, probably!

# Our Wedding

> "Happy marriages begin
> when we marry the ones we love,
> and they blossom when
> we love the ones we marry."
> —**Author Unknown**

September 3, 1960, the day of our wedding dawned warm and sunny. Aunt Anna, cousin Margaret, and Norma Smith came to help with the last minute preparations for the meal. At eleven o'clock, they sent me upstairs to have a bath and to prepare myself for the wedding. For once I filled the bathtub and had a nice soak.

When all was ready, the family left a little earlier, and Norman came for me. Perhaps Menno and Esther were there too; I can't remember that detail. I do know that Norman asked if we could have prayer before we left for the church, and I know how thankful I was for that request.

As we walked up the aisle, toward the front of the church, things seemed a little unreal. The service we had carefully planned began well. The hymns we had chosen felt right. The time came for the ceremony, and we were called to face the bishop. All went as planned, and we kissed each other to seal our vows, even though the bishop had not invited us to do so. We waited for the song we had requested to be sung to finish that important part of the service before we sat.

"You may be seated," said the bishop.

We tried to signal with our eyes, "No, not yet."

"You may be seated," he repeated.

Again we waited, hoping the song leader would begin as instructed.

"You may be seated." Finally, after the third order, we sat.

Some of our friends, not knowing the plans, teased us that we were too enamoured with the idea of being married to hear the bishop's instructions!

The bishop continued with his little time of instruction that had been planned to come after the song, then announced both songs together. I was extremely disappointed, because we had carefully planned it to be meaningful as possible within the boundaries set by the church. We had cleared it all with the bishop before—all, including having the song sung while we were still standing. He, perhaps, was a little reluctant to do it thus, but agreed. I felt let down. I guess part of me wanted our ceremony to be a bit different. We had first hoped to have a quartet sing, but that wasn't allowed, so we had thought this would do.

However, we were pronounced 'Man and Wife' and happily walked down the aisle, hand in hand. As we neared the back of the church, I saw tears in Norman's eyes, and his chin began to quiver. How touched I was to see the depth of his feeling. People streamed past us wishing us well. It was an awesome time!

I had asked Elsie Jones, our sweet, soft-spoken neighbour, to take pictures. I wondered why she wasn't outside the church to take them. We found out later that she had come to the church door with her camera, and someone had told her she couldn't take pictures at the church. They, of course, meant inside, but she, being unfamiliar with our old-order Mennonite practices, felt embarrassed and left. She was at the house to take photos there.

We had tables set up in the front lawn. The head table was just in front of the verandah, with smaller tables and chairs scattered across both levels of the lawn. As we sat down, I wondered if it would be too hot in the sun for those seated there. Just as we began our main course, a dark cloud loomed in the northwest. Soon the wind began to pick up, and it felt as though it was blowing across an ice field. People began to search out more sheltered places and ask for sweaters or blankets. Most of the older people moved up on the verandah or into the house. It was quite cold before we were finished, not quite how we had envisioned the occasion. Who would have thought it would turn that cold on the third day of September?

Mark had been born to Eva and John just a bit more than three weeks before, so Eva spent some of the time in the house with him. One of our poor guests got so cold she ended up with pneumonia. We were really sorry about that, yet we were blissful in spite of the weather.

During the reception, Enos, John Drudge, Mary Ann and Elizabeth Baker sang several numbers. It did enhance the day.

After a suitable time, we changed into our "going away" clothes and left with not much fanfare and barely a flake or so of confetti. Dad and Mom Smith had just bought a brand new Ford Falcon, and they generously let us take it on our honeymoon. Perhaps most of the confetti that was thrown landed in that car, and some of it stayed as long as they had it.

## OUR HONEYMOON

Finally, at almost nine o'clock, we left to head towards Barrie. It was a long day, with emotions running high. We were two rather young and naive newlyweds, and so sleep did not come easy. Finally we sat closely on chairs looking out over a moonlit lake, and there I fell asleep with my head on my new husband's shoulder. Tenderly, he led me back to bed. I thrilled to wake up several times through the night to find his arm still around me.

Our rising did not come with the sun! It was 10:30 a.m.—an unheard of hour in my thinking— before we were ready to leave the motel to cook our breakfast at a park beside the lake. To my abashment, I had forgotten to pack an egg turner. I was quite proud of the way I could fry an egg to perfection—over easy. I tried with a spoon, but ended up breaking the yoke. How humiliating! However, Norman seemed to enjoy them anyway. Perhaps it was because we sat so closely on the same side of the picnic table that his mind was elsewhere!

That evening saw us at New Liskeard, with a room at the Wheel-Inn Motel—at about five o'clock. We cooked supper beside the lake and turned in early. The next morning there was frost on the table at Kap-Kig-Iwan Provincial Park when we wanted to make breakfast.

"Why don't you just scramble the eggs, if you don't have a turner?" Norman asked. Henceforth, eggs fixed by scrambling them directly in the pan became 'Honeymoon eggs' forevermore.

We spent our next night at Hearst. There was no park or place to fix our supper, so we pulled into a lane nearby that led into the forest and made do. We spent the night at a little motel on the outskirts of the town. The family at the restaurant where we ate our breakfast was sending their children off on their first day of the new term. In spite of them speaking French, we ascertained that for the youngest, it was her first day ever, and she was quite nervous.

Kakabeka Falls was a lovely spot and we found our motel right next to that tourist place. We spent some time at the falls, holding hands and revelling at the togetherness we felt. The falls were secondary attractions.

At Kenora the following night, we found a cozy cabin on a cliff beside the lake. We decided to rent a rowboat and go out for a bit. It seemed we hadn't gone far, but when we turned to go back to shore, the wind had come up and was driving us away. It took a lot of rowing on Norman's part to get us back—probably three times as long to get back as it had to go out. We were glad to get our feet on land again. That night, in a mood of domestic bliss, I made a potato soup on the stove in our cabin, which pleased my new husband. I didn't realize just how much he loved potatoes, but they sure went over well.

After looking around Winnipeg a little bit, we headed on west to Portage La Prairie for the night where we found a nice little park and we cooked our supper there. We always stopped early enough to have a leisurely evening meal and relaxation.

Through the flat prairies, we travelled a little longer that next day to reach Regina. There weren't many accommodation options until we reached the city.

We spent quite a while trying to find a motel but finally had to take one that cost a whopping $10.00 a night! That was the most we had paid and it seemed unreasonably expensive. We asked if there was a park somewhere where we could cook supper. They said there was one at the Parliament Buildings but didn't think there were picnic tables there. Again, we drove around looking, but couldn't find anything. We thought we'd drive out to the country again and park in a laneway to a field or something. When we opened the car doors, it didn't take us long to discard that idea. To our horror, the ground was covered with grasshoppers—road and all. They even jumped on the car as soon as we stopped, and on us when we stepped out. We bought our supper that night.

During that time of searching, I noticed that every time I got out of the car, people would stare at me. They probably had never seen anyone in Mennonite garb. It made me feel very self-conscious. Although I loved being Norman's wife, I had the fleeting thought that if I was a man, I wouldn't be noticed with such curiosity.

We had planned to go to the Duchess, Alberta, church on Sunday, so we found a small motel in Brooks, just a little south of Duchess. I guess it was a Saturday night in cowboy country. There was a bar beside the motel and wild parties going on in the parking lot much of the night. We even had one inebriated person try our door. We didn't get too much sleep that night, but we did find the church and we had let Johnny Groves, former neighbours of Norman`s, know we were coming, so we had lunch with them. That was an interesting visit. We got to know their children too. Their oldest, Gordon, was six going on twenty! He was quite a talker. He repeated several times, "In ten years I'll be sixteen, then I can get my license. I can hardly wait!"

When he was told that Norman had grown up right across the road from his Grandpa Grove, he got a bright idea.

"I'll get packed and go to Grandpa's with you."

"They're on their honeymoon, Gordon," his father reminded him. "They're not even going straight home from here. They're going further west yet."

"That's okay with me," Gordon said, but we tried to let him down gently.

That afternoon, John's mother-in-law, Mrs. Lauver, called and insisted we come there for supper and the night. She wouldn't take 'no' as an answer. When we got there, she had invited another daughter and her husband, as well as a neighbour to share supper. The neighbour had come to Alberta as a young man when it still was the 'wild west.' He told us all kinds of stories. We weren't sure we should believe all of them.

The son-in-law, Kenneth Torkleson, asked me, "What was your maiden name?"

"I was a Nighswander," I told him.

He broke out in laughter and kept at it for a long time as though it was the funniest name he ever heard. I was a little insulted. I thought a man with a name like Torkleson had no right to laugh at Nighswander.

The next morning we headed first to Calgary where Norman fulfilled one of his dreams—he purchased a ten-gallon hat, which he enjoyed wearing. I'll never forget our first glimpse of the mountains from there. At first I thought I was seeing things—that it must just be a cloud formation on the horizon, but no, there were mountains in the distance. We couldn't believe how far we still had to drive until we finally reached them. Several times, we stopped so Norman could use the binoculars he had purchased to bring on our trip. We found a motel right in Banff National Park and went hiking on a trail on a mountain just south of town before we retired for the night. The next day we went to visit beautiful turquoise Lake Louise.

In a park with plenty of picnic tables near that lake, we decided to cook our supper. Norman got the camp stove going and then said he was going to the men's facilities. I was cooking vegetables and frying meat when several large birds lit on the branches of a tree right above the picnic table. Further and further down toward the table they came. I tried to shoo them away, but they were quite bold. I was getting increasingly nervous, because I had a phobia about birds in close confines. All of a sudden one dropped down on the handle of the pan. The bird was too heavy for it and the pan flipped to the ground. Several more birds joined the first to eat the meat that had spilled and then congregated on the table. They were too close for comfort. I turned to retreat to the car. To my horror, we had left the car door open and there were several more of them sitting on the open door. I screamed, "Norman! Come quick."

From the facilities, Norman heard the desperation and fear in my voice and ran, expecting to see a bear after me. I doubt whether a bear would have produced more terror in me, but my dear husband didn't know about my phobia, so he laughed as he chased the birds away! I didn't think it was a laughing matter. As soon as the birds left the car, I got in and shut the doors. Norman had quite a time getting all the birds to leave. I can't remember if we actually ate there or not, but I know I was shaken, and Norman probably wondered what kind of a woman he married. I later found out those birds were Canada Jays.

In spite of, and perhaps because of the trauma at the park, our cabin at Radium Springs provided another opportunity to learn to know each other better as we increasingly became more intimate.

From Radium Springs we turned down to Montana and to Yellowstone Park where we were treated to a view of the grizzly bears. We had reserved a motel room in West Yellowstone. The owner wondered if we'd like to go to the town dump to see the grizzly bears. He said there was a gentleman who guided the tourists so they would be safe. I was a bit fearful, but both of us thought it would be an adventure, so we put in some time in our motel room waiting for the tour to begin at dusk. As we gathered in front of the motel, we were given strict instructions about how to proceed. Several cars followed the guide. We had been told to park fairly close together about four or five feet from the rim of the dump. The guide constantly shone his floodlight toward the dump, to the sides, and to the rear of us. Before long, he whispered, "There they come—over the far end of the dump."

A female came first, followed by a cub. Several others came from the far side, and a huge male lumbered over the edge, flattening large gallon cans and everything else with each step. Nosing around to find tasty morsels, he made his way to the drop, right in front of our feet. Someone took a flash picture which made him raise his massive head. He was not more than three feet from us. We had been warned to go to our cars immediately if the signal was given, and to leave as fast as possible. I thought we should run when he raised his head and seemed so close, but he soon lost interest and went on with his scavenging. It is an experience we'll never forget, but it was perhaps more dangerous than we realized as well. Not too many years after we were there, someone was hurt in just such a tour, and the tours were ended.

We saw Old Faithful gushing on its regular schedule. We just happened to stand beside Norman Maust and his family. He was the director of a choir from Virginia that sang for the Mennonite Hour radio program and we recognized him from some of their visits to Wideman's Church.

From Yellowstone, we headed east again, through clouds in the high mountain ranges, slept in Billings, Montana, then travelled through rain to Wasta, South Dakota. That day we couldn't cook our own meal but ate at a snack bar. Because we could find no motel, we slept in a vacant apartment a garage owner consented to rent for a night. We spent a night in Minnesota then the next night at our friend's, Norman and Marion Wenger, in Indiana before we headed back to Ontario.

## CHAPTER 21

# Home Again to Married Life

> Being in love is a wonderful feeling,
> but being loved and appreciated in return
> can be the most wonderful experience
> that can happen to your life.
> —**Cathy Bustos**

We stopped in at Norman's folks on the way home, arriving an hour or so before supper.

"Guess I'd better add potatoes to the pot." His mom reached for the bag and got out at least a half dozen.

"Oh, we haven't been eating that much, so you don't have to do too many more," I said in my naivety.

"If you think that, maybe I still know your husband better than you do," she said quietly.

I was a little hurt by that, but tried to let it go. She was proved right when I saw the amount of potatoes Norman consumed.

Coming home gave us a rather weird feeling. We had become a unit while we were away. Our apartment at Allan Wideman's wasn't completed, so we slept in Grandma Nighswander's spare room the first few weeks, but we didn't really belong there. In the early morning, Norman left to do chores and I went down a little later to do painting in the downstairs of our apartment. Some evenings we would eat supper at Allan's, sometimes at my parents, and occasionally at Norman's parents.

The first night we ate with Allan and Elizabeth, she made fried potatoes. Allan helped himself first and then handed the dish to Norman. I thought he was going to empty the dish and felt almost horrified at the amount he was taking. However, there were lots for Elizabeth and me yet. In that moment, I concurred with his mother and realized that Elizabeth also knew my husband's eating habits better than I did. In the ensuing years I, too, became used to the fact that Norman loved his potatoes, would eat great mounds, no matter how they were fixed, and if there were any left on the table, he would be apt to finish them after dessert.

Allan and Elizabeth accepted us almost like part of the family. Allan was very good to work for. He and Norman were alike in some ways. Neither of them had to say a lot or would explain too much. They trusted each other. Norman was especially flattered that Allan asked him to plough the front fields where the neighbours could see his straight furrows, because he said Norman could plough straighter than he could. They were very generous in sharing their garden space, and let us have the walnuts from one of the trees and many more kind gestures.

Five years we lived on that farm and its beauty always fascinated me. In the front of the white stucco farmhouse was a broad expanse of lawn dotted with blue spruce. Looking toward the road from the house, an apple orchard grew on the left, or west side of the lane, and a garden on the right, between the road and the lawn. On the south or back side of the house were a neatly trimmed lawn and wide flowerbeds along the foundation of the house. A broad, covered verandah enhanced our end of the house on the east, a covered porch at the centre front door, which was seldom used, then an enclosed verandah at the west side led to the main house. Further to the west was a big woodshed and the lane came in right beside that. A pump on top of a well stood close to the sidewalk that led to the main house, and just south of that was a gazebo covered with a grapevine. Just a bit further south and a bit to the west, the hip-roof barn housed a herd of Holsteins. Three very large English walnut trees shaded the lawn to the eastern side. A garage, also to the south and toward the east end of the lawn, offered a convenient place to shelter the cars.

With two weeks of hard work, the downstairs of our apartment was finally finished, enough that we could move in. Once the fridge and stove were delivered, I began my housekeeping. Since our bedroom and bathroom were still not complete, Allan and Elizabeth let us sleep in their upstairs room another month or so until we were finally able to live completely in our apartment. What delight it was to set up our little space the way we wanted and to settle into our life together.

At our community shower, three weeks after our honeymoon, Dad came and whispered, "I left a book, in a brown paper bag, on the front seat of your car."

*Bless him!* I thought, *even if it is a little late!* I eagerly opened the bag on the way home. A little paperback booklet fell out. *So, You're Getting Married.* The information was not what I expected, nor did it arrive when I needed it. It was written more for engaged couples and saying very little about the marriage relationship and nothing at all about the physical union. Still I've always been glad that I at least asked. Years later, when they moved to Barwick, they left the book they had purchased as newlyweds. I was thankful they hadn't given me that one! Although written by a Christian author, that book was not espousing what God intended for a loving marriage relationship. It treated sex as only a way to reproduce and put a guilt trip on anyone who wanted it for more than that. I honestly believe it caused a lot of friction, guilt and discomfort in my parents' marriage. How sad that they, being open-minded enough to try to educate themselves, would be influenced by the kind of thinking that saved the marital relationship for procreation only, and espoused the idea that anything more was animal lust! I was glad we had been given the book by our friends, which was much more helpful in beginning our lives together.

Norman was used to going to bed much earlier than I was, and since he also insisted that I need not get up when he had to go to do the milking, I gradually felt like a different person. From 5 a.m. to 10:30 p.m. days filled with hard work, like I'd been used to, three to four hours more sleep and much more relaxing days seemed a luxury. I felt as though I was seeing the world through different eyes.

Although I continued to help Elva on some days, much of that first year I spent putting our wedding gifts into place, providing the finishing touches to our décor and completing the friendship quilt that I hadn't quilted before we were married.

We often took long walks in the evenings—especially on moonlit evenings. Norman loved the moonlight, and I didn't mind the romantic moods it evoked in him. I loved sharing how I was feeling about different happenings or things we were experiencing, but when I asked how he was feeling, he would tell me, "I don't know—I don't really have feelings." We were getting to know each other, and one thing I was finding out was that I needed to help him recognize his feelings.

Grandad Nighswander often came that first year too, to help Norman finish up the trim on the upstairs rooms and hall. In June of 1961, Grandad and Grandma and Allan and Elizabeth planned a trip to Maryland to look up some of our Nighswander roots. The morning of their departure, Grandad came to the door to say "Goodbye." I was touched and so happy that he took the time to do that. It was only a week later that the telephone rang just after Norman and I had gone to bed. We were shocked to get the message that Grandad had taken a heart attack as he visited a cemetery in Maryland. He was taken back to a friend's house and the doctor was called, but he died there. Poor little Grandma had to travel home alone with Allan and Elizabeth. She looked so lost and forlorn, and there was quite a bit of red tape to get Grandad's body back home.

The funeral was held at the Altona Missionary Church as there was a little more room there than in the little Mennonite Meeting House. He

144

had been a frequent attender there any way. Rev. Sargent had a part in the service too. One of the songs that were sung was, When I've Gone the Last Mile of the Way (by Johnson Oatman, Jr.).

> When I've gone the last mile of the way
> I will rest at the close of the day
> And I know there are joys that await me
> When I've gone the last mile of the way

It was a fitting song to say goodbye!

About a month after Grandpa's death, I knew I was pregnant. I felt as though one of my most cherished dreams was coming true. I felt elated all way through. What joy it was to prepare a layette, to fix up the small room next to ours as a nursery. I papered one wall with a pattern that showed deer beside a brook and made a plastic padded top for a dresser to use as a place to bathe and change our baby's diaper. The top drawer was filled with baby soap, powder, Q-tips, oil and everything I thought I would need to attend to the wee one. I hemmed and folded diapers and lovingly stitched wee nightgowns and stacked them neatly in the middle drawer. The bottom drawer held extra bedding and shawls. We went to Toronto to buy a crib and had it made up ready.

I had calculated that the baby would arrive March 14 or 15. The doctor thought my due date was the 7th. The 7th passed and, finally, the evening of the 13th, one of the warmest March days I remember, I began to have contractions. By 11, I knew this was it. We went to the Brierbush Hospital in Stouffville and by soon after midnight I was bearing down. I thought I was going to have a short labour.

My mom had told me having a baby was like "walking through the valley of the shadow of death" so I was steeled for real torture. It was hard work. I had asked to have the baby by natural childbirth without the aid of anesthetic. By three o'clock, Mrs. Middlemiss, the nurse was asking if I didn't want a small whiff to help me. I didn't! I think she felt really sorry for me.

Suddenly, when Mrs. Middlemiss asked once more, Dr. Button said, "Don't ask her again." He said he was going to have to make a small cut so I wouldn't tear. I was too busy to wonder why, but at about 4:20 a.m., he told me that when he asked me to push, I was to push as hard as I could, even though I was tired. The reason for his caution was that our son came bottom first, and it was natural for my body to feel the job was done. But it was urgent to push the head out before the baby tried to breathe. Push I did, and at 5:30 a.m. when our 8 lb. 1 oz. son was laid on my stomach, I saw a perfectly shaped head and a cute little Steckle chin and I cried with joy. I caressed his cheek and kissed his forehead. I could hardly wait until Norman could see his son. In spite of the hours of hard work, and that he was born double breach, it did not seem like the valley of the shadow of death and I was thrilled with the whole process. We named him James Stuart. With a surname like Smith, we figured there would be fewer J. Stuart Smiths than Stuart J. Smiths.

Of course, in those days, fathers were not allowed into the delivery room, but Norman was pleased when they finally met. He'd had a sleepless night and after spending a bit of time with us, he left to get some rest.

Instead of rest, he came home to a house that smelled strongly of skunk. It was almost too overpowering for him to sleep there. He opened all the windows in the house and turned on fans. The kitchen and dining room part of the house had no basement, and the skunks had crawled in under the front verandah and burrowed into the crawl space. Allan and Norman waited until the night when the skunks were out, then they filled in the holes with fresh soil mixed with red pepper to discourage them from going in again. Each of the days I was in the hospital, Norman boiled vinegar and tried every method that people recommended to reduce the effects. He didn't want to bring his wife and new son into a smelly house, however, when I did come home, the house still smelled—not much of skunk, but quite strong of vinegar!

The Brierbush Hospital was mostly nursing home, but the downstairs included a combination operating and delivery room, a recovery room for tonsillectomies, a nursery and a room for new mothers. Because there had been no births for a while, the heat in the nursery had been shut off. The night that Stuart was born, the weather was unusually warm, so it wasn't noticed. Through the next night, the temperatures dropped drastically. The morning of the 15th, I heard a nurse say, "Oh my goodness! That poor baby was almost blue! We forgot to turn up the heat." Someone else said, "Shh-hh!" The door to my room was promptly closed. I didn't have the nerve to call out and ask to see my baby, but I could hardly wait until they brought him in so I could see for myself if he was all right. I don't know how they warmed him up, but when they brought him in at 6, he seemed to be okay. I often wondered though what it did to his psyche and if that was why he seemed to struggle with feeling accepted and secure.

I knew that our old neighbor, Hugh McIntosh, was upstairs, so that first morning when the nurses were taking the breakfast upstairs to the seniors, I told them to say *Cimar a thathu?* (sounded like Cimarachi) to him. The nurse came downstairs beaming.

"Mr. McIntosh says, "*Tha gu mat*" (Sounded like Hakuma) and wants to know who is here in this room."

The next afternoon when Mrs. McIntosh came in to see her husband, she stopped in with a card and a wee silver spoon engraved with an 'S.' They were extremely pleased I had remembered the Gaelic greeting.

## BECOMING A PARENT

When Stuart was born, Alan and Elizabeth realized it was going to be difficult to heat as much water as we needed to do baby laundry, so they put in a hot water tap in the cellar way. I still had to fill pails and carry the water through our dining room and small kitchen into the wash house at the back, but it was better than heating it on the stove. We didn't have a camera to record the stages of our new son's life, so Anna—Allan and Elizabeth's unmarried daughter—offered to loan us one that she no longer used. We were extremely thankful. In fact we had that camera until after we moved away. When we finally could afford another, we returned it to her.

Our poor little son seemed to have a lot of troubles, one being severe colic. After I breast-fed him, he'd sleep perhaps twenty minutes, then he would awake, screaming. Grandmas, Great-grandmas, Aunts and Great Aunts and just about everyone else had advice. Most of them thought I probably didn't have enough milk and that I should supplement it with Pablum. That didn't work either. No one even thought of suggesting that he might be getting too much, nor that I weigh him before and after to see how much he was actually getting. By summer, he had a fissure that caused him a lot of pain with every bowel movement. He cried so hard he gave himself a hernia. Dr. Button wrapped him up with a heavy bandage. It was hot and humid at the time, and that extra padding gave him a heat rash. I should have had the book which I got later from La Leche League. He didn't sleep more than a half hour, day or night, and I was extremely tired. Norman had to work during the day so I didn't want to bother him, although at times when I could hardly walk the floors anymore, because I felt as though I was going to fall asleep, and was afraid of dropping our son, I woke him to ask if he could take a turn while I grabbed a few minutes of shut-eye. We tried to keep him away from the other end of the house so he wouldn't disturb the Wideman's, but at one time Elizabeth did ask if Stuart was ever awake and not crying. I didn't want to tell her, but those times were very minimal in the first three or four months of his life.

Stuart also developed a food sensitivity. He had been eating from the table since he was seven months. At nine months, he developed severe diarrhea. The doctor told us to take him off of everything except milk, cottage cheese and beef. Now I think those were odd choices, but that was the advice we got. It was hard, since he already knew what he wanted, and I had to try to feed him at a different time than when we ate so he wouldn't beg for some of our food. He started early to teethe, but each tooth came through with great difficulty. Often the teeth would break through then the gums would swell up and close in again in a great blue bulb over the emerging tooth, so that each tooth had to break through not once but up to three times each. When his two year molars came through at 18 months, he turned into a different child. He was still very active and mischievous, but now he was happy!

This beloved little son of ours didn't want any proverbial grass growing under his feet. If I hadn't written it in his baby book, I would be inclined to disbelieve what I know to be true. He didn't begin crawling like most babies; he pulled himself up on anything he could—preferably a chair, which he could shove to where he wanted to go. The first time he climbed the steps was when he was seven months old. I happened to be talking to Elva Nighswander on the phone when he disappeared up the steps. When I told her I had found him three steps up, she said, "Teach him how to come back down to minimize the possibility of falling."

I did that, but it just increased the area for him to explore, although I did try to keep the stair door closed. By the time he was nine months old, he was walking a few steps from one chair to the other. But one day, his older cousins came to play. He sat watching them push the toy trucks and tractors while on their hands and knees. One could almost see the light-bulb moment when he caught on to that method of travel. He took off on his hands and knees and didn't look back. Forget walking! He could now get to where he wanted without the bother of going through the faltering process of walking. And he did—onto desk tops, over the lawn, into the fields, from room to room, as far as he could, whether I was watching or not. In fact he seemed to go twice as fast if I wasn't!

He loved when I read him stories. Somewhere he had received a small poem book. I memorized all of them so that when he turned to a certain page, and gave me a hint, I would "read" the poem from wherever I was, putting lots of emphasis on the different parts. For instance,

The airplane taxis down the field,
It heads into the breeze,
It lifts its wheels above the ground
It skims above the trees.

It rises high and higher,
Away up toward the sun,
It's just a speck against the sky
—and now it's gone.

With each line, my voice rose then levelled off with the next line. He loved those poems and they were repeated often until he, too, could repeat them—often with the same expression.

He wasn't quick in talking more than one word at a time, but he got his messages across. The first time he put a phrase together, at eighteen months when we were travelling, he announced, "Gate big tuck," when a semi was approaching.

I was always very conscious of the fact that it must have been difficult for Anna to have a happily married young couple living at one end of the house while that experience still eluded her. However, I had long admired her and it was great to have that contact with her. She often came over and visited a while. When Stuart was old enough to be outside, she often took him with her and let him "help" plant or weed her flower beds. He, in turn, adored her. When Allan and Elizabeth's grandchildren came, they readily included Stuart in their play and they became almost like cousins.

At one point, Anna decided she wanted a dog. Allan thought one would get lonely, so they ended up buying two border collies—Scotty, tan and white, and Laddy, a black and white. They became Stuart's friends too. In fact, it was the dogs that led him on several adventures. Stuart loved to be outside. Before he could walk, I put gates across the two openings to the wide verandah. It made a lovely place to play. One day I hadn't heard him for a while, so I looked out the door. The verandah was quite empty. The gates were still in place, the toys I had put out for him were there. Where was Stuart? He was still not walking, so where could he be? My heart was in my throat as I opened the gate and started to look around on the lawn. Just then, Norman came to the barn door. I called out to him. "I've lost Stuart!"

"You've lost Stuart! How could you do that?"

"He was playing with his toys on the verandah, the gates are still closed, but he's gone!"

"He can't walk, so he can't have gone far."

Together we called and kept looking. Finally, on the far side of the garage in the tall grass, we found the dogs, and Stuart crawling on all fours, heading further afield! After that, I watched him on the verandah. The posts of the railing were far enough apart that the dogs freely went in and out. Stuart must have learned from their example and taken the same way of escape. That was the last of feeling he had a secure place to play in the out-of-doors he so loved.

When he finally began walking at fourteen months, it became even more difficult to keep watch. He wanted to go beyond any limits I would set, and it seemed to take him no time at all to get there. If it had been our place, I would have probably decided to build a fence. But it wasn't and I have a hunch that may not even have stopped him—he probably would have found a way to climb over it. I began to dress him in red, so we at least could spot him easily. Once, Norman came carrying him, dripping wet. He had gone around the barn where they had dug a trench to drain the liquid from the freshly filled silo. Being close to the barn yard, it also contained a bit of manure juice. Wouldn't you know it? Stuart had stepped right into it. Luckily, his scream reached Norman's ears. He was just inside the barn milking. Stuart could very easily have drowned in the vile stuff, but Norman vaulted out through the open window and rescued him. Stuart had his little white leather shoes on at the time, and they plus their wearer were thoroughly soaked—the shoes beyond rescue.

One time Scotty led him over the rise in the southeast field. By that time, we knew the best way to find him was to call the dogs. Scotty came running, and Norman took off in that direction. Stuart was at the very southeast corner of the farm, right at the fence!

In the house, he discovered he could make a circuit from the dining room to the living room, in one door of the downstairs bedroom and out the other to the dining room again. One time he was merrily making the rounds while I got a meal ready in the kitchen. When I brought the food out to the table, I saw that on one of his passes, he had grabbed the end of thread from the sewing machine I had in that bedroom. I don't know how he did it without breaking the thread, but there were about seven orbits of thread, round and round the circle. It took quite a while to wind it back onto the spool!

When my sister Esther graduated as a Registered Practical Nurse, I had a party for her on our front lawn. The men were digging a hole for a new telephone pole near the end of the lane. I had just gone into the house to get more refreshments when, suddenly, Martha took off over the garden following Stuart, who was headed toward the hole. He got there before she did and, thankfully, he went in feet first, but there he was, almost six feet down in the hole.

*The farm where I was born and lived until I was married,*
*and for five years during my marriage.*
*The addition on the right was where my grandparents lived.*

*Apple blossoms across the lane from our house.*

*Hugh McIntosh home across the road at the end of our lane.*

*Altona Public School, SS#17, Pickering,*
*where I attended. It occupied an acre off our farm.*

*The trees my great-grandfather planted. Crozier house on right.*

*Grandparents' return from their Western trip in 1947.*
*Eva and me on the welcoming committee!*

*My sister Eva standing beside me in high chair.*

*Eva, me (4 years old, with doll, Toddles), and Enos.*

*Back row: Me (7 years old), Eva, Mom Front row: Enos, Esther, Anna Mary.*

*The six Nighswander Children: Eva, Me, Enos,*
*Esther, Anna Mary and Martha.*

*Me, grade six.*

*On the Quinte Loyalist during a family trip when I was fourteen.*

*Marriage to Norman Smith, September 3, 1960.*

*Our Family in 1979:*
*Stuart 17, Wilma 16, Beth 13, Loralyn 8.*

*Our Farm House near Ailsa Craig.*

*Our grown family in 1993 including first two grandsons.*

*My Dad and I.*

*My wedding to Paul Meyer.*

*The Smith/Meyer clan:*
*8 children, 18 grandchildren and now three great-grandchildren.*

## CHAPTER 22
# One After the Other

> "Whether your pregnancy was meticulously planned, medically coaxed, or happened by surprise, one thing is certain – your life will never be the same."
> —Catherine Jones

When Stuart was six month old, I missed my period and I knew another child was on the way. It's not what we had planned. I was still very tired, and at first my whole body and mind resisted the idea. I was still getting no more than a few hours of sleep at a time. I felt guilty at not being happy about it. I had always wanted more children, but I was so tired out and not fully recovered from my first pregnancy. The morning sickness that was nonexistent with Stuart came on full force. I couldn't even stand the smell of boiling water.

Finally in an attempt to reconcile my feelings with the facts, I began to sort Stuart's out-grown baby things into piles of what could be used for another. In touching and handling those things, my outlook subtly changed and I began to treasure what was happening in my body.

I knew in my heart that I wasn't the only one who would have trouble with the idea of having children 14 months apart. I dreaded telling my mother who had been quite clear on her opinions when others had children that she perceived as being too close together. I kept complaining about gaining weight for a while, but finally thought I needed to tell her. She was spending a day a week at Grandmother Reesor's, so I chose to go there one day close to Stuart's first birthday to break the news.

"Mom, I thought I should tell you that we're expecting another baby." I said it as softly as I could. Immediately I could tell by her eyes that she was calculating the months and Stuart's age.

"How far along are you?" she asked.

"Five and a half months." I almost whispered.

There was a moment of hesitation then, "Oh, Ruth! Ruth!" She looked as though she was about to faint and that it couldn't have brought more shame to her if I was announcing my pregnancy while unmarried. "Couldn't you have waited a little longer than that?"

What was I to say? I paused a bit. "Mom, it's not the way we planned it, but it's the way it is, and we will welcome this new one into our home and into our love."

I hoped that she, too, in time could accept this new grandchild.

We decided we should plan to get someone to help a few weeks after the baby was born. We tried several girls who did that kind of work. No one was available. Finally someone suggested Margaret. *Oh, no!* I thought. *She always makes me feel so naïve and stupid. I don't think I can take having her in my house for three weeks!*

However, since we could find no one else, I called to ask if she would consider coming. I thought perhaps she would already be spoken for in that period of time.

"Let me think about it, and I'll get back in a few days," she said.

Two days later, she called to say she would take the job. Even though I really needed the help, my heart sank.

There was no room in the nursery for two cribs, so we planned that the new baby would sleep in a smaller crib in the hall at the top of the steps for the time being. My due date was the beginning of June, but the last day of April, I began to have contractions. When I visited Doctor Button, he timed my contractions and sent me straight to the hospital. He thought if Stuart was born in six hours from beginning of labour to a double breach birth, he didn't want to take any chances. All afternoon and most of the night, the contractions came quite strong and five minutes apart. At four-thirty a.m., they began to subside and when the doctor visited, he said I might as well go home.

Not everything had been prepared, so I hurried to finish what I needed in case baby decided to come early. Part of that was sewing a few more outfits for Stuart. Almost daily, I wondered, *Is this it?* False labour frequently kept me living in uncertainty. We made plans to take Stuart to my parents when the time came. June 4, I had planned to make Stuart's last outfit. Soon after breakfast I was certain my contractions were the real thing. I finished the outfit, sewed on the buttons and after lunch told Norman that I think I'd better go to the hospital.

In spite of a lull in my labour, Wilma Kristine made her debut at 4:20 that afternoon. She did well in the very beginning, sleeping through most of the night and only fussing a bit in the evening. I thought I was blessed and on easy street.

Margaret had come the day I arrived home from the hospital. She was a little aloof the first few days, but soon we were getting along great. One day I told her, "I think we are becoming good friends. I don't know why, but I always sensed that you thought I was—well, maybe not as good as you—so I dreaded thinking of having you here for three weeks right after I had a baby."

Margaret burst out in laughter. "Did you really?" she asked, her eyes wide in astonishment.

"Yes I did. I don't know why, because I think quite differently now."

"The reason I'm laughing is that when you called me to see if I could come, I thought exactly the same as you. I always felt as though you thought you were better than me! I tried to find a good reason not to come, but I couldn't, so I said I would. Now I feel so different about you too!"

We gave each other a hug and agreed that perceptions aren't necessarily right. We did become good friends—and it taught me that I should befriend people to whom I felt inferior because it just might be that I'm having the same effect on them.

When Wilma was just a few weeks old, she began to projectile vomit after each side of breastfeeding. She even started losing weight. Something was wrong. I tried pumping my milk and giving it to her in a bottle. With that she was alright. I felt a sense of rejection that she would take my milk from a bottle but not from me. When I finally was advised to weigh before and after feeding, I found out what her problem was and knew it was the same issue that Stuart had. She was getting eight ounces on each side! It was way too much, of course, so up it came. Poor Stuart couldn't do that, so his stomach just ached. When I thought of it, I could hardly stand to realize pain he must have suffered.

What a little comforter Wilma was. She reassured me I did know how to care for a baby. Once we had figured out the problem of overfeeding, she slept between feedings and through the night quite early. Stuart loved helping to care for her. Once when I was in the kitchen getting a meal ready, while Wilma slept in the carriage and Stuart was reading his books, I suddenly heard Wilma crying. What was wrong? Stuart had peeked in the carriage and was overwhelmed with the desire to kiss the baby. There he was, a foot on each wheel of the side of the carriage. Not being able to reach in far enough to kiss her, he lifted her head by her ear to administer that sign of his affection!

When she was old enough to be in the Jolly Jumper, Stuart was delighted to sit in front of her, encouraging her to jump. He loved bringing her toys. However, when she learned to crawl and get around on her own, she headed for the toy she wanted. Almost immediately there was a howl of indignation from big brother. "She took my toys!" This was soon followed by a cry from little sister because the toy she had succeeded in reaching was unceremoniously grabbed from her little hand.

It was immediately obvious that there was a major crisis in Stuart's mind. The toys he had become accustomed to having on his own were now in jeopardy of being claimed by another.

I gave Wilma one of her own toys, then quickly gathered Stuart's toys, and put them in a box in a corner behind a little gate that had been used for other purposes. It was low enough that Stuart could easily climb over, but high enough to keep Wilma away from his treasures. I explained to our eldest that his toys were now safe, and little sister would only play with the ones he wanted to share with her. The relief on his face was plain to see. With every one relaxed and happy, I returned to my work and kept watch from a distance.

It wasn't long until the little man climbed over the gate, carefully looked over his stash, chose a toy and climbed back to present it to his sister.

"Here, you can play with this."

He sat and smiled to see her play with the toy he had shared. In a minute or so, the action was repeated. He chose another toy and brought it over the gate to share. Before long, the box behind the barrier was almost empty, and the two siblings sat on the floor sharing and playing happily with all the toys.

Where Stuart had taken off from the porch to far-off points of interest, Wilma, when she was old enough to play outside, even without gates, wouldn't venture further than the little square of cement in front of the verandah. The sandbox, under a shade tree across the lawn, was not far away, but if she wanted to play there, I had to carry her over the grass to the sandbox. When she was ready to come back, she'd call out for me. I never had to guess where she was. Her traits also made it safe to keep her in the crib at the top of the steps, because she wouldn't dream of climbing out herself.

Far from Stuart's waiting to talk, Wilma was talking a blue streak from the time she was less than a year old—at home. When we were away, she was very quiet and shy. One Sunday when she was two and a half, she came to me after church to ask a question. The woman to whom I had been talking remarked, "Oh, Wilma's talking now?" We laughed about that, because she could babble on endlessly about anything and had been for a long time.

## CHAPTER 23

# Maturing with My Children

> "You have to do your own growing
> no matter how tall your grandfather was."
> –Abraham Lincoln

Soon after Wilma's birth, I began to have trouble concentrating. My reactions were slow and I felt tired much of the time. After several visits to the doctor about the same problems, Dr. Button decided to start me on thyroid medication which helped a lot.

In 1964 when I was twenty-four, and Wilma was just over a year old, I began to have blackouts which gradually worsened. When I began to wake up to blackouts, my usually calm family doctor became alarmed and made a rush appointment with a neurologist, fearing a brain tumour. We had two children under the age of two. Wilma wouldn't even stay alone with her father, much less her grandmothers, and I felt it a real blow to be faced with such a possibility. I spent a sleepless night, and in the early hours, I went down to the kitchen and began to pray. I earnestly told God how much my family needed me—that I couldn't even be spared long enough to have tests, much less major surgery and possibly death, at the worst. After pouring my anxiety and anger out, I felt a distinct presence in the room and a touch on my shoulder. I heard Jesus asking, "Ruth, I love your husband and children more than you do. Can't you trust me to care for them with or without you?"

He seemed to stand waiting for me to answer. Although humanly understandable, my anxiety suddenly looked entirely superfluous.

I finally said, "Yes, Jesus, I trust you. Do what you know is best."

I was filled with a quiet assurance and not surprised when, a few days later, the specialist found nothing and concluded it to be a type of migraine. That experience was a turning point in my growth.

Although that quiet assurance ran like a deep stream through my life, now I thirsted for more and more of Jesus. Several books at this time were real growth experiences.

While searching the Scripture helped me grow in my understanding, I also found myself feeling boxed in by the life patterns the church dictated. As I did when I was younger, I began again to feel God was calling me to more of a leadership role or possibly even teaching or preaching. That set up real conflict, since there was no place for such service in the church we were attending. I was distressed over the disagreements in the church over so many outer things, when it seemed the more important issues were ignored.

While the Preacher's Kid pressure was somewhat relieved, I began to realize that in some aspects, the box I sometimes chafed against had become a comfortable nest to a certain extent. God gently led me to understand that if Jesus was to be Lord of my life, as I deeply desired, I was going to have to be willing to leave that nest. It was at this time, that I wrote the following poem.

As the Eagle .... So the Lord
—based on Deuteronomy 31:11

The eagle hovers o'er the nest
With ever watchful eye,
As eaglets venture forth to test
And give their wings a try.

And when from nest at last they push
Should they falter in sudden fear,
The eagle dips 'til beneath
And safe on pinions bears
The eaglet to the nest again,
With tender, loving care.

So, too, my Heavenly Father
Hovers with watchful eye,
As I His bidding follow
And give my wings a try.

When from nest at last I push,
And I falter, in sudden fear,
I feel my Father's arms beneath me,
And upward, safe, He bears
My spirit to His throne again,
With gentle loving care.

But if the eaglet cowers—
Refuses to try the air—
It misses the richest blessing
Of knowing the eagles care.

And even so, if I refuse
The task my Father bids,
But shrink and hide from
Something I've never tried—
I'll miss the richest blessing, too,
Of knowing my Father's care.

—**Ruth Nighswander Smith Meyer 1964**

Now, instead of hunting for proof texts, I read the Bible to meet Jesus, and let him guide me. It became an exciting journey that led to a new understanding of all the Holy Spirit could mean to me. Jesus said he would send the Holy Spirit to be our Comforter, our Guide, and to fill us with his power. I found this to be true, as I grew closer to my Lord.

Again, books also played a large part in my growth. *Shadow of the Almighty,* by Elizabeth Elliott, and *Beyond Ourselves*, by Catherine Marshall, are just two that helped change my life.

## PRAYER GROUP

In 1963 or '64, the women of our church began meeting for study and prayer. Most of these were in the 25-40 year range, but there were a few of the older ones as well. The first evening we got together, we began, one by one, telling the story of our spiritual journey. To people who had never had the chance to put into words and share this journey aloud with others, it was a freeing experience. Just the telling and the affirmation of each other was the impetus we needed to get serious about our growth in our relationship with Christ. We studied several books on deeper life in Christ and one on conversational prayer that opened up a whole new experience.

With the women's prayer groups, which I so enjoyed, a subtle change took place in my relationship with Norman. At first I shared my excitement with all that happened. Gradually I sensed a tension that grew with each meeting, it seemed. I asked if he didn't want me to tell him about it. He just shrugged his shoulders. So I tried to tone down and tell less about our time together. The tension increased.

It probably was partly due to the development in the prayer group that the young married couples with small children wanted their children to experience Sunday School. We met with the ministers asking if we could begin a Sunday School in our church. In spite of many meetings and well-thought-out approaches, the idea was flatly refused.

We began meeting in homes on Sunday afternoons and broke up into classes according to age for Bible Study and activities. We also prayed for guidance because we hesitated to break away from the Markham-Waterloo church. The more we studied and prayed, the clearer it became that to be able to follow God as we felt we should, that would have to happen. The entire time, we kept up communication with the leadership. Finally we decided to form a new congregation under the Ontario Mennonite Conference, as it was then called. Ontario Conference churches at Wideman's, Cedar Grove and Hagerman were already in the area, but accommodating all of us would have taxed their capacities. We were allowed to use one of the three existing church buildings of the Markham-Waterloo congregation. For a time we met at Almira, but then we settled into the Reesor's building and called ourselves Steeles Avenue Mennonite Church. I don't think it is often that churches separate into two congregations with as little animosity as it did in this instance. Relationships remained steadfast. I'm sure there was some grief on the part of those who stayed with the Markham-Waterloo church, but we continued meeting with the sewing circle and kept attending special services with them. At about the same time, my father and another young minister began a congregation associated with the Conservative Mennonite movement. That left only the Bishop in the original body.

When Wilma was between 2 and 4 years of age, I taught a Sunday School class of 5- and 6-year-olds. I would set her on an over-turned box in the corner of the room near my chair and give her a few toys. She never moved off that box for the entire hour, nor did she interrupt my teaching.

Teaching Sunday School to the children, and later the adult women, and leading singing in church began to fulfill the longing I had felt for years, but also awoke the desire to take more leadership roles.

Soon after the prayer group in our church started, Margaret Britton, who lived across from Elva and Harvey Nighswander, began a morning prayer group for community women. Elva invited me to be part of it. Several of us had small children, but there was a room next to the one in the basement where we met that was well stocked with toys and the children played quite nicely there. I came from Mongolia, and there were several local women and some from Claremont and

Stouffville. Although I had attended services in other churches for some years, it was the first time I had met with the possibility for that kind of personal contact with women from other denominations. There were Anglican, Pentecostal, Missionary, United members and Mennonites to begin. I found it to be a horizon-widening experience. These people who we always looked at as being on the outer edges of Christianity, I found to be struggling with many of the same issues and longing with all their hearts to become all God created them to be. My life was definitely enriched and I grew in my understanding. We chose a passage of scripture to read over and over again throughout the week. When we came together, we quietly sat reading the same scripture, making or adding to notes of what we gleaned from the passage. It always amazed us how many different thoughts came from 5 or 6 verses.

It was during that time that Earl Doner, our Raleigh salesman, told me about Margaret Gibbons, a woman who had moved into a house north of the Mongolia corner. She had just been diagnosed with MS and had two small boys. He wondered if I could visit her, since she had moved from the city and was quite lonely as she tried to adjust to the knowledge that she was a victim of this disease.

I did go, my children in tow, and had a cup of tea with Margaret. From the beginning, I liked this English woman who had quite an accent.

"Would you be interested in going with me to a women's weekly prayer meeting?" I asked.

"I'd love to, but I have the two boys and I can't afford a babysitter, even if I knew one."

"Oh, you can bring them along, Margaret. There's a play room right next door to our meeting room with lots of toys and other children to play with."

That started a friendship of long-standing. Margaret freely shared her search for meaning in life. It was soon evident to us that she had been caught up in a cult. I happened to have a book on cults, so after a few weeks, I asked if she would like to read it.

The next week, she exclaimed, "How could you girls sit here and listen to me going on and on about the group in which I was becoming interested? You didn't even argue with me or tell me I was on the wrong path!"

Margaret B. smiled. "Would you have listened if we had told you right away? Would you have come back the next week?"

"No, probably not," she answered. "Thank you for being patient with me and showing me a better way. But thank you, Ruth, for lending that book to me."

As Margaret G. grew in her faith, she began to just glow as she enthusiastically shared her faith with others. Her very looks changed. Even though she sought healing from her MS, and it never came, she lived a fruitful life of service right to the end. When her husband died and she couldn't find enough help, she had a house built that would house five or six handicapped people. They pooled their available funds to hire 24-hour help. Forty-two or forty-three years later, about a year before she died, I visited her again. She was blind and in a wheelchair, but she was still praising the Lord, her face aglow!

## A RELUCTANT MOVE

The time in our first home on the Wideman farm was idyllic. I loved that place and always felt as though I was living a storybook life while we were there. The grounds were beautiful with many trees, the lawns nicely kept. I had large flowerbeds to lovingly tend and fill with a variety of blooms. The huge walnut trees south of the house bore a huge crop one year. Allan and Elizabeth said we could have the crop from two trees nearest our end. We gathered bushels. It was a messy job taking off the hulls, washing them off and drying them. Norman built several large boxes with wire bottoms to stack in the wash house so they could dry naturally. Once they were sufficiently dried, we put them in burlap bags and hung them from the rafters. Many winters after that, we often spent the evenings cracking nuts, putting the nice halves in one container and the broken ones in another. Many dishes and baked goods were enhanced by those home-grown walnuts.

We were quite happy living at the Wideman's and anticipated being there for a long time. However, early in 1965, Mom and Dad began talking about moving to the Rainy River District—the Barwick area—where a few families had already moved. There was a native reservation there where a man from Minnesota held regular services, but he wanted to retire. From the time he was a young man, Dad dreamed of going to India. He perceived this as a call and an opportunity to pursue such a dream. They asked Norman and me if we'd like to rent the farm at Altona and perhaps consider eventually buying it.

I, myself, had always dreamed of going to some far-off place. We had even talked of farming in Alberta. Going back to where I was born didn't seem inviting at all. However, I told Norman if this gave him the chance to farm for himself, I was willing to do it. He talked it over with Allan, who told him he had visions of Norman taking over his farm someday, but he felt that if my parents had given us the chance, we should take it. I would far rather have stayed where we were, but we started making plans to move.

We borrowed money from the Credit Union to buy the cows and machinery. Norman had already bought three pure-bred Holsteins. Most of Dad's cows were non-registered or grade cows, as they were called. Even though some had come from pure-bred stock, Dad hadn't always bothered registering the calves.

As we loaded our possessions from our honeymoon house, my heart cried, but I tried to keep it inside, as Norman was excited about having his own farming business. Dad and Uncle Joe had always worked together in putting the crops in and harvesting, so Norman agreed to continue that practice with Joe.

In May of 1965, my parents left for the north with a truck and cars laden with their earthly goods. There was a whole garage full of items they left behind, plus some items in the house and in the woodshed upstairs.

We moved in and began farming. With our move into my parents' house, other expectations settled on our shoulders. It was still "home" to my siblings. Esther came there on her days off and/or weekends.

Enos, too, lived there much of the time until his own marriage. Martha stayed to finish her year in Pickering High School, then left with two of her friends to take the train to her new home in Barwick. We inherited apple customers, and our home was their headquarters whenever my parents came to visit. Much as Norman enjoyed farming on his own, he began to feel as though the farm would never truly belong to him— there was a whole other family who still felt ownership.

That spring, I did what I long had thought would be nice to do. I mowed both sides of the lane right to the road and made small flower beds outside the posts, one each side. I'm afraid I took it as an affront when one of Mom's good friends made the comment, "It already looks ragged and messy around there." I think it was her loneliness that caused that remark, because not only had I beautified the entrance to the property, Norman had cleaned up the long-standing "junk" piles beside the implement shed and between the corn crib and henhouse south of the barn. Those had been there as long as I remembered! So I knew that we had improved the looks of the place, not let it go.

I began to help with the milking morning and night. When fall came, there was that big orchard full of fruit trees that had to have their abundance not only picked, but sold or preserved. That duty mostly fell to me, because it coincided with harvest and corn-picking. After the second year there, Norman's folks sold their cows and Norman rented their farm too. Norman's dad began to come to help out. I don't know how I would have managed the apple-picking without him. The apples still needed to be sorted and sold to customers who came to the door, or delivered to those who were used to having them brought to their doors in Stouffville. The culls were made into apple butter which we also sold. Often, customers came at inconvenient times. I ladled the sticky sweet substance into their containers, weighing it in order to know how much to charge. Often, just as I got things all cleaned up, another customer appeared. Our three- and two-year-old children had to come along with me wherever I went.

My grandmother still lived at the other end of the double house. By this time, she was quite forgetful and couldn't really be left alone. Aunt

Mary and Uncle Joe and Dad arranged live-in care for her. Norman's two maiden aunts—Clara and Eva— took turns staying with her. Although Uncle Joe and Aunt Mary were basically in charge of Grandma's care, I still was the go-between in many cases and looked after Grandma when her companions had a day off. On those days, I brought her over to our end of the house, or took her to the garden with me. When she sat in a lawn chair under a tree, I kept an eye on her as I worked. Often I brought a stack of children's books so she could read stories to our children, just as she had read to me. That worked inside or out, most of the time.

She grieved Dad and Mom's absence though, and as time went on and her mind deteriorated, she began to resent my presence because she associated my coming with Dad's leaving. She often grumbled about the lawn not being mowed or the flower beds not being kept up, when I'm quite sure they were done just as regularly as they were by my parents. Dear little woman—she just found it hard to adjust and ended up feeling lost most of the time. As an adult, I knew that, yet it hurt to have my special Grandma so out of sorts with me.

There were some happy times too. Sometimes she would help pod peas or snap beans and we would sing while we worked. I treasure the fact that Stuart and Wilma were able to get to know her. Occasionally, Grandma would be reading to them and would get tired. She would drop the book and shove the children away. At first this action hurt and confused them, but they got to understand it was just time to give Grandma a change, because she was tired.

One day we sat together in her end of the house while I did mending. I had made a bowl of popcorn for her and the children. She sat eating hers when all of a sudden she began to chuckle.

"What's so funny?" I asked.

"Oh, I was just thinking of David and Cindy."

"What was funny about them?"

"Cindy was working for David's mother and she thought she had him wound around her little finger. But one day Abe Reesor took me to Markham Fair and we met David and Cindy there. I winked at David—and I got him!"

It was a side of my grandmother I hadn't seen before, but I could imagine she might have been a bit of a flirt!

On Wilma's third birthday, she received money from her grandparents. I suggested we go to the five and ten store, so she could choose what she wanted. I went to the toy aisle with her, thinking that would be where she would find her heart's desire. However, there was nothing there that caught her interest. In the next aisle, she spied a little white straw hat with a pink ribbon around the crown, and that ribbon was long enough to tie under her chin. That's what she wanted. She still had money left, so she asked if she could have the little white gloves she found, white socks, a small teapot and a juice glass. She was very happy with her choices.

I had just made her a flower-strewn pink gingham dress with a large lace-edged white collar. The hat, gloves and socks set it off beautifully. The first Sunday she wore her whole outfit, we were invited to George Reesor's for lunch. The children stayed out to play on the swing. Anna and I were working in the kitchen, when Ernie, a few years older than our children, came in and tugged at Anna's skirt, wanting to tell her something. Finally, Anna asked him what he wanted. In an awed tone, he said, "Mama, Wilma is so-o-o pretty, she looks like a princess!"

It became obvious that we needed someone to stay with Grandma all the time. Soon after Aunt Eva Smith came to stay with Grandma, Norman had an extra-long day in the fields with some break-downs of equipment. It was late to begin milking, so I went to the barn and fed the cows. I managed to clean out the gutter behind the first row of cows, and began the milking. When Norman arrived, he was extremely embarrassed that I should have been pitching manure. He cautioned me to never ever do that again. The next day, Aunt Ina called and said she heard I'm working quite hard and admonished me to take care of myself. I asked her what she meant, and when she told me that Aunt Eva had told her about me cleaning the stables, I said how embarrassed Norman was and please not to tell anyone else.

When I got off the phone, I went directly to Grandma's end of the house and asked to talk to Aunt Eva. I told her that living so close to each other, we may find out things about each other that we wouldn't necessarily want everyone to know. After explaining what I heard and how embarrassed Norman was, I asked her to please not repeat things like that again, and I would try to offer her the same courtesy. She apologized profusely and promised me she would do that. We got along fine after that and reached a level of friendship that amazed both of us.

I saw underneath her usual rather gruff and critical exterior a side of her I had never seen before. The next Christmas, I gave her a soft, plush rug to lay beside her bed. On the gift card, I told her that it represents the soft tender side of her character that she had allowed me to see, and which I so appreciated. She came to me with tears in her eyes and told me no one had ever said anything so nice about her. No one had ever bothered to look that close at who she really was. After that, we had an even stronger bond. That experience taught me to do that for others whom I had seen as harsh or outspoken, and I believe it helped me discover some other hidden gems.

CHAPTER 24

# The Family Grows

> "A mother's joy begins
> when new life is stirring inside...
> when a tiny heartbeat is heard for the very first time,
> and a playful kick reminds her that she is never alone."
> —**Author Unknown**

round Christmas of 1965, I knew there was another baby on the way. I was happy about it, even though I didn't know how I was going to manage. I began to gain quite a bit of weight. Mid-March of 1966, my water broke one night. The doctor was as alarmed as I was. He ordered me to stay off my feet as much as possible. He said I should only get meals and go to the washroom. Stuart had just turned four and Wilma wasn't quite three. I had never yelled at my children, but with the doctor's orders, when they got into trouble, I sometimes resorted to yelling. I got help to do the cleaning and laundry, but it was a long wait. The doctor, with each visit, kept urging me to hold on for another month and then another, so the baby would have more chance of survival. It was uncomfortable to sit, because the baby didn't have the usual fluid cushion. I worried that something was wrong and the doctor admitted that sometimes a miscarriage happens because that is the case. I struggled because a child with special needs seemed a big responsibility that I wasn't sure I could handle. Finally I told God that if he was going to allow that to happen, he would have to have a big bundle of extra grace with which to endow me. But I yielded it to him and found a measure of peace.

Six weeks after I had been ordered to stay off my feet, Aunt Ina called to ask if our trio (My sister Eva, Norma Smith and I) would sing at the spring mission meeting. I explained that with my condition, I couldn't do that. She wondered what condition. I smiled to know that Aunt Eva had taken my advice so seriously that she hadn't even told Aunt Ina of my difficult pregnancy, bless her.

The months crept by and still the baby kept growing. I got so big that the doctor started wondering if it might be twins. That could have explained the problems I'd had. He thought he could discern two heartbeats, "But," he said, "That sometimes happens."

During that summer, Stan Thompson died. I thought I could manage to go to the visitation. John greeted me with a huge grin and remarked, "You're looking …full of life!" That was probably the kindest thing anyone could say to a woman so very large in pregnancy!

About a month before my due date, the leaking of fluid stopped. My due date arrived and I was still sitting around and became quite impatient. Saturday, August 13, I'd had enough. I got up and cooked a large ham, a pot of potatoes that could be fried, and baked desserts—still no labour pains. Finally after supper, I got on my hands and knees and washed the kitchen floor, waxed and polished it. I gave up and went to bed.

Eleven thirty, I awoke feeling a little pop! I also knew I was in labour. When I got up, I saw flashing lights at the corner north of us. Norman called Uncle Levi and Aunt Ina, who lived across the road, to come stay with the children. Not wanting me to see the accident at the corner, Norman headed south to circumvent the scene, and we were on our way to Claremont and up to Uxbridge Cottage Hospital from there. At six-thirty, Beth made her way into the world. Dr. Petrie was there in Dr. Button's place.

"You've got a big baby girl," he announced.

"Is she alright?" My voice almost trembled.

"Well give me a chance to count her fingers and toes, but she looks like a beautiful little girl to me!"

When they placed her on my chest, I marvelled, as I did for months afterward, at her perfect little features. I was amazed and filled with thankfulness, because I had been prepared for some kind of physical handicap or perhaps Down's syndrome. Nothing like that appeared to be the case.

When we came home from the hospital, there was a whole row of welcoming committee sitting on the front verandah: Grandma, Aunts Clara and Eva, Aunt Amelia Nighswander and her daughter Edith and, of course, Stuart and Wilma. Wilma's ankle was bandaged, because in my absence, she was teaching Stuart to jump off the verandah and she had sprained her ankle. But they were anxious to see their little sister.

It was nice to be able to move around again and resume a more normal life, but with Beth's birth, I lost only a very small amount of weight and size that I had gained during pregnancy. I visited the doctor again to get his advice. He put me on a 1500–calorie diet to which I adhered religiously. I didn't want to remain at the weight I had attained. When a woman stopped by one day the conversation drifted to weight. I said how much I wish I could slim down.

"Oh, you shouldn't worry about that now. You'll lose it when the baby comes."

Between the two of us, I don't know who was more embarrassed when I told her I already had the baby and she was six months old. I struggled to know what to do about it.

One Sunday morning when Beth was eight and a half months old, she woke up hungry. I took her downstairs and got a bottle from the fridge. I tried to turn the nipple right side up, but was having trouble with it, so I set her in the high chair, turned to the counter no more than two or three feet away, fixed the nipple and turned back to see Beth sitting on the arm of the high chair. Before I could grab her, she fell, the back of her head hitting the floor with a smack. I picked her up and felt for a bump on the back of her head, but could feel nothing. Finally satisfied, my hand came to the side of her head and my finger dropped into a definite depression that felt at least a half inch deep and perhaps 2 inches long. My heart almost leapt into my throat. It was a Sunday morning, but we took her to see the doctor. He said the impact had caused the one bone in her cranium to bend inward at the impact and she would need surgery to pull it out into place. However, there would be no harm in waiting until the next day. It was a long day! We watched her play and do her usual climbing, but kept her from falling again.

Monday we took her to the Scarborough Hospital. She cried when they took her away, and my heart bled for her. We saw them pushing her crib from the recovery room to the room where she would be staying. She was sitting up, leaning forward to prop herself up with her hands. Her head was swathed in bandages, her cheeks flushed red, and her bright eyes trying to figure out where she was. They motioned that we should wait, and thankfully she didn't see us, so there was no crying out for us. Finally, we were allowed to go to her and she was indeed glad to see us, but after awhile the nurses urged us to go home, as she was still groggy from the anesthetic. There was a shower that evening at Harvey Nighswander's for my brother Enos and his new bride, Arlene, who had just returned from their honeymoon. I must say my mind wasn't much on the festivities.

The next morning we got a call to say we could bring Beth home. That scared me almost as much as the thoughts of having her stay in the hospital.

When we got to the hospital, Norman stayed at the desk to fill out some necessary papers while I went to her room. The nurse was holding our daughter and I could see that Beth had been crying. The doctor had just visited, which probably upset her again. Beth took one look at me and extended her arms. When I took her into my own, she laid so close to me as though she couldn't get near enough. I got her dressed and went out to join Norman. As soon as she saw him, she called out "Daddy!" She paused then repeated in a quieter but relieved and thankful tone, "Daddy." It was the first time she had said more than "Da-da" in reference to him.

We took her home, but she slept almost with one eye open. It seemed she was afraid we wouldn't be there when she woke up. A few nights later, she had a fever and I noticed the bandage at the top of her head was bulging outward. We took her to the doctor. There was a swelling, and Dr. Petrie took out a few stitches from the incision to drain a blood clot. He didn't think there was any under the skull but couldn't be sure. In the next day, when the blood gathered up again, he sent us back to Scarborough. We arrived there about 8:30 p.m. and waited a long time before the doctor came in. After taking a look under the bandage, they asked me to leave the room while they again opened a few more stitches to drain the blood and take a closer look. I refused to leave, though they asked again. When I asked why they wanted me to leave, they said it was because they were afraid I'd faint. I told her if my 8½ month old daughter had to go through the pain, I was going to be there to help her. I wouldn't faint, and I would hold her during the procedure. Poor little darling! She cried, but I kept reassuring her that I was there and loved her. The doctor left, saying he was going to consult with some colleagues.

After quite a while, the nurse came and said she had to take Beth, but couldn't say where she was taking her. We waited in the room over an hour, getting more and more concerned with each passing moment. Finally, Norman went to see what was going on and where Beth was and when she would return. He was told that she had been admitted and asked him to sign the papers. When we asked why and for what reason, the nurse said that the doctor had left the hospital and he was the only one who could tell us. She told us to go home, and if we wanted to know more we could come back in the morning.

The next four days, I was in the hospital by nine in the morning and stayed until nine at night. Every morning I was told the doctor had already made his rounds and wouldn't be back until after his office hours. The nurses just kept saying they couldn't tell me, and that the doctor was the only one who could tell me why she was being kept there. The only times the nurses ever came into the room was to check her temperature twice a day. I closely watched, but they did nothing else. I fed her, changed her and walked the halls with her.

When one of the nurses saw her walking, she said, "If that was my child walking at that age, I would put her on the floor and put the playpen upside down on top of her." She thought she was far too young to be walking.

On the fifth morning, I waited until nine when the doctor's office hours started and called. The nurse said, "He's with a patient and cannot be disturbed."

I told her my story, and said I would wait on the line until he was available.

"That won't be necessary. He will call you when he is available," she said.

"Pardon me, I have waited four days to speak to him and he never found time to call me to respond to my concern, although I left messages for him to do so. This time, I will wait."

"It may be quite some time before he's done with his patient."

"That's all right. I've already waited four days."

Within moments, the doctor was on the line. "Mrs. Smith, we are keeping your daughter in for observation to make sure the blood isn't forming a clot underneath her skull and putting pressure on her brain," he said, sounding impatient and condescending.

"Can you tell me when that observation takes place and what they are looking for?" I asked.

"The nurses observe her throughout the day and night, when they feed her and change her and answer her calls. I try to stop in each day on my rounds. We check her pupils to see if they are normal size, see if there is swelling at the site and observe her actions to see if they are normal."

"Doctor, I have been there twelve hours a day. I have fed her, changed her, put her to sleep and played with her each and every day. I was never told what to look out for. The nurses only checked her pulse and temperature a few times a day. I've never seen them check her pupils. If she needs observation, could I not be informed what to watch for at home and even bring her in once a day to see you, if you need to do that? It seems to me that it would be far easier on her, me, and the rest of the family."

It took a bit more talking, but he finally agreed, so I spent one more day with her, and by the next day, he had signed her out. She was far happier at home. They had shaved off all her hair, except a four- or five-inch circle on the right side of her head. There was a scar of a near circle perhaps 1 ½ inch in diameter on the left side of her head. But her sparkling eyes were as bright as ever and the whole experience had not dimmed her enthusiasm for life and exploration.

The activity didn't stop with her hospitalization. When she was two, she climbed up on the counter, and with the aid of overturned bowls, got access to a cupboard I thought was way out of her reach. I had cough medicine the doctor had given me, of which a ¼ teaspoon dose made me very sleepy. She had consumed almost half the bottle by the time I found her. Within minutes she was like a rag doll. Even a finger in her throat brought no response. I had no car, so I called the doctor's office. The one on call was one I did not trust. He said, "She may sleep four or five days, but she'll be alright."

I didn't know what to do. I felt God nudging me to lay her on the couch, put my hands on her and pray. That I did, then I asked, "Now what, God?" She had shown no signs of improvement. "Go get supper ready and trust her to me." It was a hard thing to do, but I did, and even began singing a praise hymn to God. Underneath I was restless, but still that whisper came, "Just trust her to me and believe." Five or ten minutes later, she slid off the couch and began her usual merry chatter. I could only give thanks in utter amazement.

Those experiences, too, helped me, personally to grow in my trust and acceptance of what God allows, and in the ability to feel praise in the face of what seems to be adversity. That lesson was soon to be put to the test.

## CHAPTER 25
### Relationship Woes

> "Life is a school.
> Problems are simply a part of the curriculum."
> —**Anonymous**
>
> "I am the only one I can change.
> So if I'm unhappy about the way things
> are going between me and another person,
> I can either continue in my misery
> or change the one I can change!"
> —**Ruth Smith Meyer**

Uncle Joe, Aunt Mary and Dad continued to find it almost impossible to get a live-in companion for Grandma. When the Smith aunts couldn't handle it anymore, Mrs. Parsons from Toronto took over the duties. Anne Harvey came on Mrs. Parsons's days off. When Grandma needed heavier care, it was decided to put her into the Brierbush Hospital and later into Markhaven. I tried to visit her there, but she got almost violent and very upset at the sight of me. Because I had moved in where, in her mind, Dad should have been, she blamed me for her present situation. They finally asked me not to visit because it was so hard to settle her down after we left. That hurt me deeply. It wasn't my decision to place her in a home, but with Beth a young baby, I couldn't manage helping with the milking, the garden and orchard, and looking after Grandma too.

With our move to Altona, the tension between Norman and I had grown and sometimes felt unbearable. I often felt caught between my family of origin and my loyalty to my husband. Although we lived there, and it now was our home, it felt to my parents and to my siblings like "the home place" to which they had a right to come when they needed to. I wanted to make them feel welcome, but Norman was a more private person who needed his space. I didn't know if that was the problem because he wasn't able to say what was bothering him. I could only guess. Any time I got courage to ask what was wrong, I would get the same answer spoken through clenched lips, "Nothing!"

Beth's birth eased the tension somewhat, but soon it returned. With so many close neighbours, women often stopped in to visit. If Norman happened to come into the house, they, too, felt a certain tension and often stopped talking until he left again. That seemed to only make him more suspicious. I assumed that he wondered what were they talking about that couldn't be said in front of him.

When Grandma moved out, her end of the house was rented to John and Delores Jennings. They had two children, Vincent, who was Beth's age, and Jeanine, a few years younger. They became close and very good playmates. Delores and I had a lot of good conversations and also became close. Norman seemed to resent that too, although he never said so. The tension was obvious when he came into the house and Delores happened to be at our end. I felt as though I was walking a tightrope.

Living in Altona once more, I determined if I had to live there, I wanted to be more involved in the community than my parents had been. I was already involved in the prayer group at the Britton house, but soon after we moved back, the school districts were amalgamated. The by-then two-room schoolhouse off the farm property was closed, however, Art Latcham bought up many of those abandoned buildings and turned them over to the communities they had so faithfully served. A committee was formed to oversee the upkeep and plan ways to use the building for the good of the community. Both Norman and I got involved. He served as a board member and after a while as president, and I got involved in the social committee. We often organized suppers, pancake suppers, concerts and such activities.

In 1967, several of us decided a nursery school would be a good experience for our children. There still was no kindergarten at the Claremont School where our children would be going, and so we formed a co-operative to begin the school. I served as chair of the committee, and we hired Patricia Housten, a qualified teacher living in the community. Again, my horizons were broadened. I worked closely with Patricia. Parents were all expected to give of their time and take turns to help the teacher. After awhile, on days when Patricia couldn't be there, I would fill in for her. I longed to take courses to become fully qualified for such a job, but my days were too full. Since I was helping with chores, looking after the orchard, a large garden, it just wasn't feasible.

With all the possibilities opening up, I could see other places my talents could be used, and I began to see a bigger world. That started to interfere in our marriage. Norman felt left out while I was growing in my understanding and expanding my world. He felt rather threatened by my wish that I could do other things. I still felt that motherhood was my highest calling, but I wondered if I couldn't incorporate something outside the home as well. I had always felt inadequate at smoothly running a household, and I found some of these other newer tasks to be very fulfilling, because I felt much more capable of doing a good job. I loved it! When I noticed an advertisement for a TOPS Club (Take Off Pounds Successfully) beginning in Stouffville, I thought that might help me get my excess weight off. I had already been successful in losing about twenty pounds but had levelled off and couldn't seem to lose beyond that number.

The association with a whole new group of people not only helped me keep my eyes firmly on my weight-loss goal, it also widened my horizons again. The doctor lowered my caloric intake to 1200 calories, and again, I stuck to it faithfully. When the weight recorder resigned, I took over the task. I shared my enthusiasm and encouragement with others who were discouraged. I wrote notes and made phone calls and thought of many ways to keep them going.

In spite of my faithfulness in my intake of food and my morning exercise, the weight didn't fall off me as it did with many. Often my loss of the week was a half, one pound and very occasionally two or three. In between there would be gains of one or two, making the overall progress very slow. I had fashioned a paper chain—four links for each pound I wanted to lose—and festooned it around the kitchen wall as a visible sign of my progress. It was discouragingly slow.

Once, at one of my stand-stills, when I had made an appointment with the doctor to talk about my weight loss, a different doctor was the only one available. He inquired about my eating patterns.

"Are you aware of the calorie count of the foods you eat?"

"Oh yes, I keep close count on everything."

"How many calories are in an egg?"

"Seventy calories."

"Aha! Did you think of the butter you fried it in?" he smiled with a smug look.

"Oh, Doctor, I don't fry my eggs. I either poach or boil them."

"What about a slice of toast?

"Sixty-seven for a slice of white bread."

"How about the butter or jam you put on it?"

"One hundred and two in a tablespoon, but if I do use butter, I don't use more than a measured teaspoon full."

He paused. "It seems you have a good handle on calorie count. All your body really needs is a poached egg a day. Why don't you try that for a month?"

"I won't harm my health by doing that?

"No, you won't. Drink lots of water too."

In my day, most people believed their doctor knew just about everything about health. I went home determined to give it my all. The entire month of February, my daily intake was—one poached egg and lots of water.

I lost eleven pounds that month. I was delighted, but it didn't seem as great a weight loss as I expected from all that deprivation. I returned to the doctor and asked, "What do I do from now on?"

"Add a small salad at lunch with 2 or 3 ounces of chicken or tuna. Gradually increase up to 250 calories a day and stay on that until you've lost your weight. "

The first week after adding the small salad, I gained back six pounds, but then I did very slowly begin to lose bits at a time.

Now although I had three preschoolers and regularly helped with the milking twice a day, plus the housework and large garden and orchard, my life and my thinking more and more revolved around my weight loss, the TOPS club, the nursery school and church involvements.

Admittedly, I found it hard to set priorities and harder yet to refuse an opportunity to stretch my wings and try new challenges. As Norman saw it, I was spiralling out of control, not able to do everything because I was doing too much. Although there was more than an element of truth to that, I perceived him as being uncooperative in helping me become all I could be, wanting me to be nothing but a housewife.

Norman found it difficult to express himself, so instead of sitting down and talking about it, we began to draw apart. When I asked how he felt, I thought he wasn't answering. I later found out that he was just mulling it over in his mind so he would say it right! He didn't want to make a mistake. By the time he was ready to speak, I had moved on to something else, thinking he didn't care to talk about it.

Things came to a head soon after our ninth anniversary. Late one tension-filled night when the children had taken way too long to settle, I was dead-tired. Norman had gone to bed much earlier. I crawled into bed looking forward to finally getting some rest.

When I was almost asleep, Norman blurted out, "I don't plan to leave you and the kids, but you might as well know I'm finished with our marriage. Don't expect me to put any more effort into our relationship."

I was immediately wide awake! Hurt beyond belief, I was momentarily dumbfounded. *What effort?* I wondered to myself. I had come to feel that I was the only one trying or caring about our relationship.

"So are you saying I am to be only your housemaid and nanny for our children?" I finally asked.

He turned away to hug the other side of the bed and answered, "Suit yourself!"

I went to sleep with tears running down my cheeks. Norman didn't budge from his side of the bed.

The following days were a deep freeze. We got up in the morning without our customary hug and "Good morning!" Conversation took place at meals, but only about items of daily living that had to be addressed—appointments, the children, parts he wanted me to pick up at the farm machinery places.

*I'm obviously still useful for such mundane tasks*, I muttered under my breath when he asked me to do that.

My attempt to ask if we could talk about our situation got no reply on the first dozen tries. Finally he answered abruptly, "Nothing to talk about."

After several weeks of this stalemate, in early January, I formulated a plan. With a lot of prayer, but without consulting Norman, I asked someone to take over milking the cows for a long weekend, and a sister-in-law to stay with the three children, now seven, six and two. I packed our bags and informed him on Thursday night that we were leaving the next morning.

"What for and where to?" he asked in a flat voice.

"To a motel, where we will stay for the weekend and where we will talk," I answered.

No comment.

I wasn't sure Norman was going to cooperate.

The next morning we did leave and I drove.

We rode in silence except for the odd comment on the winter landscape or the kind of truck he loved when we saw one along the four-lane highway. After a few hours, we drove into a raging blizzard.

Bucking drifts and peering through the blowing snow, we finally reached an exit to London. The radio informed us that all major roads were closed. We had to manoeuver around road closure barricades to reach a motel with adjoining restaurant. The wind kept blowing. It was obvious we weren't going to be leaving any time soon.

Since there was nowhere to go, there was nothing to do but sit staring at one another or talk. Most of the next day, we did more of the staring than the talking, while I desperately prayed in silence.

Finally Norm's words came spewing out. Wow! He made it clear that all the changes I had made over the years had been misguided efforts—the very things that fed his frustration, insecurity and anger.

Norman never yelled, but the intense anger and frustration were evident in the controlled emphasis of his voice.

"You never tell me anything anymore." His brows were furrowed with pain. "You're always talking to your women friends on the phone or going to their place. I know you are telling them things you don't share with me. I don't even count in your life any more. I think you'd rather be with other people than me. Whenever I try to tell you how I see it, you argue back and make me feel I'm all wrong."

I wanted to explain why those things were happening. That he didn't seem interested in what I was doing or felt threatened by it. Oh, I had a million explanations, but I kept listening, because it was the first time that he had shared any of his feelings. Much as it hurt, I needed to know.

After another day and a half of finding out all that I was doing wrong, bit by barbed bit, I was decimated. I still had no clue what he *did* want. The list was long. I talked too much; I tried to help him finish his sentences if it took him too long to get the right words. I praised other people for the things they did, but he felt only disapproval from me. I could do anything I turned my hand to, and he had only a few strengths he felt were worthwhile. I could speak in public and his legs shook at the very thought of it.

Since explaining my side came through to him as arguing or saying he was wrong, I tried to keep silent. Through the bit of night remaining after his outbursts, he slept. I tossed and turned, trying to think how I could get him to express his needs while still acknowledging my own—pleading *God, help me out here.* How could it all fit together? It truly was a very long weekend, made longer by the fact that because of the snowy roads, we had an extra day before we could get home.

Norm finally had shared what was wrong, and I was thankful, but he still hadn't verbalized what he wanted of me, if there was anything he did like about me, or how I could still be myself. Furthermore, his discontent had made every strength I thought I had feel like a weakness. I felt so devastated by his revelations—listing everything he didn't want—I had no idea where to go from there.

Finally, the storm had let up outside so we could go home, but a new storm raged within me.

During the next year, there many agonizing prayers and long hours of talking far into the night before Norm could express his desires. His revelations often made me cry, which upset him. I kept telling him, "Even if it makes me cry, I need to know what you are feeling."

That was true, but I didn't know how to hear it without filling me with guilt. I knew his feelings had to come out, but I no longer knew how to voice mine for fear of making him quit. At least Norman seemed willing to work at our marriage again, so I listened when he was willing to talk, and I tried to encourage him to voice what he was thinking when I sensed that something was bothering him. Sometimes that took a long time.

There were moments when I felt total despair. One day on the way to Markham, I saw a big truck coming toward me. Unbidden, the thought crossed my mind, *If I swerved toward the truck at the last minute, all this struggle could be over.* That scared me. I knew that wasn't the answer. Even though I had come to feel that there was nothing good about me, I still was the mother of three children, and Norman was trying again. I changed my thoughts to *Lord, show me the way through this, and guide me to becoming what you want.*

## CHAPTER 26

# Getting Ready to Move

> "Life is not about waiting for the storm to pass,
> it is about learning to dance in the rain."
> —Vivian Greene

Meanwhile we had other issues to face. When we moved to Altona, the plan was to eventually turn our rent into payments toward the farm to make it our own. However, at about the same time as our marriage was crumbling, a threat to that plan was taking form. Developers devised a plan for *Century City* on a vast acreage in Uxbridge Township right north of our farm. They were planning to use the pond on the McNair property across the road for a sewage system. Of course, land prices skyrocketed.

Norman was anxious to have a farm of his own and to get started making it the way he wanted it to be. We started looking around at farms 25–30 miles away. So many farms had ramshackle houses and barns that would have to be completely renovated to house Holsteins of the calibre that Norman had and wanted. It was important to him to have a good house, since he said a barn would be renovated to make money so we could live, but a house could be put off and he was afraid it might be years before we could afford renovations to a home.

Several days we spent looking in the Uxbridge/Sunderland area. Another factor was choices of churches. We didn't want to have to drive almost an hour to a church in which we felt comfortable and where we wanted to be involved.

On our way home from our stormy London weekend, we stopped in at a real estate office to see what farms in the area were available. Several of them were to the north and west of the city. We decided to call on Peter and Ada Bunnett just south of Ailsa Craig since we were very close. Norman told Peter about looking at farms and he immediately took us to his neighbour's who were thinking of moving back to Belgium. The farm had a huge square light brick house with a large wing to the south. The moment I saw it, I exclaimed, "Not that house for me! That is way too much house to keep clean and tidy!"

We did like the area, though. It was close to a fairly large city, but reminded us of the Stouffville community 15 or 20 years prior to that time—still very much a farming community. We arranged to visit the Bunnetts again on a weekend and had Wayne Schlegel, a real estate agent, show us a few farms. There were a few of them that we really liked. On the way back to Stouffville, we also looked around the Kirkton/St. Marys regions.

The spring of 1969, Peter called. "My neighbor is ready to sell his farm and move to Belgium. Would you like to come and have a closer look at it?"

We arranged another trip and had a look at the 208–acre farm with the Ausable River making a large 'S' through it. There was quite an acreage of river flats with deep top soil. Some farmers may have felt the land to be cut up by the river and large banks of thorns and scrub trees. Norman and I saw it as a place where there would be lots of wildlife and beauty as well as good farming land. The barn was solid, but the stables would have to be enlarged as our registered Holsteins were much bigger than the grade cows the farmer had in them. The house was well built and solid, but the porch needed replacing and the bathroom was in need of major redecorating. Otherwise it was a good house. There were thirteen rooms in the main and second stories. Besides that there was a full basement divided into three rooms, with lots of head room and a beautiful attic that could have contained an apartment with the addition of dormers or skylights—but who needed that with all the room that was already livable? The kitchen had new cupboards—twenty-six doors and seven drawers! Although it was nice, I groaned inside to think of keeping all that space organized and tidy.

There was one problem though. The farmer wanted to sell it lock, stock and barrel—the grade cows, quota and machinery, as well as the farm. The cows we didn't need, because we already had our herd. We had much of our machinery too. We wanted only the farm, and so we went home without making an offer.

A few weeks afterward, we got a call from Ailsa Craig saying they would sell us only the farm, quota and machinery. Norman didn't really want the machinery; much of it wasn't what he needed. The negotiations went back and forth. We finally reached a deal that suited us, but we had to get our funding in place. Just when we had that ready, the farmer called to say the deal was off. They decided to stay in Canada. Since early in the process, we prayed that God would show us definitely if this was the farm for us. Although we were a little disappointed, since we had the financing in place, we told God we'd accept that as a "No." We felt quite peaceful.

Twice more, we got calls. "It's on again, we'll take it."

"No, we can't, it's off."

It felt as though we were on a roller coaster. Each time there was a real letdown and feeling of disappointment before we could finally leave it in God's hands again. We almost gave up on that being the place God had in mind.

It was busy summertime, so we went on with our usual work and didn't even start looking again. In early September, the farmer called again and said, "We decided to go to Belgium—and this time it's for sure. If you still want the farm, come out next week to our lawyer in Parkhill and we'll sign the deal."

They would have a farm sale to sell their equipment and household furnishings on the 15th of March and leave for Belgium the next day. We would have possession the same day. We made the trip to Parkhill, signed the papers, and went to look at the farm again to let the reality soak in. I noted the garden had six-foot pigweed covering most of it.

We came home, our emotions a jumble of jubilance, jitters and panic. Jubilance, because we finally had something concrete in our plans; jitters because it meant moving away from our home stomping grounds and source of support, and the knowledge that it was a large commitment; panic because moving 150 miles with household goods, farm equipment and livestock was going to take a lot of packing and planning.

Meantime we still had corn silage to put in, gardening to finish up and the produce of 48 apple trees to pick, process and sell. After talking about it, searching for a place and thinking about it, we were actually doing it! We were also still struggling with getting our feelings out in the open, dealing with our different perceptions and re-building our marriage. We hoped the move would bring us closer together as we began again in a new community.

That Christmas we told our children that the gifts would be small, because we would need to save all the money we could to buy our farm. Stuart had his heart set on a Hot Wheel set with all kinds of tracks and several cars. Bless his heart, he came one day and said, "Mom you don't have to get me Hot Wheels, if we are buying a farm."

"Thank you, Stuart!" I gave him a hug. "There will be something for you on Christmas Eve, but it will just have to be small this year."

"Could we have a little bit of money to get you and Dad a gift though?"

"Perhaps a little."

"Could Aunt Eva help us buy it?

"I think she could do that sometime, when she comes up to Stouffville."

I smiled at the way our children were growing up. I remembered the previous Christmas when we had opened our gifts on Christmas Eve.

The children were happy with their gifts and exclaiming over them. All of a sudden, Stuart grabbed Wilma's hand and took her into the hall at the bottom of the steps and shut the door behind them saying, "Don't come in here. We'll just be a minute."

We were curious to know what they were doing that would have taken them away from their new toys. Finally the door opened up and they shoved a large box into the living room. "This is for you, Mom and Dad. We thought you should have something too!"

We opened the box to satisfy our curiosity and smiled as we saw it filled with clean laundry that had been waiting on the stairs to be taken up with the next trip. I still say that is one of the nicest gifts I received, because it proved that our son was growing up and becoming aware of the desire to give as well as get.

Christmas came that year, and when the children opened their gifts, they were undoubtedly elated with what they found. Stuart got one length of Hot Wheels track and two little cars. His gratitude was as deep as if he'd got the whole set. In fact when his friend Danny called to say that he had received the whole set and expressed sympathy for Stuart because he got so little, Stuart told him, "Oh no, you don't understand, Danny. I didn't think I would get any because we're buying a farm. I'm really glad for what I have."

The girls got new home-made clothes for their dolls and were quite happy with their gifts too.

When we opened the gift the children gave us, we were happy too. It was *Kerplunk*; a table game they all thought would be fun. Our family did have a lot of fun playing with it in the years to come.

After Christmas, the packing and planning began in earnest. Every spare moment I had, I packed those things we could do without. I still helped milk twice a day and although I was trying to withdraw, there was continued involvement in the nursery school where Beth now took part.

The children got sick soon after the New Year. I had also been suffering from a cold. When I had to take one of them to the doctor on call, I mentioned my own cold and told him my inability to fight it off may be due to my strict diet. When he heard what I was eating, he cautioned me to not continue. He felt that unless I was trying to become a model for bikinis, I didn't need to lose more weight. My goal had been set at 150 pounds and I had reached 164. He gave me a letter to change it to 160, ordered me to increase my calorie intake to at least 500-700 and gradually increase it to 1000. Furthermore, he ordered a bone-marrow test to make sure I hadn't ruined my health.

I was rather shocked, because I had been following doctor's orders and thought I was doing a good thing. I did gradually increase my calories and didn't gain weight.

I began to pack in earnest. There were not only our possessions to decide whether to take along or get rid of, but also pieces that Mom and Dad had left behind that needed to be evaluated. First I needed to know if they still wanted them, then to decide if I wanted to take along what they didn't claim, or to ask my siblings or get rid of those too.

By the end of February, my sister Eva came to help. I had long ago promised myself that I would someday give Eva a birthday party, because she was always doing things for others but never got much for herself. I figured I could make it a real surprise by having it early. I asked her if she could come on a certain day to pack everything in the spare room which was away from the road and the lane, so she couldn't see people arrive. I invited all the ladies from our prayer group and a few others to come in the afternoon. Eva went up to get started and I told her I'd be up as soon as I could. Everyone got into the living room without detection and I called, "Eva, could you come down here and give me a hand?"

When she opened the hall door, everyone called out, "Surprise! Happy Birthday!"

My dear sister was absolutely surprised and flabbergasted! She had to quickly sit down because her legs were weak. We had a nice afternoon and I think she enjoyed it. I'm so glad I took the opportunity while I could.

A move of a few blocks is a lot of work, but this move would be 150 miles and would include not only household items, but our farming operation, lock, stock and barrel.

Emotional attachment and need to disengage was a reality as well. Even though from early childhood, I had wanted to move far away from the place of my birth, I was now leaving behind all that was familiar. My support system would no longer be in close proximity. The uncles and aunts, cousins and second cousins who surrounded me in Pickering and Markham Townships would no longer be a part of my everyday life. Even the doctors, lawyers and other professional people to whom I was accustomed would no longer be available. Many of these people had been involved in my life and that of my family for generations. Added to that were the involvements that I so enjoyed—the nursery school, Sunday School teaching and song leading—all things for which I'd had no opportunity to do in my younger years.

Still in the 1970s, many people were born, grew up and continued to live in the same community all their lives. The growing metropolis of Toronto and the implications of that giant octopus reaching out its tentacles into the surrounding peaceful farmland changed that for many families who had deep roots in the countryside.

There was also a very real excitement in preparing to move. Norman's mother, although she was going to miss us, took some satisfaction from knowing we were moving back to within a half-hour's drive from where she grew up in the Zurich area.

As originally planned, the owners of the Ailsa Craig farm had an auction sale on the 15th of March, 1970. Norman and I drove out to be there. It was a lovely spring day, the snow was mostly melted and the lawn was very soft. As I watched vehicles turn around on the lawn and make deep ruts, I wondered if we'd ever get the lawn in shape again. We stayed until it was over, had a few words yet with the former owners and collected our keys, because they were leaving that night for Belgium.

It had been a long and emotional day, but although we'd had someone to do the evening milking, we had to be back to do it in the morning. We were so tired and sleepy that we switched driving several times on the way home. Coming up Markham Road from the 401, we were close enough that we began to relax—which made us all the more sleepy. In that stretch, we changed perhaps a half dozen times. We really should have stopped and had a nap. However, we did get home safely.

A week and a half later was March break. We packed mattresses, one bed, food and cleaning equipment and headed west to spend that week in our new abode.

When we arrived, we were shocked to find the TV aerial missing (it had not been sold at the auction), every light bulb in house and barn was gone, and the water bowls in the pig barn were cut off and gone. We had to go into town to buy several packages of light bulbs for the coming darkness.

The front unheated entrance made a wonderful refrigerator for the week. My sister Eva had baked a big batch of cookies and sent them along in a bread bag. Those I left on the counter top for the night, along with a few other containers of food that didn't need refrigeration.

We set up a bed in a room upstairs and laid mattresses in two other rooms—one for Stuart and one for the girls. When we were all settled for the night, there began a racket in the attic that made us wonder what in the world inhabited that space. It sounded big enough that it must at least be squirrels, and it thudded as though they had a bowling alley in the attic.

The next morning, what had been a completely full and untouched bread bag of cookies was now literally completely empty except for a few crumbs. There was a medium- size hole eaten through the bag, but otherwise untouched. The cookies were gone. Evidence on the counter around the bag let me know it was mice. But how many mice would it take to eat that many cookies in one night? I shuddered at the thought. I'm not as afraid of mice as my mother, but the image of there being that many was rather daunting.

I went to the hardware store in Ailsa Craig and bought ten mouse traps and great packages of mouse poison. I also acquired steel wool, fiberglass insulation and plaster of paris. Every night, I set all ten traps. Every morning all ten traps had caught a victim. The mouse poison, too, had to be replenished each day. Sometimes the traps even snapped on victims through the day. I looked through the cupboards along the floorboards at every corner, nook and cranny where a mouse may find entrance. I stuffed in steel wool and fiberglass insulation and sealed it off with plaster of paris. We washed out cupboards; we washed down walls and vacuumed the papered walls. We polished windows and did our best to prepare for our move in May.

Norman arranged with the milk inspector to come look at the barn and milk house from which we wanted to ship milk and get his specifications as to what needed to be done.

At the end of the week, we set all ten traps again, made lists of all we needed to do, both house and barn, and left again for Altona to get things prepared at that end.

We would have to make several trips to put in the seeding and prepare the barn for our cows. The stanchions were not long enough for our cows, so we ripped out what was there; John Reesor and Claude Kerr came to help us install new ones in the main part of the barn. Eventually we wanted to convert the attached pig barn to cow and box stalls, but that would have to wait until later. The spider webs had been hanging down to head height when we saw the barn so those had to be cleaned and the walls whitewashed before we could ship milk.

When we returned, with Norman's parents for another five days the beginning of April, all the mouse traps were full and there were even two mice that had jumped into a plastic pail I had used to wash walls and floors. They had obviously not been able to get out again because they had expired there. Again, we kept setting traps each night until it finally slowed down and not all were full every night.

On that visit, which was over Norman's birthday on the 11th, I asked Norman to plow the garden so I could plant. I didn't know when I would be back, so I planted everything, thinking I could replant if it got frozen off.

We made several shorter visits to keep things progressing at the farm. When we called the milk inspector to come again, he was pleasantly surprised. He said he had thought to himself on his first visit, "They'll never make this barn fit to ship first grade milk." But he was pleased with the changes we had made.

By the second visit, I knew that my garden was going to require a great deal of attention. It appeared to have been generously seeded down with pigweed. In spite of frequent trips through with the garden tractor and hoe, a few days later, the total coverage of green would once more blanket the entire garden.

CHAPTER 27

## The Move

"It was an image Melody would never forget.
Or was it the emotions the image conjured—
hope, excitement, and fear of the unknown,
all three tightly braided together, creating a fourth
emotion that was impossible to define.
She was getting a second chance at
happiness and it tickled like swallowing fifty
fuzzy caterpillars."

—Lisi Harrison

Back at Altona, many people came to help us get ready. There were farewell parties—church, community and TOPS club. On moving day, John had his big truck; Paul Meyer offered to take a load and several others did the same. John and Norman took machinery, Steve Wideman took the cattle, and several other trucks and cars took up the cavalcade. Norman and I left in our vehicle, a little earlier than the others, so we could be there to guide those unloading to get things in the right place. It was a hectic afternoon and evening getting things into some semblance of order. The first priority in the house was to get beds all set up ready for a good night's rest. Of course, the cows had to be milked right away.

I didn't even think that day or for a long time afterward, that we should have provided a meal for those who so generously helped in the move. There were no pizza shops or fast food places anywhere near Ailsa Craig at that time, but surely we could have planned to bring sandwiches or something and at least make a big pot of coffee!

Since there was only a month and a bit of school remaining, we left Stuart and Wilma with John and Delores Jennings to finish off their Grade Two year. They came to Ailsa Craig the week before school ended so they could try out East Williams and get to know at least a few students, so not everything would be new in September.

Several families from the Nairn Mennonite Church brought us dishes of food, and the first Sunday before we even got everything unpacked, Hank and Hildegard Thiesen dropped in to welcome us to the community. A few weeks later, we were accepted as members in that church.

At our farewell parties before we left, we had invited people to come see where we were living. They did! Between June and the end of November we hosted 190 guests. A few just came for a call, more stayed and enjoyed a meal and many came for a weekend. In fact, we had only a few weekends without guests in that time and those were usually the ones when we went back to the Markham area for Saturday and Sunday to see family and friends. In August, we hosted the entire youth group from Steeles Avenue; they spent a weekend with us. George and Anna Reesor were the youth sponsors and they came along. What a wonderful weekend that was. Sleeping bags were stretched out from one wall to the other in the big room above the kitchen. The girls slept there. A few boys slept in the living room and family room in the house, but more of them wanted to sleep in the hay mows in the barn. However, there was only one bathroom for, I believe, it was 26 people in the house those three days.

It was so nice to have the youth of the church so interested in where we had moved—enough to spend a weekend with us. Of course we had known them from the time of their birth and I had taught many of them in Sunday School.

On the Saturday night, we planned a wiener roast. After everyone had their fill, someone suggested that we should have had marshmallows.

"Norman, would you get my wallet and go to the Variety Store in Ailsa Craig to pick up a few bags of marshmallows?" I asked.

I had just cashed the family allowance cheque, so had the funds to do it. When he came back, he handed the bag to whoever was at the table where we had laid out the hot dog fixings.

Monday morning I needed something in town and looked for my wallet in my purse. It wasn't there.

"Norman, where did you put my wallet Saturday night?"

"I put it in the bag with the marshmallows."

My heart sank to my shoes. After scouring the house, I went to look in the ashes left from the bonfire. There I found the metal parts of the wallet, but my grocery money for the month, my license, my birth certificate and other important papers were gone!

We lived very frugally the next month, and our meals consisted of what we had in the garden and freezer plus milk from the milk tank.

We were glad for each one of our visitors, but it did make a busy year. I was helping now, not only with milking the cows and washing the milking equipment, but also with the haying and field work. We were not flush with money that first year, so it took some ingenuity to find food for all those meals. Some weekend visitors did help by bringing food along or shopping for some groceries to help out.

CHAPTER 28

# A New Community

> "You are my hiding place;
> you will protect me from trouble
> and surround me with songs of deliverance.
> I will instruct you and teach you in the way
> you should go; I will counsel you with
> my loving eye on you."
> —**Psalm 32:7-8, NIV**

Anxious to become involved and get to know our new community, I threw myself into anything I could find to do. My first effort went to finding another TOPS club. There was one meeting in Parkhill, so I weighed in there the first full week we were in our new home. The rest of the members couldn't quite share fully in my joy when the scales revealed I had reached my goal. They didn't know of my long trek toward that finish line. It may have just been the difference in scales, but I had hung around the last three or four pounds above my goal for months. To have reached it was quite a feat. The association with the members in that club was a tremendous help in getting to know the people in the area.

That summer when it was time to refill my thyroid prescription, I looked at the pills and told the druggist they didn't look like what I had been taking. He said they were probably just from a different company, but they were what the prescription required. I was apprehensive but took them home and began using them. In ten days, I had gained twenty pounds. My long-awaited goal weight had disappeared. I called my family doctor in Stouffville. He had made a mistake and quickly corrected it. The gain stopped, but I could not rid myself of those pounds that had come flooding back.

In September, school started. At Claremont, because Wilma had the advantage of nursery school, they thought she would get bored in kindergarten, so they moved her up to Grade One, but into a different class than Stuart. At East Williams there weren't enough children to have two classes of one grade, so Stuart and Wilma ended up in the same room. We felt some concern, but tried to talk to them and prepare them for it.

We got a notice about a Meet-the-Teachers Corn Roast. There, too, we met other parents in the area. One couple invited us to come to the Home and School meeting later in the month. That was another opportunity to get to know the parents of those in our children's classes and to feel a part of the community.

That fall, we saw an announcement in the bulletin about a Marriage Enrichment Weekend to be held at Chesley Lake. Even in our busy life, we were still struggling with our relationship. Both of us thought it may be a good idea to go. Another couple from the Nairn congregation also wanted to go, so Norman and I scraped together the cost of the weekend, made arrangements for someone to do the chores, the required four milkings, and went. The cost was difficult to manage, but our relationship was worth trying our best.

The input at the weekend was excellent and the discussions in the whole group good, but a little intimidating. They weren't conducive to sharing the deeper wounds and areas needing healing. We also met in smaller clusters—but we were rather distressed that those groups were set up so that husband and wife wouldn't be in the same one. I was afraid to say too much, because I couldn't check with Norman if it was okay to share it.

We could request a private time with the weekend's resource person, a psychologist and counsellor from Indiana. I did that and told him about Norman's giving up on our marriage and the weekend I had planned to get us talking. He applauded me for my effort, which was very affirming to me. Years later, my sister-in-law saw the same man as a counsellor for herself. At one point he told her she should get her brother's wife to take her to a motel for a weekend. She had to ask me what that was about.

It was the first time, though, that Norman was able to identify some of his deeper feelings and unlock the treasure chest of his true self, even if it was only a crack. I was elated and honoured to have him reveal that treasure to me. When we came home, something had definitely changed. We felt hopeful, but it was difficult to continue on our own.

Meantime, farming on his own was taking its toll on Norman. Up until now, he always had worked with his Dad, with Allan, and then with Uncle Joe, especially in the busy times. He longed to have someone to work with and became quite depressed. I was really concerned when it seemed to be hard for him to wake in the morning, get out of bed and get going. He started chores later and later each morning. This was the man who was very particular that the cows should be milked regularly every twelve hours. After lunch, he'd lie on the couch and, instead of falling asleep and waking, ready to go in ten minutes as usual, he would stretch his rest to an hour. We thought of hiring help, but he wished he could arrange it so that they could be more like partners—that the other man would have a vested interest in the farm. I think it seemed more and more impossible to find the right combination, which just made him feel more hopeless. I tried to find ways to help more with the farm work, but with a large garden and my feeling that I should also be doing all the sewing I could to save money, it made my load almost too heavy.

It was when we were filling silo that year that an incident made us super aware of how fast things could change. I was driving tractor in the corn field while Norman took the loads to the barn to put them in the silo. The old John Deere 630 had a cranky clutch that sometimes didn't cooperate. Once when I was backing up with the harvester to hitch on to the wagon, the clutch grabbed unexpectedly, pinning him between the tongue and the harvester. He yelled in pain and I quickly went forward. Thankfully, it was no more than bruises, but I felt shaken for the rest of the day and Norman made sure after that to stand to the side.

The fall of 1971, we worked on incorporating the ell that had been a pig barn into more stabling. That entailed a lot of hard work with the air hammer— it was back-breaking work. John Reesor and Claude Kerr, who had helped get the barn ready for our cows, now helped with the renovation of our barn. We also had decided early that spring to enlarge our family. The new little one was due the middle of November. It probably wasn't the best timing.

I kept asking if he could manage if I had the baby at home. At the birth of each of the children, my labour slowed down between home and hospital. I thought it could be exciting to just stay home for the birth. Norman was not at all inclined to have that happen even if he was well experienced with helping cows give birth.

Saturday, November 6, I'd had contractions all day. I was tired of being pregnant. When we got into bed, I asked Norman, "Is it okay if I go into labour and have the baby tonight?"

"Oh, if you have to, but if you could wait one more week, the barn would be at a better stage," the poor tired man said.

The next Saturday night, I asked the same question.

"I guess you were good enough to wait a week, but it would be nice to have at least a few hours of sleep."

At midnight, I awoke and knew I was in labour, but not wanting a repeat of what had happened before, I waited until the contractions were five minutes apart. At three-thirty, I gently shook him and said, "I think it's time for us to go to the hospital, if you are sure you don't want to deliver the baby."

He was out of bed, pulling on his pants while he asked, "What time is it and how far along are you?"

We had arranged for Uncle Levi and Aunt Ina Smith, who had also moved to Ailsa Craig, to come and stay with the children when the time came. I went to the telephone—Aunt Ina said they would be there in a few minutes—while Norman went to get the car warmed up. We got to St. Joseph's Hospital in London in record time. He was taking no chances. When we got to the hospital, they settled me in and examined me.

"It won't be for a while," the nurse assured me.

I felt let down, but resigned myself to another wait. Norman came into the room and almost before he sat down, I told him, "Go get the nurse! The baby is coming."

The nurse came with a look of forbearance on her face. She lifted the sheet, I'm sure, with another speech ready to placate me.

"Oh my goodness!" She hastily replaced the sheet, loosened the brakes and started for the door, "It is coming!" she said as she hastened down the hall. She stopped at the door outside the delivery room long enough to tell the doctors, "If you want to be there to deliver the baby, get your gloves on and get in there!"

They each got one glove on before the newest member of our family made her debut fifteen to twenty minutes after arriving at the hospital, and perhaps a minute after the stretcher was in place. The name was to have been Steven Christopher John, but after some consideration, we settled on Loralyn Kaye which seemed more suitable for a girl.

Grandpa and Grandma Smith came out to care for the family until we got home a few days later. Stuart could hardly wait to take me into the living room and inform me that a sister wasn't part of the deal he wanted. He was willing to have a little brother, but another sister? He was not happy at all. However, after a good cry and my telling him what a wonderful thing it is for a young girl to have a big brother, and how special he could be to her, he settled down and began to think of ways to develop a special relationship with her—and he did.

Beth found it a little difficult in adjusting to no longer being the youngest in the family. A few days after Loralyn and I were at home, she was on edge, so since I needed something in town, I took her along. When we got settled into the car and headed to town, I looked over at her.

"Do you want to tell me how you are feeling?"

"Oh, Mom! I don't know." Tears came to her eyes. "I'm not little any more, but I'm still too little to be big!"

*What an astute observation for a five year-old.* "Oh, Beth, you don't have to be big all the time yet. Sometimes you'll want to be big sister to Loralyn, but sometimes you'll still want to be our little Mary Beth and that's alright! You can take your time to grow up."

Tears streamed down her face as she said, "Thank you, Mom!" As typical of our happy little girl, she sighed deeply, smiled in relief and chattered merrily about something else.

That year, we were asked if we would provide a place for a woman who had spent quite some time in the psychiatric hospital and needed a half-way house before returning home. Magella came to live with us. She was a big help, especially through the early stages of my pregnancy. She had four girls just about the same age as our children. I think it helped her at times when she missed her own girls. She struggled a lot with insecurity and fear of traumatizing her children the same way she had been impacted when her father experienced mental illness in her childhood. At those times she became suicidal. When she started taking a real interest in our morning Bible readings, we had good conversations about what a personal relationship with God could do for her. She was beginning to read and pray on her own and we rejoiced to see a new confidence in her. That continued until her supervisor brought her superior to visit. When Magella told them how she was finding new self-assurance and meaning for her life in a developing relationship with the Lord, the supervisor's superior began scolding her like a little child.

"Now, Magella! We've been trying to get you to walk alone," he said, patiently, "By doing that you are just substituting one crutch for another."

I was horrified and saddened to see her wilt right in front of my eyes. I had to speak up.

"With all due respect, even if faith in Christ was a crutch as you suggest, sometimes when we are hurt or broken, a crutch is a good thing. However, what Magella had told you about isn't a crutch, but Someone who has been giving her self-confidence and has made her feel more whole."

The damage was done, though. A few nights later, she came downstairs confessing that she had taken a whole bottle of pills. I raced her to the hospital to have her stomach pumped.

Again, I gently tried to encourage her, build up her self-esteem and I tried to tell her the gentleman didn't know what a relationship with Jesus could be. He was mistaken in his ideas, and she should continue reading her Bible and pray, because I could see the difference it made. She really struggled with it because she wanted so much to get well. She was afraid she would end up like her father, spending his last days in a nursing home, long before he was the age most people are in such facilities.

A few weeks later, I had gone to a meeting. The children were playing outside, when Magella came to the kitchen door with a towel wrapped around her arms and told the children to get their father. He was down the back lane fixing a fence, but they ran to get him.

She had doused herself in nail polish remover and set herself on fire. Norman called Peter Bunnett to accompany him to the hospital with Magella. Good thing he did, because she would have opened the car door and tossed herself out on the way. At home, there were bits of charred clothing in the hall and a few places where it had burned into the wood. She was in Strathroy Hospital several months while her wounds healed. I visited her regularly. I was distressed when her caregivers sent her to a nursing home in St. Jacobs when she was ready to be released. I tried to advocate for her, because I knew she would feel that was the end of the road.

Several months later, I received a letter from her sister saying Magella was sent on a bus for a weekend to go to her home near Waterloo, but she never arrived. She had taken another bus to Niagara Falls, left her purse and a message on a park bench and had thrown herself over the railing into the churning waters above the falls. Her body was retrieved later from the water below. Her message said she felt it better for her family if her life was ended.

## LIFE KEEPS HAPPENING

There's something to be said for experience. Our first three children were born within four years. When you start at age twenty-one, you learn parenting on the job while you, yourself, are still maturing. When Loralyn was born almost ten years after our first baby, we had done a lot more living. We both, but I especially, was much more relaxed. However, there was one thing I was insistent on—this baby would be harnessed firmly into the high chair any time she was placed in it. One Sunday when Loralyn was almost eight months old, I asked the others in the family to take Loralyn into the house while I went to cut a head of cabbage to use for lunch. When I came into the kitchen, Loralyn was crying and crawling toward the family room where everyone else had settled. Right away, I noticed a swelling on the whole right side of her head. Touching it, I felt the puffy, fluid underneath her skin. Whoever had brought her in had set her in the high chair—without the harness! She had fallen out and was crawling to join the rest of the family. No one saw it happen.

A trip to St. Joseph's Hospital and an x-ray showed a hairline fracture from which some of the fluid was leaking between the skull and the skin. They wanted to keep her in for observation. Because of allergies our children developed, I was breastfeeding and only introducing foods very gradually. Loralyn had already shown intolerance to wheat products, so I told them to feed her nothing but rice Pablum and that I would be in to breastfeed her by nine in the morning.

The following morning, when I arrived, I knew by the smell of the diaper and the colour of its content that she'd had wheat products. I had to remind them again and again.

She was in for a few days, but having learned from previous experience, I soon asked if I could be told what to watch for and do it from home. I was granted that privilege and Loralyn progressed well—

probably better than her mother who was dealing with guilt feelings, having allowed two of her babies to have fractured skulls!

The spring of 1974, we made another change in our farming routine. Jim and Bea Bender—Lorne and Katie's son— had been married the year before we moved out to Ailsa Craig and had gone on a two-year volunteer assignment with Mennonite Central Committee in Winnipeg, Manitoba. When they returned, Lorne and Katie built a house in Ailsa Craig and Jim and Bea moved onto the farm. Jim really wanted to go into dairy but felt he couldn't afford everything he would need. We invited them to come to our place and presented them with a proposal to enter into partnership. There was some hesitancy on their part, fearing that such a working relationship may end up with hard feelings that could affect our church life. I assured them that Norman was used to working with someone, and that he wasn't one either to get hurt easily or to insist on his way of doing things. It was agreed that Jim would look for a herd of Holsteins of comparable size; we would buy more quota and roll the equipment both of us owned into the partnership. The milking would be done on our farm and the young cattle housed in Jim's barn. That meant enlarging the barn for a bigger herd. There were several more weeks of back-breaking work, breaking up cement, shaping the new stalls and gutters ready to accommodate more Holsteins.

That spring, the doctor decided I should go in to the hospital for a week to do extensive tests regarding my thyroid. I kept gaining weight and was tired and sluggish much of the time. I often told Norman, "I wonder if I'll ever feel slept out again. I seem to be tired first thing in the morning as soon as I wake up."

Norman's parents came to cook for the family and care for two-year-old Loralyn while I was gone. They wanted me to go off of my thyroid medication several weeks before. That really slowed me down.

On arrival at the hospital, the doctors immediately ordered blood tests and other procedures. A doctor and team of students came to my bedside one day to test my reactions. They asked me to close my eyes and tell them when I felt a pin prick. They started with my face and continued downward on different parts of my body. Each time I said "Yes," when I felt it. When they got down to my legs, one of the students laughed out loud when I answered.

"What's so funny?" I asked.

"It's just that I prick you with the pin and there's a long pause, then you say 'Yes.' It's taking a long time for the message to get from the prick of the pin to your brain."

They put me on a very high calorie diet. I was told to eat it all. Big servings of potatoes, pasta, vegetables and meat ending with a generous helping of sweet, sweet desserts—things I hadn't eaten in years. I couldn't always eat it all. Still I was urged to eat up.

I gained ten pounds in those five days in hospital. They came to the conclusion that I didn't need thyroid and that I should go home on a 1200 calorie diet. I was thunderstruck!

"After two years of 250 calories a day and several years at 500 a day, taking thyroid, and still not losing weight, how do you think I'm supposed to maintain, much less lose weight on that?"

"We'll send a dietician to help you know what to eat. Try it and see how it goes."

The dietician came. She asked me what I had been eating and wrote everything down. She asked a plethora of questions and said she would be back.

Later that day she did come back. She pulled up a chair close to my bed.

"I have examined what you say you have been eating. You are quite right on your calorie count. If I would have been asked to plan a 500–calorie a day diet, I couldn't have done a better job of balancing the necessary nutrition a body needs. Since the doctor ordered a 1000 calorie diet, I have made some additions that I suggest you try."

I again voiced my fear that I would gain weight.

"You may not have had enough calories to burn off fat. It does take some calories to do that. Give it a try and see how it goes. The doctor has made an appointment for you to come back in nine months to check on your progress."

Those nine months, I religiously stuck to the diet menu that had been given to me. I was pleased that I didn't gain weight, but at my appointment I was down only one- half pound when the nurse weighed me.

"So how are you doing," the doctor asked when he came in.

"Not very good. At least I didn't gain, but I didn't lose either."

"What do you mean by that? You were down a half a pound!"

"You must be joking, doctor! If it takes nine months to lose each half pound, it would take at least 15 years to take off the ten pounds you put on me the five days I was in hospital."

"I'm not joking, and I want you to continue as you have been." His voice let me know he was insulted. I also perceived that there was no use to argue or even plead. He was done. He had finished his time with me. I waited until I got into the car, then I cried all the way home.

I did as instructed, but without thyroid, my mind slowed to a crawl. It took inordinately longer to do even easy tasks like doing laundry or loading the dishwasher. Every action became a separate effort —pick up plate, turn toward dishwasher, place in rack, turn toward table, pick up dish…each punctuated with a long pause until my brain kicked into gear. Norman wouldn't allow me to drive the car, and he had to pick up on many of the tasks I usually did. Finally after almost a year of that, he said I had to call the doctor at the hospital and tell him he had to do something, because my family could no longer live with me as I was.

When I finally got him on the phone, he listened then said, "Don't worry, we'll fix you up. Call your family doctor and he'll have a little something up his sleeve that will help."

"A little something up his sleeve? Can you tell me the name of that little something?"

"You don't need to worry about what it's called. Just call your doctor."

I didn't want any kind of "speed" medication and pled with him to know what he was recommending and wondering if it wouldn't be better to do further investigation to see if we couldn't find the root cause, but nothing was forthcoming.

I told Norman I wasn't comfortable with taking something I didn't know what else it might do to me. He said, "We have to do something. Ask your family doctor what it is, and if he thinks you should take it."

What was prescribed was called DBI and my doctor, thinking it might help, encouraged me to try it. It did seem to help a bit, but it became a way of life that by evening my brain was too slow to be able to get a meal together. The older girls took over the work of the evening meal with me just pre-planning and supervising if they needed help. Life settled into a new kind of normal.

Probably because of her older siblings, Loralyn seemed to be anxious to catch up and be doing what they were doing. She reminded us of her older sister, Wilma, in her ability to talk, and talk and talk from a very early age. Although I didn't allow too much television, she loved Mr. Dress-up and learned a lot from him. One time when I was folding laundry, she asked if she could do the towels. I made a pile of them on the end of the couch. She took one and laid it out flat, carefully folded the whole length in thirds, brought the ends to the middle then folded it in half.

"Where did you learn to fold them like that?" I asked, in amazement. I had never ever folded a towel thus.

"That's how Mr. Dress-up says you do it. He showed us how yesterday."

Her favorite pastime was "betending" that she was Susan, Mr. Dress-up's frequent visitor. When she was finished eating, she'd find a scarf, put it around her neck and perhaps find a pair of my shoes and knocked at the door between the dining room and kitchen.

"Come in," one of us would call out.

"Hello! I'm Thuthan!" she'd chirp merrily with her distinct lisp.

"Hello, Susan!"

From there she'd repeat some of the show she had watched just before lunch, ad libbing to suit her taste. When she ran out of material, she'd go to the other side of the door and do it all over again. She never seemed to tire of it.

## CHAPTER 29

# Fostering and Flames of Fallacy

> "It is not the strength of your faith that saves you,
> but the strength of Him upon whom you rely"
> —Charles Spurgeon

Stuart enjoyed his little sister, but he still at times wished he had a brother, so when Ed Driediger, who ran Nairn Family Homes, asked if we'd consider taking a foster child for a while, we thought perhaps it would be company for Stuart in a household of so many females. The boy Ed had in mind was actually seventeen, but developmentally more like an 8–12 year-old. We talked it over and Stuart was enthusiastic about it. That summer, Stuart was scheduled to go to Fraser Lake Camp for a week. While he was gone, Ed called and wondered if we could take Ken right away. We should have waited, but we didn't know all the circumstances. Stuart didn't have the best of weeks. Some rather negative things had happened and he was anxious to unload his unhappiness when he came home. When we picked up Stuart at his drop-off point, Ken was along, so Stuart felt forced to hold it all in until he had his parents alone. To add further to the tension, Ken had always lived in foster homes, and took Stuart to be a new foster son.

But since Ken thought he had been there first, he felt he had the edge on Stuart. Things were off on the wrong foot from that moment.

Ken had no concept of being born into a family and always having the same family. When he realized that Stuart had already been in our home before camping week, he kept asking how long he'd been with us. No amount of explaining could help him understand. When Ken first heard about and then met the children's Smith grandparents, he finally began to perceive the relationships. Often he would look sad after one of the children talked about their grandparents.

"What's the matter, Ken?" we'd ask.

"I don't think I have a grandma or grandpa. I don't even know if I have a mother or a dad. I don't belong to anybody."

We tried to assure him that he did belong to our family now, but we weren't sure if he believed us. Because of his experience in foster homes, he found it very disconcerting when I asked him to do one job and one of the others something else. He thought we should all be doing the same thing. He was very comfortable helping with dishes or cleaning, especially if two or more would do it together, but outside work didn't go well at all. He felt much more at ease joining Loralyn with her activities than exploring outside with Stuart. As a result, the two boys got into arguments and got quite testy with one another.

Eventually, Ed found a job for Ken with a crew in the area, because Ken would soon be aging out of Child and Family Services. He seemed happy to be considered adult enough to have a job. Saturday, October 19, 1974, over a year after he came, he was to have been picked up to go to work at 4:30 a.m. We never found out why, but they didn't show up. He was angry and disappointed. He and Stuart were niggling away at each other so Norman said he'd take Stuart with him to another farm where he was ploughing and Ken could throw straw from the mow and bed the cows.

Again, Ken was unhappy, because he was doing something by himself. However, he finally went to the barn. Perhaps a half hour later, he came running into the house.

"There's a fire in the straw mow!"

"Are you sure?" I asked, as I ran out to see. There was!

I called the Fire Department and quickly got into the car to race down to get Norman. In the heat of the moment, I wasn't thinking clearly. I should have taken the children along. When I got over to the sideroad west of our farm, I could see the end of the barn was in flames. By the time I got Norman's attention and we got back to the farm, the barn was almost engulfed, the fire truck was there and the lane was full of cars. Poor Beth had been so overtaken by fear that she began to run out the lane. Wilma, with Loralyn on her hip, was in pursuit to bring her back when some kind soul picked them up and stayed with them until we returned.

The cows were safe in the pasture field. The men pulled the bulk tank out of the milk house, freed the calves that were in the barn, and took the milking and whatever other equipment they could rescue, out of danger before the top of the barn collapsed into the stable. Thankfully, the wind was from the right direction and blew the flames and smoke away from the house and the silos. What heartache to see all the work we had put into the barn, the feed for the coming winter and the means of our livelihood, go up in smoke. I had called Norman's parents after I got home and they arrived a few hours later. The one-story part of the barn that had housed pigs before we turned it into stables was still standing, but it would hold only ten cows. The Surge Milker agent came while the firemen still battled the flames and set up a make-shift milking parlour and hooked up the tank outside in order to milk the cows that evening. Several men from the church and neighbourhood came to corral the cows and lead them in to the ten stalls to be milked four at a time.

That night we sat around the table in the kitchen staring at each other and wondering where to go from here. Jim, just newly involved in the dairy farm, thought our milking days were over, but Norman assured him that we could begin again. Before we went to bed, Norman and I went out and walked up the barn hill that now ended abruptly at a smoking abyss. We stood, arm in arm, surveying glowing embers of the ruins. It seemed so unreal and unbelievable. Norman took a big breath.

"I've heard farmers who lost their barns say that in the end it was the best thing that ever happened to them, because they could build the kind of barn that answered their needs. That may be so, but it's sure hard to see it right now. All I can think of is the back-breaking work that we did to re-do the barn, and I would have been happy to live with that."

"Do you think Ken started the fire?" My heart hurt to think it, but I did wonder.

"It crossed my mind." He paused. "I don't want to think that. I don't even want to ask him. We'll just wait and see. As they say, 'give him enough rope and he'll hang himself.' You know he can't keep things a secret very long. He'll come out with it if we give him time."

We walked slowly back to the house through the darkness that felt both comforting and strange at the same time.

The next week was a blur of telephone calls, visits of people who sympathized with us, and with insurance agents, banks, builders, electricians, plumbers and all the businesses that needed to be involved in building a new barn. The first priority was to bulldoze the remains into a heap so the ground could be levelled where the new barn was to be erected.

We couldn't believe the help that came. The same men who helped with the milking that first night came every morning and night to make the job easier. The call went out further afield, and each morning a carload or two of men came to help in the clean-up and later in getting the forms ready to pour the foundations.

Two weeks later, I thought I could finally carry out my plans to visit my sister in Kitchener the way I had planned to the Monday after the barn fire. I had the urn full of coffee and left lunch for the men who were working on the foundation. Ken said he'd finish up the dishes before going to see if he could help Dad. I left with Loralyn, to pick up something in Nairn, then to stop at the bank in Ailsa Craig before I headed for Kitchener. When I came out of the bank, I met our friend Belle. Her face was pale and she looked as though she were about to cry.

"What's the matter, Belle?"

"You'd better go home, Ruth. There's another fire at your place."

"Oh no, Belle, that was yesterday. The bulldozer working on burying the ruins caught fire."

Belle's eyes clouded with sadness. "No Ruth. It's a fire in the house this time."

For a moment I just stared in disbelief. When the horrible reality soaked in, I ran to the car. The distance from Ailsa Craig to the farm never seemed so long. When I got there, the windows to Stuart's rooms were broken out, the smoke was pouring out of the gaping spaces.

The mess from Stuart's room had been shovelled out on the lawn. I shrivelled in embarrassment. I was trying to get Stuart to keep his room tidy. I had read in a magazine, about one woman's attempt to help her child. She told him that she couldn't stand going into his messy room so if he had clothes to wash, he'd have to bring them to her because she didn't want to even see his room. He was also to keep his door closed. It was week three of the experiment, and I had been determined to leave it until he saw the need for some semblance of order. Now the local fire brigade had seen the results of this experiment and literally shovelled it out the window! Would I ever be able face those men or their wives again? I could just imagine them telling their wives what they had seen that day.

I entered the house and saw the water pouring down the stairs as though it were a waterfall. Several women came to give me a hug.

"They've got the fire out now. It started in Stuart's closet."

"What would have started it there?"

"They say there was a chemistry set in there that may have been the cause."

Upstairs the paper from Stuart's ceiling was hanging to the floor. The inside of the closet door was charred, the carpet in the room a soggy mess.

"I have to go get the children at school. I don't want them to find out from someone else before they hear it from me."

I left and went to the office at the school, asking staff to have the children come there. When they arrived, I told them the bad news. Stuart and Beth wanted to come home, but Wilma said she'd stay and come home on the bus.

When I got back, Ruth Arnel met me at the door.

"Quite a few people have come to clean up. We want you to go to the paint and paper store in Parkhill and pick out what you want for Stuart's room."

*What in the world is she thinking? How can I choose paint and paper when my house is a soggy, smoky mess? I can't possibly do that!*

"Just go!" She almost pushed me to the door. So, numb with shock, Stuart, Ken, Beth, Loralyn and I went. It took quite a while to find something suitable. Stuart was more into it than me. I just couldn't concentrate. Finally we left for home.

Imagine our surprise to see new panes in the windows when we drove in the lane.

Ed Driediger, director of Nairn Family Homes through whom we had received Ken, was waiting. He said he was taking Ken to town for a bit and he could spend the night with them.

When we went into the house, we found the stairs were wiped dry. The paper was off Stuart's room and much of the hall. The scorched, partly burned closet door was gone—our dear friend Fred had taken it to his shop to sand it down ready to be repainted. The closet was cleaned; the hole that had burned up through the attic was repaired. I couldn't believe how much had been accomplished in a few hours.

Before Ruth left that evening, she said there would be women there each day until the job was done. The big hall, the living room and dining room all needed to be repapered because of the water damage. The cellar had several inches of water in it.

The Bunnetts offered to have the children at their place for the night since it all smelled so smoky yet.

Ed came to tell us that he had questioned Ken about the fire, asking if he had started it. Ken had answered, "I wouldn't do that to Mom and Dad!'

He kept adamantly denying it through prolonged questioning. Finally, Ed came back toward the farm. In plain sight of it, he stopped and said, "All right, Ken, do you want to tell me the truth now?"

Finally, he admitted to setting the fire in both the house and the barn. How our hearts grieved. That admission was almost as hard to take as the damage the fire had done.

"It's not quite what I had in mind when I said after the barn fire, 'Give him enough rope and he'll hang himself.'" Norman sighed. "I just thought he'd eventually admit if he did it. I never thought it would take another fire."

We had tried so hard to help Ken grow up with the hope that he could find a way to live and support himself. Just a few weeks before, I had asked Ed if we were pushing him too hard, because I was having doubts as to his capability. It seemed as though we were asking an eight- or nine-year-old to act like an adult. Ed encouraged me to continue. "It may be his last chance," he said.

Every morning for the next two weeks, Norman and I, after breakfast, stood crying on each other's shoulders as carloads of men and a half dozen or so women came armed with not only what they needed to help build a barn and redecorate the house, but they also insisted on bringing meals for themselves and us. We hadn't been in the community that long, but we were embraced and supported in a way that we marvelled at. Cousin Emily came from Stouffville to help for several days too. All that assistance and backing was such a gift to us.

As I sat one morning, seeing if I could find a scripture to give me a measure of peace, I opened my Bible and the first words I read were, "When you pass through the waters, I will be with you; and when you pass through the rivers, they will not sweep over you. When you walk through the fire, you will not be burned; the flames will not set you ablaze" (Isaiah 43:2).That passage brought not only the peace I sought, but comfort as well.

In two weeks the house was finished and in order. Six weeks after the barn fire, the cows were together in the new barn with no need to be milked in shifts. It took a little longer for us to feel grounded and oriented to a new perspective.

## MORE UNEXPECTED DIFFICULTIES

The following spring, I began to have trouble with my periods, spotting between times. I had no idea what was wrong. One morning I hemorrhaged quite badly. The children went to call Norman and he raced me down to Strathroy Hospital. Neither he nor I thought we were going to make it in time. I slipped in and out of consciousness all the way there. They examined me quite thoroughly, but when I told them I was dieting quite strictly, they decided my blood sugar was low and told me if I feel like that again to drink a glass of orange juice and lay with my head hanging over the bed.

The entire next month, I didn't feel well at all. One day in April, I started having cramps. When I went to the washroom I passed what I thought must be a large clot. When I inspected it, I saw that it was a fetus! A baby? I hadn't known I was pregnant. I was so shocked I flushed the toilet and immediately felt a huge wave of horror and regret. I had just flushed my baby down the toilet! I called the doctor and he said that I had better go to the hospital for a D&C. He thought they might as well, at the same time, do the tubal ligation that had been scheduled in May. When I awoke after the procedure, I was informed there was another fetus in the tubes, and I was lucky that one miscarried because it could have burst at any moment. I was surely thankful! Had it happened, I probably would have had a glass of orange juice, laid with my head over the edge of the bed, and I could have died. At the time, I felt considerable relief, because we thought our family was complete with the four we already had. I wasn't prepared for the dreams that haunted me years after. Dreams where I suddenly realized I had forgotten to feed the twins, or sometimes I couldn't find my babies. I'd wake up crying and feeling so guilty for being such a bad mother. I had those dreams for many years, so for a long time, I grieved what I hadn't even known.

## CHAPTER 30

# A New Career and Interruptions

> "This time like all times
> is a very good one if we but know
> what to do with it."
> —Ralph Waldo Emerson

When Loralyn was going into Grade One, I noticed a Langs Bus Lines ad requesting applications for driving school bus. Norman wondered if I'd like to do that. My first thought? *How would I ever keep twenty or thirty children quiet and still drive safely?* In a classroom it would be difficult enough, but in a bus? I didn't think that was my kind of job.

Norman, though, kept urging me to think about it. I was surprised, because he usually cautioned me about getting too busy. When he mentioned that the extra money could help, I wondered if he thought I wasn't holding up my end of things. I called and asked about the job and next thing I knew I was in training for work I never had dreamed of doing. Stuart was planning on leaving that fall for college and, with Loralyn in school all day, I could be free to do something part-time.

I got my training, took the examination and was granted my bus license. At that time, Langs provided transportation for the Vacation Bible School at the Nairn Mennonite Church in July. Doug Langs thought it would be good experience for me before I had an actual school route. In September, 1979, I started a route that led to Valleyview School in Coldstream, with the understanding that I have one day a month off to attend the Family Life Commission meeting in Kitchener. For several years I had been a part of the Mennonite Conference of Canada body that encouraged the strengthening of marriages and family life, and I didn't want to quit what I felt was a lack in many churches.

My new career took a sharp turn in January of 1980. Eva, Esther and I were planning to fly to International Falls at the time of the spring break. I was cooking and baking ahead so the family could manage on their own while I was away. One morning I had a big pot of chili, one of stew and a hamburger and cabbage dish on the way. I kept being interrupted by people coming to the door and the telephone. Just as I got back to my cooking, the telephone rang once more.

"Oh, no! Not again!" I grumbled.

*Accept interruptions as opportunities.* The thought was so vivid it almost felt audible.

Startled, I took time to let it soak in a bit before I reached for the receiver. "Okay, Lord, if you say so!"

It was Audrey, reminding me that the Careers Guidance committee had a meeting at one o'clock. It had completely slipped my mind.

"Lord, this seems more like an obstacle than an opportunity, but thank you for the privilege of serving on this important committee. And please help me get these dishes done before lunch."

As I went to the meeting, I gave thanks for this warm, sunny January day. The sun had warmed the snowy farmyard of my fellow committee member. I parked the car and went to the house. The meeting went well and we accomplished much of the planning we needed to do. Suddenly I realized it was almost bus time.

"I have to leave right now!" I told the ladies. "It will be after three when I get back to the bus yard and we leave at ten after." I rushed into my coat, said a quick goodbye and ran to my car. My heel slipped in a little hollow of ice, my leg twisted and I heard a crack as I fell to the ground. When I tried to move, I knew I had broken my leg.

## DEALING WITH INTERRUPTIONS

"Okay, Lord, what are we going to do with this interruption?" I asked as I turned my face heavenward. I called out, but I knew the ladies probably couldn't hear me with the door closed. My only alternative was to scrunch along on my seat toward the car, just a few feet away. Every move hurt, but I was able to open the front door of the car and reach up to lean on the horn. It took several attempts before Mary came to the door.

"What happened?" she asked.

"I slipped on some ice and broke my leg. Would you please call the bus depot and tell them I won't be able to take my bus run? I'll need help to get up, though."

When they all came out, one of them said, "Maybe it's not broken. It might just be sprained."

"No," I told them, "I'm sure it's broken. I heard and felt the crack."

I instructed my friends to open the back door, then if one held the bottom of my leg while the others helped me raise myself up, I'd try to heave myself in the back seat. Together we made the effort, and I got onto the seat even though I almost fainted from the pain.

Audrey offered to drive me home and Mary said she'd follow to bring Audrey back again. When we got there, Norman thought we should stop in at Dr. Hoch's to see what he said.

"I'm sure it's broken, but we can go. Just bring me a big towel to support my leg while we drive."

Dr. Hoch came to the car to examine my leg. He concurred that it, indeed, was broken and that I should go straight to Emergency at the hospital.

When I got there, they cut off my boot and my pants and sent me to x-ray. It revealed that I had broken my tibia twice, spirally, and the fibula was snapped off at the ankle. I was put in a toe to hip cast. I had been thinking I would be off work six weeks but was told it would probably be more like six months. The first few weeks I had excruciating pain every time I moved to a standing position. Lying flat on my back was very uncomfortable, so Norman went and bought a recliner which became my bed for the first while. Four months I was severely restricted in what I could do. I couldn't put any weight on my leg for several months. Every time I felt like chafing under the sudden change of plans and my lack of ability to do much of anything, I remembered that whispered phrase, "Accept interruptions as opportunities."

I found out that all the committees I was on kept operating without me. It reminded me of a poem by Saxon White Kessinger I had noted years before. It suggested that if you're feeling indispensable, you should fill a pail of water, insert your hand and stir as much as you like. When you withdraw your hand the remaining hole will be a measure of how much you will be missed.

My recuperation was a time of learning this lesson, of letting go and adjusting my sense of values.

I decided to use my time to write a lot of letters, make decorated stationery and do embroidery. When I got really bored, I painted flowers on my cast from my toes up past my knees. In May when the cast was cut down to my knee, the doctor asked if I wanted to keep the drawing. I declined and said that I can draw on something else if I want to keep my art work.

Even four weeks later when the whole cast was taken off, I still had to walk with crutches for a month or more. The hospital staff offered me no physical therapy, so it took quite some time to regain the level of use to which I had been accustomed.

I resumed my bus driving again the next September. I soon got to love the children who rode my bus morning and afternoon. I kept the rules to a minimum but stayed firm on those. On special days like Thanksgiving, Hallowe'en, Christmas, Valentines and Easter as well as the last day of school, I always took a little treat for them. Several times when I found out that a family was going through a difficult time, I'd take a container of soup for their supper. I congratulated the children on their successes and comforted them when they were down. I never sent those who misbehaved to the office, neither did I scold them in front of their peers, but instead told them to stay on the bus after the others got off at the school. When we were alone, I had a heart-to-heart talk with them, explaining the need for safety and for keeping my eyes on the road rather than on miscreants. I expected their cooperation and their best, and they respected me.

One Friday night, on the way home, Kevin, as I shall call him, acted up considerably. When he got off the bus, I told him that on Monday morning he should stay on the bus when we got to school because we needed to have a talk.

"What about?" he asked, drawing up his shoulders.

"We'll talk about it Monday morning."

Sunday we had just settled down to have lunch when the phone rang.

"Hello."

"Hi. Is this Ruth?"

"Yes, it is."

"This is Kevin." His voice was so low I could scarcely hear.

"Oh, hello, Kevin. How can I help you?"

"Ple-e-ease, Ruth," he pled, "Can you tell me what we have to talk about tomorrow?"

I smiled. "Well, Kevin, I need to talk about how we can keep all the children on the bus safe. If I have to watch in the mirror to make sure you are staying in your seat or not pestering the other children, I can't keep my eyes on the road. If an animal would dart out in the road or a car would suddenly appear, I might not see it in time. That could cause an accident that might hurt you and all the other children on the bus, wouldn't it?

"Ye-e-es."

"Do you think you could help me drive the bus safely by sitting in your seat and keeping your hands to yourself?"

"Yes, oh yes, I will. I promise."

"You think you can remember that?"

"Yes I will." He paused. "Do we still have to have that talk tomorrow?"

"No, if you can remember to behave, we don't need to talk again."

The few days to think about the possibilities had done more good than if I had been able to do so the next morning. Kevin did remember, and if he momentarily slipped, all I needed to do was look at him kindly and say, "Kevin!" Immediately he would respond with "Sorry!" and stop what he was doing.

As time went by, I got to know the children very well. Some of those students spent their whole public school life on my bus. Many heart-warming and sometimes funny things happened and often I wondered what parents would say if they knew what the children shared with me. In fact, I found out some of the children thought I spent my whole life on the bus. While in a big store in London one evening, I met a family whose three children rode my bus. When little Mark saw me he looked quite concerned. "Ruth! What are you doing here? You should be on the bus!"

"Did you think I'm on the bus all the time?"

"That's where you belong." His head nodded to emphasize his distress.

His mother took over and explained that I have a home where I live most of the time and driving the bus is like the job his daddy goes to in the day, but he comes home at night. We could imagine, through his facial expression, the wheels turning in his brain, but it was obvious he was having trouble changing his understanding.

After eleven years, when the time came that I needed to quit that job, those dear children were genuinely grieved to see me go. They made up a scrapbook of pictures of all of them, and one of the Grade 8 girls, who had started off as an extremely shy little kindergartner, wrote a lovely thank you, including gratefulness that I didn't even talk to her or look at her too much those first days of school, yet she knew that I understood and cared for her. Except for the days I went to Kitchener for the Family Life Commission meetings and a few sick days, I was on that bus route every school day.

A bonus to driving the school bus each day was the nature I observed along the way. A great blue heron nested in a tree along a little stream, a snowy owl inhabited the same few blocks for three winters in a row. I saw a red-tailed hawk frequently as well as red-headed and pileated woodpeckers, rose-breasted grosbeaks and many more smaller birds. Once I had almost too close an encounter with a turkey buzzard that suddenly flew up out of the ditch. I thought he was going to come in through the windshield and had already pictured him inside the bus with me, when he grazed the top of the bus and flew on. I saw animals too—foxes, beavers, deer and even a wolf or two.

The early morning sunrises at different times of the year delighted me. As I started my route, and turned the signal lights to *automatic*, I always prayed, *Lord, turn the switch on in my life so that if the doors open, your light will always come on and let people know you are here.* I often used the drive from the bus depot to my first pick-up to converse with God.

I'll never forget one morning as I sought his peace for something that was going on at the time. The trees were covered with a thick frost and it was still a little foggy or misty. I came over a rise, and there in front of me was a stretch of road bordered with over-hanging branches. The sun was just coming over the horizon and it cast a rosy hue on the silver arches and even the mist that hung between them. The beauty was so serene and almost surreal, but it spoke volumes to my soul about how situations that might be negatives in life (like frost and fog) can become things of beauty if we let the light of Christ shine on them

CHAPTER 31

# A New Kind of Marriage— a New Me

> "Being heard is so close to being loved
> that for the average person,
> they are almost indistinguishable."
> —**David Augsburger**

It was during the years on the Family Life Commission that our group asked the Marriage Encounter organization that was based in Kansas, if they would hold a weekend in Ontario. The first one was well attended and there was demand for more weekends. Norman and I were getting along much better, but we had learned to avoid those things that still caused conflict. It seemed to me that there was no use bringing those things up, because Norman couldn't express how he felt about them, and then it would just be me talking, so I stayed quiet. I wondered if a Marriage Encounter weekend would help us and began to suggest that since I was on the committee promoting these weekends, that I should experience one so I knew what I was encouraging others to do. His comment was: "Perhaps some time."

After about the third weekend, he finally gave permission for me to register. As the time came closer, he got quieter and quieter. I knew he was nervous about going. The day we left, he hardly spoke a word—and that is the way it was all way down to Niagara Falls.

I think after Friday night, he would have liked to return home, but he stayed on. By half way through Saturday morning, his attitude had completely turned around.

We had a full weekend where we were not only given tools to improve our communication but also the time to practise with those tools. We were taught that while our feelings were our own legitimate response and responsibility, sharing them with our spouse helps us to understand one another and to respond with compassion and love. What a treat to have Norman write down some of his innermost thoughts to share with me. With the new listening skills Marriage Encounter taught, I could hear and accept how he was feeling. He began to feel free of the burden. Instead of seeing only his own perceptions and needs, he began to hear mine too. I heard and acknowledged his pain, and he did the same for mine. It was exquisite delight.

On the way home, we talked about the wonderful communication the weekend had brought us. I suggested, "Maybe we should write talks and become presenters for Marriage Encounter."

"Dream on!" he said. "You know how I like writing and how hard it is for me to speak in public! But I would like if we could go to a weekend every five years or so—whether I want to or not. Go ahead and make me go."

"You're a man! You can decide on your own that we should go, now that you know the benefit."

When we came home, we sought to allow each other our own strengths. We began to accept responsibility for only our own feelings. That freed us to accept the other's feelings for just what they were, not something we had to fix or change to fit our way of thinking—just to truly hear and understand more about each other. Oh, we hit more bumps on the road, but as we learned to share and listen—not to just the words we spoke or wrote, but the cries of our hearts—understanding of each other deepened.

We began to see how our separate and diverse personality traits really were a gift to each other. For instance, I learned that every last detail didn't *have* to be shared; he learned that he didn't have to have everything *totally* and *completely* worked out in his mind before he put it into words. I began to celebrate his ability to see underneath the obvious to the crux of the matter and often asked his help to clarify my thinking through an issue. He also began to fully support me in my more public roles. He even learned to share some of those. He joined me in reading scripture during the church service, several times we shared in a devotional time at a meeting, and together, we took a position on the board for Marriage Encounter.

The weekend and the conversation about ourselves and each other brought me to realize that I had some unresolved feelings from my childhood. After attending an information session about aging, where I heard that much of the repetitive and undesirable behaviour of elderly people was their way of dealing with those lingering, unsolved issues from earlier life, I determined to do something about my own. I asked my doctor for a reference and got a wonderful counsellor whom I saw regularly over the next year.

I told her about my desire to hear my Dad say he loved me and my attempts to resolve that issue. I told her I had thought of it for a long time after we were married, so after much prayer, I gathered up courage to ask Dad outright.

"Dad, you probably do love me, but for years I have longed to hear it out loud. I don't know why it is so important to me, but I decided rather than let it continue to bother me, I would just ask if you could assure me by telling me that you do."

Immediately I felt the mounting tension. "Why would you have to hear it from me?

Should you not just trust that it is so..." on and on went the explanation that felt more like a scolding, but he couldn't say the words. I felt devastated.

When I confessed to my counsellor the burning need that hounded me most of my life, she let me talk, handed the tissues to me when

I cried, and let me talk some more. Finally she spoke. "It sounds as though the need to hear your father express his love for you has left a big hole in your life."

Dabbing my eyes as the tears once more spilled, I nodded my head.

"Oh yes—a big hole."

"Sometimes there are holes in life that, for one reason or another, can never be filled," she gently suggested. "At such times, we just have to accept the holes and learn to live with them."

That day, on the way home, I pondered her statement.

"Okay, Lord. I have this big hole in my life. What can you help me do with it?"

The car was empty except for me, but I heard a distinct voice. "What would lace be without holes?"

I was stunned! I mulled it over in my mind.

"All right, Lord, I hear you! So help me find a way to tat around the holes of the relationship between Dad and me and make lace out of this need to know he loves me."

"You can start by assuring him that you love him."

"But Lord, he's my dad. Shouldn't he be the one to start the process?"

"Do you want lace or do you want holes?"

"Lace, Lord. I do want lace," I whispered. I took a deep breath. "So where do I begin?"

"Just start telling him, in your letters, that you love him."

I began to include that line in my weekly letters, even though at first the words seemed less than truly genuine. After a while I felt nudged to tell him qualities I appreciated about him—lessons he had taught me by word or example; his love of reading and books; his longing for knowledge and information; his love of solving problems with creative ideas; his desire to help others to find faith; how he stood for the right whether it made him popular or not; his ability to put together sermons that touched and inspired others.

In their yearly visits to us, or our visits to them, I began to hug him. He stood straight and tense, afraid of the physical contact, but I kept on. Something was happening—and surprise—it wasn't all in him. My heart began to feel tender toward him. I grieved that he was unable to let himself show love or accept and return hugs. I slowly began to accept him as he was and, in turn, I was able to better accept myself.

## CHAPTER 32

# The Nest Begins to Empty

> "Enjoy the little things,
> for one day you may look back
> and realize they were the big things."
> —Robert Bault

Meanwhile a transition was taking place in our lives. Our children started leaving the nest. Stuart, on finishing his Grade 12 year, decided to go to Hesston College in Kansas the fall of 1980. That college had some training in agriculture which he felt would be his calling. He was also able to get computer training which was of great interest to him. We went down together to see the college. That visit confirmed in his mind the conviction that it was the school he wanted to attend. He looked forward to the atmosphere of a Christian college.

We took him to the airport in Detroit and saw him off to a new stage of life in Hesston, Kansas. At the beginning, he called often and early October a bout of homesickness hit him. If he would have had a car, he probably would have high-tailed it to Ontario. With a lot of encouragement and a promise that if he still felt he couldn't do it when he came home for Christmas, he could change his plans, he did stay. By Christmas he was thoroughly enjoying life at college and had gathered a whole group of friends, most of whom would stay friends forever. At the end of the school year, he came home to be employed by Peter Twynstra and Merlon Bender before returning in the fall.

Wilma stayed on at North Middlesex District High School for her Grade 13 year. She turned seventeen at the end of that school year and had set her sights on going to University of Waterloo for a Bachelor of Arts degree, then she planned to go on to Teacher's College to fulfill her dream of becoming a teacher.

After a summer of her work at the ball diamond concession stand, I took Wilma to Waterloo, to register at the university. She had found a place to board with her cousin's friend who had a house on University Avenue, not too far from the campus. It was hard on Mama's heart to leave my little barely-eighteen-year-old to fend for herself. It was difficult for her too, so I had to put on a brave front.

When Beth left to go to Rockway High School in 1983, although she came home each weekend, it left us with only one child at home most of the time. To ease the transportation back and forth, Norman bought an older Ford Granada that Wilma and Beth drove back and forth many times, accompanied by two friends from Parkhill. Now we only had our youngest at home. Life took on a more relaxed mien, and it made us begin to wonder what the rest of our life could hold. We talked of the possibilities.

On a routine visit to my doctor, when I shared how I still was experiencing some distressing symptoms, he suggested that even though my thyroid levels were in the normal range, that they were on the low side of normal and it might be helpful to try a bit of thyroid again to see if it made a difference. He said some people's normal might be different than others and I may be one of those who didn't fall in the usual normal range. He gave me a prescription, and I began taking them early in the week. That weekend, the girls came home with a few of their friends. Norman and I went on a bus trip with farmers for the day and came home around four o'clock. I got supper ready for the gang and called upstairs to tell them it was time to eat.

"Who got the supper ready?" they asked when they came downstairs.

"I did," I told them, wondering why they asked.

"How did you do that?"

It wasn't until then that I realized that I had done something out of the ordinary from what I'd been doing for several years. They were used to having me unable to do that.

What a change! My life became much more manageable and satisfying. My ability to enjoy life and take part in more activity was enhanced.

The year 1985 held a lot of transitions in our family. That year, in March, my parents celebrated their fiftieth wedding anniversary, and Norman's parents, their fifty-fifth. In September we celebrated 25 years of marriage. That fall Wilma graduated from University of Waterloo and went to Althouse Teacher's College, Beth finished at Rockway Mennonite High School and started at University of Waterloo, and Loralyn completed elementary school and began at North Middlesex District High School.

We had long talked about taking a trip to celebrate our anniversary. Vermont and New Hampshire were locales we had never visited, so we planned to spend time there. I sent for travel information and we mapped out a plan. Money was an issue, so I accepted a job at Langs Bus Lines to take teenagers to the Chatham area to detassle corn. For almost three weeks, I left with the bus at 5:30 in the morning to get fuelled, then picked up the workers in Strathroy and Mount Bridges, to arrive in the Chatham fields for a seven-thirty start. The corn was still wet when we started up and down the long rows, detasseling two rows leaving one and doing the next two. We had a one-half hour lunch period and then we were at it again. Often it was 5:30 to 6:30 p.m. before we left the field to travel back home. I had to wash the grunge off and out of the bus and get to bed so I'd be ready for the morning again. I was paid both the time as bus driver, from Langs, and for supervising the young people from the corn company, and so we had enough money for a nice trip in September.

We stayed the first night in eastern New York where we visited our friends, Gordon and Julie MacDonald. From there we went to a reserved motel in Vermont for the first week and made day trips to many surrounding areas. At Stowe, where the Von Trappe family settled after coming from Austria, we looked around their property, ate at their family restaurant and were served by one of Maria's grandchildren. We visited castles, bowl factories, glass-blowing factories and did a lot of hiking along nature trails.

From Vermont, we went to Plymouth for the weekend. We didn't realize that a weekend there would be like a summer weekend in Grand Bend. Everywhere was packed with people—line-ups for restaurants and sight-seeing places and everywhere we wanted to go. Street parties carried on half the night. We managed to get the tour of the Mayflower replica and the pioneer village there, but headed to our reserved motel in New Hampshire with a sigh of relief.

When we registered there, we asked what kinds of sights would be good to visit. The motel registrar recommended a pilot just up the hill from the inn who took people on a ride around Mount Washington.

"Oo-oh! I never cared for the idea of going up in small planes," I said with a sick feeling in my stomach.

"Oh, it's an eight passenger plane and he is an experienced pilot," the innkeeper assured me.

I saw the longing on Norman's face and couldn't refuse him. Up the hill we trudged, Norman almost on his toes in anticipation, my heart doing strange flip-flops, wondering if I'd see my family again. When we got there, the pilot met us.

"It looks like you're the only passengers, and it's the last flight of the day. Let's take the small plane. It's a lot more fun and you'll get a better view!"

Clunk! My heart hit my boots with the very thought. Norman inquired with his eyes if I was okay with it. I could see that he really wanted to go, so I nodded and followed the pilot to the door of the plane. I sat in the back and Norman sat beside the pilot. We donned our seat-belts as instructed by the excited aviator.

As he flew along and wove between the mountains, he pointed out places of interest. We took a circle around Mount Washington and saw the winding road below with cars inching along to the top of the mountain into a thick cloud. Having had the objective of seeing the view from the top, their long trip up would be of no avail, for the panorama obviously was obliterated by the thick fog.

"Now, for the fun part," the pilot said. "Get your camera ready, because we're going to fly over the edge of a deep canyon and between the two sides. I'll dip my wing so you can get a good shot."

*Yikes! I don't think this is what I'd call the safe, uneventful ride he promised.* I didn't have much time to think more.

"Okay, get ready." The wing dropped to the left. "Shoot!"

It was a breath-taking view, and I clicked and clicked with no time to think about being afraid. He levelled out and rose over the crest of the next hill. From there on, I just gloried in the beautiful fall splendour that looked like coloured popcorn covering the hills. Now and then a white-steepled church or farm house with accompanying red barn added variety to the trees, lakes and streams.

All too soon, we were coming in again for a landing. When we climbed out, voicing our thanks for a wonderful experience, the pilot had one more request.

"Give me your camera while you stand in front of the plane so you'll have one more way to remember New Hampshire's beauty."

From our new location, we again made day trips to see more of the beauty and history of the state, including Castle in the Clouds. Hiking trails were well marked and we made good use of several. One of the most memorable was a two-mile hike back through the woods of the White Mountain National Forest to a wonderful waterfall. We shall always be grateful for the advice of a waitress at a small restaurant that led us to Highway 112, through picturesque scenery and the Sabbaday Falls.

When it was almost time to return home, we went to Maine to visit our friends Gus and Lorna Pendleton before we headed up to Canada. By that time, a hurricane coming up the east coast started to send us rain which teemed down as we went through Montreal. Nevertheless, we meandered our way home through Kemptville, Smiths Falls and Perth, then took the #7 on home. It was a trip we would never forget and which always brought warm memories of a prolonged time for just the two of us.

CHAPTER 33

## Another Career

> "It is for us to pray not for tasks equal to our powers,
> but for powers equal to our tasks, to go forward
> with a great desire forever beating at the door of
> our hearts as we travel toward our distant goal."
> —Helen Keller

Three years later, Stuart was working and teaching at Hesston College, Wilma was teaching school in Delaware and living in London. Beth, on graduating, became manager of the Provident Bookstore in London and I quit driving bus. For some time I had been thinking of getting a more full-time job. I thought the time had come to finally go back to school, get my General Education Diploma and perhaps go to university to prepare for different work. For three weeks I attended "Woman Power," a course taught in London, where instructors helped participants discover our strengths and gave us courage to pursue our dreams. At one point toward the end, they asked us to write an essay telling about our dream job.

My job description depicted a place where I could work with and relate to people, use my creativity, have lots of variety and also do some writing and perhaps speaking. I thought it required a mixture that might not exist in any one job.

"Well, Lord, you know what I'm supposed to be doing. Open the right doors for me so that I know too."

A few weeks later, I got a call from a neighbour.

"I've been taking a gerontology course at Fanshawe College. We had a speaker from the provincial government who said there was funding available for beginning day centres for seniors to help them stay in their own homes longer and to give relief for caregivers who are looking after senior family members. I'd like to start one at Craigwiel Gardens, but I'd like to have someone to work with me. I especially need someone who likes crafts and programming, would be good at writing, wouldn't mind speaking to groups about the day centre and who could drive the handicap van. Would you be interested?"

"Tell me a little more about what is involved and how we'd get it going."

"Well, I guess the first thing we'd need to do is to see if we could use the seniors' Activity Centre at Craigwiel. We probably would have to visit doctors, Home Care, Ministers and others who work with the elderly to inquire about the demand for such a place. The next step would be to visit the gentleman in charge of dispensing the funds and probably write up a proposal to submit to him. If we get approval, we'd probably make home visits to interested seniors to explain our program and see if they would like to come. We would have to speak to women's groups to recruit volunteers and perhaps visit the township councils to ask for funding as well."

"What kind of program would we offer?"

"I was thinking of crafts, memory lane where we talk about old times, speakers on topics dealing with aging, slide shows on different countries, and perhaps some day trips with the van, going out for meals and visiting different places."

"Beth, in the course I have been taking at Woman Power, I was asked to describe my dream job. As you portrayed it, I believe this sounds very much like what I expressed!" I smiled as the door opened wide. All kinds of ideas began to flow into my mind.

The next few months in between bus runs on Beth's days off from her nursing job at Craigholme, we visited care-givers and were assured there would be quite a demand for such a place. We visited the government agency and got the information we needed to write up a proposal and worked on perfecting that. Since the government would only pay 70 percent, we also visited each of the municipal councils in our catchment area to ask for additional funds. We planned to begin in February, taking four weeks to make up posters and brochures, do home visits, and prepare a calendar of activities for a program that ran three days a week and begin on Leap Year Day, February 29, 1988.

What a joy it was to get acquainted with those wonderful seniors. There were fifteen the first day. We distributed calendars with the different activities we had planned for March. We told them about the hot meals they would receive every day they came, the availability of a bath and the possibility of foot care, if they desired that. We also asked what kinds of activities they would like to have provided and what kinds of programs would be a benefit and pleasure for them. From the very first, we were determined to work with them, not for them—giving them a lot of say in what happened.

Although we had a good number the first day, in the first few months there were some days with only two or three present, and a few days when none came. Those days we made telephone calls encouraging the ones who were enthusiastic to come at least one day a week and for some of the more reluctant ones to try a specific program. The news mostly spread word-of-mouth and gradually the attendance grew until the day of our official opening, the beginning of June, we had quite a crowd of patrons besides other people from the community to celebrate the new facility. We were open for clients three days a week, and we took one day to plan and get programs ready.

More and more people wanted to take advantage of a bath and foot care, so we hired an additional nurse who had taken the foot care course, so we could provide our own rather than have Craigholme staff do it. The hairdresser in Craigholme continued to take appointments for our clients.

The work was enjoyable and I liked thinking up new activities. In fact I sometimes felt guilty taking pay for something that gave me such joy and satisfaction. Activities I devised each month included: Expanding our Minds (learning new things), Spreading our Wings, (exploring our world), Warm Fuzzies (something that made them feel good about themselves which included things like Memory Lane or Show and Tell), Educating our Taste Buds (trying new foods, recipes or finding out about the variety of foods available), Adapting to Change (learning what is available to help through diminishing abilities) and Just for Fun (where we played all kinds of games or had a silly activity like Backward Day or Hat Day).

Each month my partner Beth baked a cake and I decorated it to celebrate the birthdays of the month. It was hard to believe how many of those seniors had never had their name on a birthday cake before. They watched eagerly as I did the decorating.

"What are you putting on the cake this time?" one would ask.

"I'm not sure yet. Do you have any ideas?"

Sometimes they did, sometimes they left it up to me. Roses were always a favourite, but I did many different designs and they were always pleased. After a while, I began to take pictures of each cake to preserve the memory of it, because so often the seniors would say, "It's so nice, it's a shame to cut it up and eat it."

Another day they enjoyed was Soup and Sandwich Day. On those days, I'd have the soup started before the seniors came so the smells would greet them as they opened the doors. Often I let them help cut up the vegetables to add to the broth. If there were left-overs, we would let them take a jar full home with them as long as they brought the container. The home-made goodness was deeply appreciated.

A few activities we initiated stand out as being truly satisfying. I created a book entitled *This is Your Life*. Each new client was interviewed about their life to introduce them to the group. I wrote up a story from the interview and checked it out with the senior to make sure I got it right and that they would feel comfortable having it read to the larger group. I took a picture of the client and put into the book with the story.

A lot happened during that story exercise. Sometimes they were reluctant to begin, but I had a standard list of questions to ease them into it. Once they got started, they shared freely and, in some cases, told me things they had never told anyone else. I always asked if there were any parts they'd rather not have shared with the group and honoured that. More than once when I read the finished story back to the client, they would say something like "You make my life sound as though it was interesting and worthwhile!" When it was read to the group, there was a tangible metamorphosis in their sense of self-esteem. One gentleman, on leaving the day his story was read, remarked, "That was better than hearing your own obituary!"

That activity also led to taking pictures before Christmas. Norman and I had taken a photography course and purchased an SLR camera with a telephoto lens. I set up a backdrop close to a window, and positioned a light on the other side to avoid any shadows, and the telephoto lens helped me get close-up shots without threatening their space. I took two poses of each person and ordered doubles. We kept one for our records and gave the seniors three prints with the option of ordering more.

Over the years I learned added ways to make it special. I asked a cosmetician to come and give the ladies subtle make-up, and a hairdresser to fix their hair before taking the picture. It became a pamper day. I found, too, that having a bedside table with a nice cover in front of them allowed them to lean forward and immediately be more at ease. So many had never had a portrait taken and were delighted to order prints to give to their families for Christmas.

For the Mothers/Father's Day Special, I wrote letters to the family of each senior asking them to write a letter, poem or anything that would explain why their parent should be mother or father of the year. Some very touching letters arrived. On the Friday before those special days, we had each of the seniors come and sit on a decorated chair, then we handed out a rose and a certificate declaring the person as the Most Loving (Caring, Courageous...) Mother/Father of the Year and finally we read the letters from their family. With each successive recipient, one could feel a tangible warmth growing stronger with each reading. Sometimes there were a few tears of joy and happiness shed. There was a visible change in just about all of them and an enlarged sense of worth and contentment that lingered. I am still convinced that the more often we can make opportunities for people to express such things to each other, the better our world will be. Too often recognition and affirmation of what a person has been to family and community is reserved until after a person dies and expressed only at the funeral.

It was such a delight thinking of ways to bring enjoyment, new experiences, a satisfactory summing- up of life, and resolution to unfinished business to those dear friends in the latter years of their life. But anything I was able to give to them came flooding back into my life with abundant blessing.

## CHAPTER 34

# *Life Changes Again*

"We should be astonished at the goodness of God,
stunned that He should bother to call us by name,
our mouths wide open at His love,
bewildered that at this
very moment we are standing
on holy ground."

—Brennan Manning

One day after the centre was going along quite well, out of the blue, Norman suggested, "Why don't you find out what is involved in writing talks and becoming presenters for Marriage Encounter?"

With difficulty, I contained my surprise and shock, and answered, "Sure, I can do that."

When we got the instructions and guidelines, much to my surprise, Norman thought we should begin to write the talks required. The guidelines provided the basic teaching, leaving room for personal anecdotes to illustrate how it works in real life. For example, when we spoke of the importance of really listening to each other as spouses, rather than hearing what we expect they will say, we had to relate a time between Norman and I when misunderstandings arose because we hadn't really heard each other.

We also shared how we experienced improvement in our listening skills since our Marriage Encounter weekend. As we worked through these talks, our understanding of each other deepened. Now and then, we spent a weekend at a motel or a park and often we camped out in our own woods for a Saturday and Sunday. We sat at a picnic table and wrote there. Those weekends were memorable—our communication intensified and our togetherness grew each time. Being outdoors in nature that we both loved, taking breaks to walk through the woods and down to the river, was a beautiful setting to not only enjoy one another, but also to be conscious of God's desire for us to find the depth of love that he envisioned for us as husband and wife. We fell deeper and deeper in love.

Finally, we had enough talks written that we were able to participate in a weekend as a presenting couple. We were rather nervous, because some parts of the sharing were deeply personal—things one does not usually share in public. We weren't sure of the response, but when couples came to us and said things like, "Thanks so much for sharing your personal lives. We thought we were the only ones having such glitches in our relationship. If you can overcome and make it through, it gives us hope too."

Norman especially was amazed at the response he got from the "quiet" spouse of the couples who attended. They really appreciated his ability to voice their viewpoint. He soon overcame his reticence and rejoiced to feel that he was finally free to use the talents God gave him.

Our life together totally changed. From that time on, we were truly married—wed together in purpose and in service with a much deeper, more accepting love. We worked together as a team and truly enjoyed each other to an extent we hadn't known before. Norman fully supported my roles and I rejoiced in his discoveries of new ways he could use his talents. Not only the couples at the weekends, but also our own children and others, saw the difference in us and applauded the new relationship they witnessed. Norman was truly transformed. The self-confidence he lacked dissipated and he started to take more and more leadership and public roles.

When we had all our talks written, we began to help out with Marriage Encounter weekends in other areas such as Indiana, Michigan and Ohio. We were appointed to Central Council and attended the meetings of the appointees from Pennsylvania, Virginia, Ohio/Indiana, Kansas and Manitoba. We established rich friendships and enjoyed not only frank talks but also a lot of fun and hilarity with those couples. And bit by bit, the relationship between Norman and me deepened and we grew more and more supportive of each other. We challenged each other to develop the talents we were given. We did a lot together, but we also encouraged each other to use our own strengths and do things separately.

In 1990, Wilma and Beth, who by this time were living together in a London apartment and were both dating young men, came home one afternoon in early spring. It wasn't long until I knew something was up. Finally one of them asked, "How would you feel about having two weddings in one year?"

To their amazement and my own, I replied, "Perfect! I got a dress a few weeks ago, so that is ready."

"What?" they asked in astonishment.

I laughed. "This is crazy, but a few weeks ago when I was shopping, I saw a dress on sale that I loved. I tried it on and it fit, but it was far too formal for what I needed. I decided that I would get it anyway and hope something would come along so I could wear it. You know that isn't like me. I don't usually get things I don't need...just in case."

"We know that!" they chimed. "Before we get to talking about the how and when of the weddings, let's go and see it."

Much talking and planning preceded the events. Beth and Peter chose August for their wedding date. The Mennonite World Conference was happening in Winnipeg, and Loralyn was just finishing up her term with Mennonite Central Committee's SALT (Serving and Learning Together) so we got plans together as much as we could, then left to go to Winnipeg, took in the conference, packed up Loralyn's things and returned home.

In late 1990, Jim Bender, with whom we had been farming, was diagnosed with cancer. He went through some gruelling treatment but bravely kept coming to help with the work much of the time. We decided to quit farming. Norman had always said that life was too short to do just one thing in your life. It had become evident that Stuart's greatest strengths lay in other than farming, so Norman was anxious to move on to something else. Jim had been wondering how long we should keep up with the milk quota as there was talk of doing away with quotas. That would decrease our net worth by a considerable amount. After much discussion, it was decided to sell the herd of registered Holsteins, and put our farm up for sale. Norman would follow another interest by taking an eleven-month course at Fanshawe College in Fine Furniture and Cabinet Making.

It was a cool summer most of the time, but Beth and Peter's wedding day was the hottest of the entire season. The wedding reception was in the hall at the church. With no air conditioning, but every available fan running, it was still so warm and muggy that the floor got wet. However it was a lovely reception before they went to New England for their honeymoon.

In the fall, Loralyn went to Peterborough to attend Trent University. Although we went with her to find a boarding place and see where she would be living, she drove herself back and forth from then on. It was a heavy year since Norman and I were elders at church. To add to the responsibility, that summer, our pastor, Karen James Abra, announced she would be quitting. In October, three of our church members were killed in a horrible accident—all three lives and that of a community woman were snuffed out in seconds. Jim, our farm partner, was going through his most difficult chemotherapy and we didn't know whether he would live through it.

Wilma and Rene were married December 22 of that year as well. The church was already decorated with cedar boughs and red poinsettias, so they just added their theme colour of purple and white. It looked lovely. They had hand-printed Christmas tree ornaments with their names and the date of the wedding as favours. Bill and Karen James Abra performed both weddings, and friends and relatives added special touches. Wilma and Rene went away for a night, came back to gather with our family on Christmas Eve Day, then left the day after Christmas to go to Germany to spend their honeymoon with Rene's mother, brother and aunt. It was good they did. Rene's mother had been diagnosed with cancer. They hoped she would live long enough for them to visit again, but in February she passed away.

In January of 1992, our first grandchild was born. Peter and Beth's Brendan was a little replica of his father and soon endeared himself to us. What a feeling to watch our daughter be a mother herself. All the moments we spent with Brendan, learning to be grandparents and enjoying this new role, were treasured in our hearts. I tried to catch as many of those moments as possible on camera. But my heart holds many more of those moments than my photograph album! Norman, too, enjoyed his grandson and began making plans what he could do with him as he grew older.

Because she wasn't accepted for the concurrent education program at Trent—her main reason for going there— Loralyn transferred to Laurier in Waterloo for her second year. She already had many friends in that area and it was closer to home and, along with that, she had more opportunities for involvement in church. By the time graduation came, she no longer was sure she wanted to teach as had always been her objective. As she had enjoyed her experience in Voluntary Service so much, she decided that right after university was a good time to give a few more years in this kind of service. She looked into several possibilities, even though quite near the beginning, she was offered a spot in Winnipeg with Mediation Services. She thought she'd like to go somewhere else to expand her horizons. Newfoundland and Texas were two places she considered, but by miraculous intervention and definite leading, she consented to the first offer. Once more, we packed up her things and went to Winnipeg.

We had been given the address of the VS Unit house on Langside Street in Winnipeg. It was a big old house right next to a walk-through alley in a decidedly dubious area of the inner city. A great big hedge at the front of the house covered nearly half of the sidewalk. It seemed a perfect place from which to be ambushed.

In the winter, she would be leaving that house in the dark to walk a block and catch her bus to work. By the time she returned, it would again be dark.

In the years she lived there, there were several murders and many police raids in the block where she resided. The inside of the house didn't make me feel any better. Security wasn't that good and the décor slap-dash at the best. It seemed to be at the other end of the earth from the farm where she grew up. It was almost more than I could do to leave my little girl there.

A few days after our return, God gave me the verse from Psalm 139:10—"Even there your hand will guide me; your right hand will hold me fast." I made a big poster with that verse on it and sent it out so Loralyn could hang it in her room. That verse came to mean more and more to both of us as the years passed.

When the farm sold, we moved to a three-acre property north of town. A few days later we left for a trip through England and mainland Europe with Peter and Ada Bunnett. We had planned such a trip the year before but had to postpone it. Now did not seem like the best time either, having just moved, but we decided to take the opportunity. It was a trip we'd never forget.

We flew to England and met Peter and Ada at the airport. In a rental car, we drove to Peter's mother's home in Norwich, staying a few days to explore the area in which Peter had grown up. Since we had known Peter from the time he arrived in Canada, it was an interesting insight into his beginnings. The narrow country lanes with fascinating names and all the houses with their own distinctive names, the walled gardens and the abundant flowers were delightful to behold. The truth of the song by an unknown author that Eva and I used to sing was clear:

How many kinds of sweet flowers grow
in an English country garden?
I'll tell you now of some that we know,
Those we miss you'll surely pardon.
Daffodils, Heart's Ease and Phlox,
Meadow Sweet and Ladies Smocks,
Gentians, Lupines and Hollyhock,
Roses, Fox Glove and blue For-get-me-nots,
In an English country garden.

There were all those and more.

From there we went to Heechem to see Peter's Godmother, stopped at the beautiful and fragrant lavender fields, and drove around Sandringham Castle grounds, up through central England and the Yorkshire moors, to just inside the border of Scotland to Otterburn and then down through the Lake Country and saw the Beatrix Potter museum. The old Roman castle in Chester was a place to be remembered as was The Vicarage, a bed and breakfast near Shrewsbury. We stayed one night in the carriage house and had a typical hot English breakfast in the main house before we left.

At Dover, we found a bed and breakfast attended by a stately and most proper gentleman in a black pinstripe suit who sir-ed and ma'am-ed us all the way to our elegant rooms. He served us tea in our own rooms on a properly laid out tray and left us to settle in. He appeared in the morning, fresh, friendly and properly dressed in pinstripe with pocket hanky perfectly placed, to serve our breakfast in style.

From Dover we left on the hovercraft to go across the channel to Calais, France. Peter wanted to hunt for the war memorial that listed his great-grandfather's name near Thiepval in the Prosiaux Forest. The vast amount of names on that memorial was astounding and disheartening. We realized that each of those names represented a family clan that had been devastated by the loss. It was difficult to fathom that this peaceful country setting could have been the scene of such slaughter and absolute horror.

In Switzerland we ended up in Langnau, the town from which my ancestors had come. At the restaurant we chose, I asked the waitress who served us, "Do you know of any Neuenschwanders in the area?"

"Yes. Why?" she asked.

"I am a Neuenschwander from Canada."

She extended her hand and shook mine with great enthusiasm. "I am one!" she remarked. "Welcome to Switzerland! Would you like to see the village from whence our name comes?"

"Yes, we would," I said, with grateful enthusiasm.

"Go south from Langnau toward Eggwil until you see a sign pointing up to Neuenschwand."

After lunch, we followed her directions and found the road to Neuenschwand was literally up—up in hairpin curves on the end of a foothill, up to the little village where the main street had barns toward the street and the attached houses overlooking the valley on both sides. We drove through the village, then turned around to come back. It started to rain, but I saw an older man coming out of a barn, and I asked Peter to stop so I could speak to him.

"Ich bin eine Neuenschwander von Canada," I said.

He broke into a welcoming smile and told me that a Newswanger family from Pennsylvania had visited there just a few weeks before. I had no difficulty understanding his dialect. I asked if there were still Neuenschwanders living in the village and he replied, "Ja, dort und dort," pointing to each end of the village.

It was quite an awesome feeling to think of my ancestors leaving this beautiful peaceful setting to travel over the sea to a new land. It would have been nice to stay longer, but it was raining, otherwise we may have walked through the village and tried to meet more people.

We visited Ballenburg, a place similar to a pioneer village that showed how people long ago lived. We travelled by rail up to the summit of Jungrfrau Joch, the highest mountain in the Alps, and took a tour through the Italian part of Switzerland before heading through Lichtenstein to Austria.

There we took a tour from Salzburg that showed the different places *Sound of Music* was filmed, and a walking tour through the city. From there we went to Schwangau, visited the Neuschwanstein Castle, on to Neckarsteinach to visit the Thiessens—Peter and Ada's friends— then along the Rhine River to the Netherlands. There we visited John Breimer's parents and the Bischops, more of Peter and Ada's friends, who took us on a nice tour. In spite of John Bischop's inability to speak much English, we thoroughly enjoyed it. We were able to take in the Floriade, an amazing, huge international flower show in Zuidemeer that happens only every ten years.

The next morning, we headed through Belgium where we were to connect with the hovercraft to take us back to England. On the freeway we were slowed down by two big trucks that drove extremely slow, one in each lane, so that no one could pass. By the time we got to the hovercraft port, we were too late for that sailing, but were glad we were able to get tickets on the catamaran. We found out later that the trucks blocking the road was a protest, and some people were stranded on the highway for three days and two nights. We felt extremely fortunate to have arrived when we did and to be able to leave for England. Otherwise we would have missed our flight home the following day.

We visited Canterbury on the way to Peter's sister's home in Greenwich where we stayed for the night. Peter and Ada—good friends and wonderful tour guides—left with his brother-in-law the next morning to catch their earlier flight, and we returned the rented car and got to the airport for our later flight. Wilma and Loralyn met us at the Pearson Airport and brought us home to adjust to Canadian time, and our new home, where we had lived only nine days before leaving for England. What a wonderful trip it had been—both connecting with our roots and widening our horizons.

## CHAPTER 35

# Settling into a New Life

"Everyday is an opportunity to have a fresh start.
It doesn't matter what happened yesterday,
all that counts is today. When you wake up in the
morning, know that today is full of opportunities
waiting to be grabbed. It is a new day, a new start,
the beginning of a new life awaits you."

—**Unknown**

From a life where we were together most of our days, we transferred to my days being spent at the Day Centre and Norman going to college. Though for many couples that is the norm for most of their marriages, it was new for us. After college, Norman built a workshop on our property and began fashioning custom-made furniture for an ever-widening clientelle.

Our second grandson arrived December 23, 1992. Nicolas Joseph Kirmse was born after a long labour. I had the privilege of spending many of those hours with Wilma and Rene. In those hours, Rene and I developed a closeness that I shall always treasure. Nicolas soon grew into a sensitive, happy little boy who readily expressed his love for the people in his life. To Nicolas, we became Nana and Papa—names and roles we were happy to accept and rejoice in.

The fall of 1993, Stuart invited us to come meet a woman with whom his pastor and wife had set him up. It took us only a few minutes to surmise that Mary Grace Scott would not only be a perfect fit for Stuart, but also for our family. I remembered the sleepless nights with Stuart when he was a baby. Those hours were often filled with prayers for every imaginable challenge he would be apt to face in life. Included in those, were prayers for the little girl who would grow up to be his wife—and for her parents as they guided her growth and development. I was glad to finally meet her. By Christmas, she was sporting his ring and plans were made for a May 1994 wedding.

Less than a year later, on March 10, 1995, Hannah Leanne joined our family. She was our first granddaughter. She was born Friday morning, and Norman and I were scheduled to help present a Marriage Encounter weekend in Niagara beginning that evening. We went shopping for a baby dress for Hannah; because I was determined I was going to be the first one to give her a dress. We stopped in to see her and her parents on our way to Niagara. What a sweet ambiance that gave our entire weekend. Hannah reminded me so much of Stuart at that age. When she was still very young, she would light up when we stopped in at their place or they came to ours. What a wonderful feeling!

Natasha Elizabeth joined Rene and Wilma's family May 23 of 1996. Nicolas accepted his little sister with joy, and it was beautiful to see the relationship between the siblings develop. She began to make strange quite early. Several times when we babysat for them, she would cry and cry until Papa would take her in his arms. Immediately she stopped crying and would look up, her eyes swimming with adoration and love. Although I would have loved to be the recipient of those looks, I rejoiced in the obvious reciprocal love between Papa and granddaughter.

That summer, my mother was diagnosed with cancer. The prognosis didn't look good, so a week after Loralyn moved home from Winnipeg, Wilma, Natasha and I flew out to that city, rented a car and drove to

Barwick, where they had now lived for thirty-one years, to spend a week with her. Natasha was already making strange and I wondered if having a baby in the house would be too much for Mom, but it almost seemed as though Natasha sensed what her great-grandmother needed. She cooed lovingly and looked mom full in the face when she was on her great-grandma's lap. She held nice and still and was so good all the time we were there.

As it turned out, the doctor discovered a tumour in Mom's breast and gave her a hormone treatment that slowed down the cancer and allowed her to return to some of her usual activities. I was still glad we had made that trip.

Norman's mother, too, had a rough year, with six of her siblings or in-laws dying within a four- month period, and she suffering a fractured hip. We found ourselves trying to support our parents from afar.

October brought another member to our family. Martin Stuart made his arrival on October 30, 1996. He was a little go-getter from almost the beginning. One day when Mary was frustrated about all the mischief he was getting into, I told her, "I'm sorry for you, Mary, but Stuart really needed a son like that!" It seemed it was pay-back time for all the shenanigans he performed in his younger years. Both of them, though, are interesting and dynamic people whom we love.

Being a grandmother wasn't enough reason for my lack of sleep those years. I had increasing trouble sleeping—after the first fifteen or twenty minutes, I'd awaken with my legs restless. I tried all kinds of things to calm them down—warm baths, hot chamomile tea, hot milk, and walking, more walking. The latter seemed to help the most, but when I needed to do that repeatedly throughout the night, it got very tiring. The condition worsened until often I'd complain at breakfast time that I felt as though I needed a good night's sleep. I worked every day, but as time went on, it felt as though I was pushing myself to the very edge of a precipice that had a large sign on its edge that read: Too much!

One day I happened on a magazine article that talked about sleep apnea. Everything it talked about mirrored what I was experiencing. I took the article to the doctor and asked if he thought that may be my problem.

"Oh, I don't know," he said. "How often do you wake up in a night?"

"On a good night, probably not more than ten times."

"Ten times! In one night?"

"Yes—that's on a good night. "

"I think it would be worth testing you to see."

He made the appointment right away, but regretfully, the appointment just to see the doctor was nine months away. That finally arrived, and it was confirmed that my symptoms made it highly likely that I had sleep apnea. The appointment for a sleep test still was another month and a half away.

I drove myself down to Victoria Hospital when the date arrived. I was wired up with all kinds of electrodes all over my body to measure the movements of my muscles, the sleeping patterns and the times I awoke.

That night was one of the longest I ever spent. My legs began to twitch and then jump. Because I was attached to wires galore, getting up to walk it off, as I usually did, was not an option. Sometimes the jerking of my legs made me wonder if I was going to knock my teeth out, they were so violent. The few moments I did sleep, I found myself moaning as the next wave would hit.

Finally, 5:30 p.m. came; the nurse came to take off the wires so I could be free to go.

"You sure put on quite a show for us!" she said, with a smile.

"I'm glad you can smile about it! It's probably the worst night of my life."

"We have quite a stack of data to analyze," she said, "but I imagine you will be called in to try out a CPAP (Continuous Positive Airway Pressure machine) in about six weeks.

I was so tired, I felt unsafe to drive home, but I made it. It was good to know there may be some relief, but those weeks seemed long.

Loralyn and I planned to go to the St. Jacob's Market one Saturday early in November, but I got a call from the hospital saying they had an unexpected opening, could I come in Friday night? I told Loralyn I could probably drive up to Arva in the morning if she would drive to St. Jacobs while I slept, if the night proved to be anything like it was when I was first tested.

Again, I was wired up as before, but this time I was attached by mask and hose to a CPAP. A few times in the night, I woke to turn to a different position. I don't think I would have wakened even then, except for the wires that had to be moved. When the nurse woke me in the morning, I felt like I hadn't for years! I felt rested and slept out. I almost sang on the way to Loralyn's house. I picked her up, drove all the way to St. Jacob's and home again—and still felt energetic. It was unbelievable! It felt as though I had stepped out from a deep, dark fog into the sunlight.

Sunday and Monday I still felt better than I had, but on Tuesday morning, I told Norman "I feel the fog rolling in again! Now that I know it's possible to live a better life, I don't want to go back to the way I've been too many years already!"

The following day, I called Dr. Ferguson's office and told them what was happening.

"Is there any way I can get a CPAP of my own before the six weeks that they need to process the information?"

"Has it made that much difference?" they asked.

"It's like walking from a deep fog into the sunlight, and now the fog's rolling back in. Now that I know there's a different way to live, I hate going back to how I've lived for way too long already."

"If it makes that much difference to you, we'll set up an appointment with the supplier of CPAPs as soon as we can. It may take a few weeks though."

"All I can do is ask you to do your best."

The very next day—it happened to be my birthday—they called while I was at work.

"We had someone cancel their appointment this afternoon at 2. Would you be free at that time?"

"I'll be there!" I said.

I went and told Beth and she agreed they would manage without me and I could leave. It was the best birthday gift I could have received.

My life changed in more ways than I could have imagined. I had no idea how many parts of the body that lack of sleep and oxygen could affect!

The back pain I thought was just a part of my life gradually cleared up, mosquito bites no longer itched for weeks after a bite, and my digestive system began to tolerate foods I had given up, and became more regular than it had been for years. The swelling in my legs disappeared and much more; I felt like a new person. My doctor suggested that my weight problem very possibly had begun because of it. However, because of the abuse I had inflicted on my body by such a low-calorie diet, it still didn't let go of the excess weight very quickly. The change made old age a much more pleasant outlook.

CHAPTER 36

# A New Era Anticipated

"Receive every day as a resurrection from death,
as a new enjoyment of life; meet every rising sun
with such sentiments of God's goodness,
as if you had seen it, and all things,
new-created upon your account:
and under the sense of so great a blessing,
let your joyful heart praise and magnify so good
and glorious a Creator."

—**William Law**

Our family was grown and on their own. Loralyn had moved to an apartment in Arva where she was very happy. We began to dream of our retirement years and planned to spend a year on the road with a house trailer, heading out east in the fall, then down the east coast and across southern United States in the winter, working our way northward as the weather warmed up and perhaps even going to Alaska the next summer before working our way back home. We started to research volunteer service projects we could do along the way.

We were still quite involved in Marriage Encounter and continued to take weekends to work and rework our talks. Those were times of growing ever closer in our love and understanding and learning to work together effectively as a team. Life seemed almost perfect.

Norman took great delight in sensing his grandchildren's strengths and interests and encouraging those. Nicolas loved helping his dad cook. For Nicolas' third Christmas, Norman built him a little stove. It was carefully built to scale, with routed circles painted silver for the burners, an oven with grates and realistic knobs for controls, a storage drawer for the little pans and cooking equipment underneath. It was large to wrap, so we covered it with a garbage bag and put on a big red bow. When others helped him to remove the 'wrappings' his eyes opened, wide as saucers, and he exclaimed with awe and enthusiasm, "Oh-h! My vewy own tofe!" That was it! He wasn't really interested in anything else that day, but spent the rest of his day cooking!"

Beth and Peter's Brendan developed the ability to read all on his own before he entered school. He was interested in the stars, so Norman found a child's book about the stars, and began to make plans to take him to a planetarium to see the stars through a large telescope.

We made a list of places we could take all our grandchildren on outings or short trips. This grandparenting thing was turning out to be a real joy, we thought.

## BIG CHANGES LOOM

In the spring of 1998, my mother began failing again. She had a lot of difficulty breathing, so she was given oxygen. She needed a lot of care.

Over the years, my mother and I had many discussions about what she saw as us straying from the truth. Probably we were both grieved. She, because of our not adhering to many of the practices we had been taught, and I, because she couldn't understand the spiritual growth that had come from seeing things in a different way.

We called regularly and supported them in any way we could from the distance between us. In July, Dad stayed at home with her from church one Sunday. She hadn't eaten much for a while, but suddenly she said she was hungry for lemon pie. There was one left over from Saturday's market day, so Dad gave her a little piece as she sat on the couch. She ate most of it and sighed. "That was good!" Dad said she moved to lay back. He eased her on to the couch and she was gone.

When we were notified of her death, the first thing that I said was, "She's with Jesus and now she understands!" Although I would miss her, my heart was glad.

We started immediately to plan to go to the funeral. My sister Eva's husband, John, had been off work for some time with a sore neck and shoulders. He thought perhaps he could go even though he was in some pain. The trip up there was tolerable.

It was a large funeral and a time for family and friends to gather. We shared many memories. It was also a time of realization that we were entering another era of our lives, with one of our parents gone. I was touched and maybe even a little surprised at Dad's deep sorrow and almost disbelief that the partner who had shared his life for 63 years was gone. Although I think their life had changed quite drastically from the time they lived in Altona, I had never seen a lot of togetherness between them in my time at home.

At the funeral and on the way home, John's pain got worse and worse as the hours went by. It was agony to watch his quick deterioration and consuming anguish. He couldn't accompany us to restaurants when we stopped for a break or a meal, and the nights were torture. We drove as long days as we could to get home as soon as possible.

Doctor after doctor gave opinions but seemed to leave both John and Eva hanging as they were sent from one specialist to another. We talked often on the telephone as they went through the frustrations. Finally, late in the fall, he was diagnosed with lung cancer. He bloated up with fluid so that at times he could scarcely bend his arms. He, amazingly, rested in his trust in the Lord and Eva did too, but her days and nights were often busy and interrupted with caring for John and taking care of emergencies. Right to the end, they kept hoping for a miracle, but on Christmas Day he died. His funeral, January 2, was attended by a huge crowd including his own parents who were well up in their nineties. Our hearts went out to Eva—a widow at 62.

Because of this, Norman and I had many long talks. We realized that just because our parents lived until ninety or past, we couldn't count on sharing their length of years. We asked our financial advisor to come and help us plan to take early retirement so we could do some of the things we wanted to do. We decided I would continue working that year yet, and then retire from the Day Centre. We began to plan our year's trip with intention.

Beyond that, Norman said he would take over household chores so I could pursue a writing career which I had long hoped to fulfill. We felt excited about the adventure of what was to come.

## A SERIOUS ROADBLOCK IN THE PLANS

How quickly circumstances can change! The year ahead certainly was an adventure, but not of the kind we had envisioned. In the summer of 1998, having experienced some lethargy, Norman did see the doctor and was diagnosed as a diabetic, which he could probably control by diet. This was not surprising, as his father had experienced this at approximately the same age. Some digestive problems following that diagnosis were, understandably, attributed to the change in diet.

When, in late February, Norman told me that the symptoms had really never gone away and explained what he was experiencing, my heart dropped.

"Oh, Norman, why didn't you tell me sooner?" Colon cancer imprinted itself on my mind in neon-bright colours. I called the doctor immediately.

Tests done in early March did indeed reveal colon cancer. Our world abruptly changed! We began to live our lives on a different level.

As we initially processed the news, Norman said, "Ruth, the hardest times in our lives have been the times we have grown the most—both as persons and in our love and understanding of each other. Let's see how we can grow and what we can learn from this time."

To that, we committed ourselves, and in prayer asked God to lead us through. Most of all, we prayed for His best, whatever that would be, and that God would be glorified through this experience.

Surgery at the end of March went well and filled us with hope. Examination of his liver, which had shown a few spots on ultrasound, looked very healthy, and the surgeon said there can be other causes for such spots on the liver. Only one of the lymph nodes showed any indication of involvement. In spite of experiencing C. Difficile infection after surgery, and infection of the incision, Norman made good progress and slowly returned to some of his usual activities.

Early in May, the doctor ordered a liver biopsy to see if the spots on his liver were cancerous. They came back negative, but the liver surgeon felt we should go ahead and remove the part of the liver that had the spots, and the oncologist concurred. We felt at peace with that, even though it meant a 6–8 hour surgery. The oncologist said even if they turned out to be malignant, it would mean a 25 percent chance of cure. June 23 was the day set for surgery. The memories of the last surgery were too vivid to make it a joyous prospect, but we realized that the only way to get this behind us was to go through it! He still faced some chemotherapy after his recuperation from the liver operation.

We were fully aware of the prayers that had supported us. Family, church, friends, Interfaith Marriage Encounter couples and their church families, people had let us know they were upholding us in prayer. It was both a humbling and most gratifying experience and something that could be felt. We experienced incredible peace in the midst of it all.

As I drove Norman to the hospital, early June 23, he remarked that he felt so at peace that it seemed he was going to "show himself to the priest." Deep within, he felt that God had already healed him. We committed ourselves to God's hand, bade each other farewell, and I, along with Beth, settled down for the vigil in the waiting room. The rest of the family was planning to join us later in the day, well before the expected end of the surgery.

Two hours later, I saw the surgeon, his mask pulled down from his face, look in the door. My first thought was, "Oh, they have found him healed!" However, when he asked us to come into the private family room and closed the door behind us, there was a chilled certainty that something had gone very wrong, even before any words crossed his lips.

"I'm so sorry to tell you this, but both lobes of the liver were extensively involved. There was no purpose in finishing the planned surgery."

My mind went on slow motion. I couldn't immediately comprehend the truth of his words. Finally I asked, "How long does he have to live?"

"It's difficult to estimate, but I would say no longer than nine months to a year."

With a few more words, the doctor left my daughter and me in stunned disbelief. We wondered what we should do first. We called Stuart, Wilma and Loralyn to ask them to come as soon as possible, and then sat there numbly looking at each other.

We suddenly remembered that Ron Falk, a member in our church and part of the small group Norman and I were in, was a chaplain in St. Joseph's and decided to look him up. He was just leaving with his colleagues for a coffee break, but quickly invited us to come into his office.

One of my first questions for Ron was, "How am I going to tell Norman. He was so sure on the way in that he was already healed."

"Ruth, I know the honesty and openness that you and Norman share. You can do nothing but tell him the truth. That's not a secret you can hide." His gentle voice helped me realize that it was probably me that couldn't quite accept the truth yet.

Ron let us talk while he listened, then he prayed with us. By that time, we could go to Norman's room to see him.

He was still groggy, but his first question was, "What time is it?"

I told him and he asked, "That's not as long as they said it would take. Is it good news or bad?"

"Darling, they found more cancer than they thought, so they didn't remove the lobe as they had planned."

"Oh!" was his only comment before he shut his eyes. Suddenly, he opened his eyes again. "How do you feel about that?"

"Well, Norman, it's not what I had hoped for, but we'll take it one day at a time."

Later, when the girls went to see him as I waited out in the waiting room, he asked how they felt too, and then he wondered how they thought I was doing. His concern was mostly for the rest of his family.

The morning of his homecoming, as I lay in bed trying to realize the truth of our situation, I saw in my mind's eye, so suddenly I almost jumped, a white light the shape of a hand, extended toward Norman. His body turned luminescent and the vision was gone, leaving me with an incredible peace. I wasn't sure what it meant, but I left that up to God.

I brought Norman home from the hospital. The homecoming was made bitter-sweet because the circumstances were so different than what we had anticipated.

The surgeon had given us some hope, saying that general health and a belief system can do a lot to slow or almost halt the tumour growth. On the way home, Norman had said he thought we should finish planning our funerals, take care of our affairs in case he should die, then concentrate on living fully each day we are given. In the days ahead, we found glimmers of hope swirling around with thoughts of despair, the ribbons of "what if's" being slivered by the sharp edges of "what if nots." Yet we were keenly aware of God's love and presence and His strong arms.

CHAPTER 37

## *Life to a Different Tune*

> "Death is nothing else
> but going home to God,
> the bond of love will be
> unbroken for all eternity."
> —**Mother Teresa**

**D**eath seldom seems a welcome guest when he first knocks at our door. That certainly was the case with us. Even with the great strides that have been made in cancer treatment, from the moment we heard the prognosis, the greater possibility of death was a daily boarder in our lives. The commitment we had made, sitting on the couch that first day, gave us strength and purpose — to be open to learn from this experience; to not fight what was to be, but to learn from it. We wanted to be open to learning from the experience, no matter the course that was chosen for us. There were daily and sometimes hourly struggles. Sometimes we wanted to push our spectral guest out the door and slam it behind him. Had not our rudder been set in the direction of acceptance and growth, the struggle would have been much harder.

I took a six-month leave of absence from my work and we began our journey in earnest. Mark Twain said, "The fear of death follows from the fear of life. A man who lives fully is prepared to die at any time." We were trying to live each hour each moment, fully.

We, along with our family, finalized our funeral plans. Deciding what form that would take, choosing a theme, scripture and hymns took some courage and acknowledgement of the reality of separation. As a family, we talked about what personal items we could display that would tell those present who we really are. We talked about what we would do about living situations and business affairs, if Norman died. That meant facing our grief head-on, but it also meant doing it together. This was a gift to each other and to our family. The closeness with each other and our family intensified. The open sharing was so much easier because of the dialogue. Allowing our immediate, extended and church family and friends to walk with us in our journey seemed a natural extension of sharing our experiences at Marriage Encounter. The benefits were not ours alone. Many people, although some felt uneasy at first, were affirmative of our openness. Our children's co-workers, among others, expressed amazement at that candour, yet, in the process, they were able to talk about their feelings and fears and hopes. There were countless opportunities to share our faith. The more we shared, the more open we became, the more comfortable with being honest with ourselves, each other and the world.

The first few weeks, some progress was made, but soon Norman was unable to sleep—an after effect of the anesthetic, they said. Countless nights were spent listening to music, giving him back rubs and massages, reading to him, praying and singing, even some lullabies—trying in vain to get him some rejuvenating sleep. Sometimes he would fall asleep in my arms, but if I would so much as move, he would awaken. I ached for him. The medications doctors gave didn't seem to help. He had only occasional ten-minute snoozes.

When I told the doctor how desperate we were getting for sleep, he recommended a large dose to really put him out. That night was sheer torture. Norman got so tired he could hardly stand it, but the minute he'd even sit down, he got so agitated and antsy that he couldn't hold still. He even got testy with me—something that was quite out of the ordinary for him.

As soon as I could, I called the doctor and I told him about our night. He paused.

"Oh no! Why didn't I think about it sooner? Ninety-eight percent of people find a sedative effective. For the other two percent it works the opposite way—it agitates them and drives away sleep. He must be one of the two percent! I'm so sorry. I'll order morphine for him. That should work."

It did, but by the time we found the solution, his health had begun a sharp decline. It was heart-rending to watch.

Even the downscaled plans for what, after his first surgery, we thought were important and the things we had still planned to do together were beyond his capabilities. We did have some precious moments along the way. We managed to make it to Ohio early in August for our last Marriage Encounter Central council meeting.

As he became thinner and weaker, our relationship with Death subtly changed, and we became more used to, more at ease with his presence. Even though we would have welcomed longer life, no longer did he feel like such an intruder.

One of our banners at Marriage Encounter states, *Henceforth there shall be such closeness that when one weeps the other tastes salt*. The truth of that statement was amplified in those months.

For instance, Norman had been doing some walking, reading and easy activities after the second surgery. One evening after an early supper, Norman went to lie on the couch. He had slept a lot that day—I became aware of the taste of salt. I asked if he was sleeping because he was tired, or to escape his thoughts. He acknowledged that perhaps it was the latter. I suggested a drive to see his nut plantation, on the corner of the farm we had leased back hoping to get a severance on which we could build a house. He agreed. Sitting in that lovely setting, we spent a beautiful two hours talking about our feelings, the distinct possibility of the limited time we had left, the implications for me and for our family. He felt deep distress at leaving me alone so soon. He also shared his grief at leaving the children and grandchildren at this stage in their lives. I suggested that he might like to borrow an idea from Marriage Encounter and write a love letter to each of them—something tangible they could keep and read often. This appealled to him right away. He began the next morning and, by summer's end, had written to each of the children and in-laws. Before he died, he also wrote a letter to each of the grandchildren. Letter writing was difficult for him. He could not have done this prior to Marriage Encounter, but those letters will be treasured by their recipients for the rest of their lives.

At one point, I had a day that I felt sheer panic at being left alone. Norman tasted salt. He gently probed my thoughts and encouraged me to share, and then listened until I had spilled all my fears and self-doubt. He just held me until I was resting in his love and care. In a quiet whisper, he told me of the strength that he saw in me, reminded me of things I could do without him, and that I would not be alone. Our family and friends would be supportive, and God, who had walked with me throughout my life, would not forsake me. In the weeks ahead, until just days before his death, he often drew my attention to more things I could do with the rest of my life.

The open house our children planned for our 39th anniversary was a beautiful time. Norman commented that he felt he was riding on a wave of love. What a way to begin the last month and a half of his life! He decided, that evening, to present the love letters he had written, rather than wait. It turned out to be the right thing to do, because it led to in-depth conversations with each of them during the following week when they took turns to stay with him while I attended the Altona School Reunion. That individual time between father and each child allowed for resolution and releasing.

The next month, many people came to share their concern, prayers and affirmation of the positive role Norman played in their lives. It felt so supportive. After a lifetime of quietly doing what he felt God nudging him to do, all the time feeling that those were just little things, I think he came to accept that those 'little things' had far-reaching effects. He thanked God many times in his prayers as the days passed for both new insights and precious friends. He kept coming downstairs through the days until the last few when the steps were just too much for him.

As strength and health ebbed, death looked more and more like a friend. Norman's sense of humour stayed intact. We had often joked that my work with seniors would enable me to look after him in the future, since he was older than me. As I helped him upstairs one night, he joked: "You're getting to use your talents with the elderly earlier than you anticipated. I'm acting like an old man, needing your help much sooner than I thought I would."

The beginning of October, at Norman's appointment, the doctor remarked at how much bigger Norman's liver was from just ten days before, and that the cancer seemed to be progressing much faster than he thought it would. Norman asked, in light of that progression, how much time he may have left. The doctor said, although one could never be sure, he thought perhaps two weeks. On the way home, I asked Norman how he felt about that prediction. Norman said, "For me, it is great relief. I know it isn't that way for you, but to me, that is how it feels."

Two weeks didn't seem very long, and I hated to think about not having more time than that with my love. After a few hours to think about it, I went and sat beside Norman.

"Norman, I've tried to do all I could to have faith and give you courage to fight and to live well, but if the time has come that you can't keep living, I will do all in my power to help you to die well. I'll let go and try to walk the last days with you and release you for the journey home. You know my love will go with you every step of the way."

We embraced as we soaked in the deep love we had for one another.

CHAPTER 38

## The Parting and Journey Through Grief

"Life is a great sunrise.
I do not see why death
should not be an even greater one."
—Vladimir Nobokov

One week later, Norman was barely able to eat alone. As I finished helping him with his meal, he remarked, "There is someone else here."

"There are only the two of us," I assured him.

"No," he said. "There is someone else here."

Several more times on the way over to our bedroom, he said again that there was someone else present. Finally, remembering other stories I'd read about someone nearing death, I asked who it was.

"I'm not sure," he said. His voice seemed full of anticipation.

"Do you think the angels are here?" I asked.

"I think maybe it is," he said, sounding relieved.

"Well, my darling, you can go with them, if they're ready to take you home," I said. Death was no longer to be feared, but a welcome friend.

In the next five days, he was in and out of consciousness, but we, his family, shared some precious moments when he was awake.

One evening as I got him settled for the night, he surprised me by looking up at me with love in his eyes.

"Ruth, I want you to know that I'd like if you would get married again."

"Norman!" I protested.

"I know that's not something you want to think about right now, but I want you to know if the time comes that you think you can love someone again, that you would have my approval. You have loved me well, and I know you have much more love to give. If you can find someone, I'd like if you could share that love with another man."

"Thanks, Norman. That is very nice and generous of you, but right now I can't imagine that anyone could be anything close to what you have been to me. You have been such a good husband and I love you so very much."

"I know," he sighed as he drifted off to sleep.

We had spent many moments that summer reading the Psalms together. Often, if it was especially meaningful, we would repeatedly read the same one, finding comfort and courage in the psalmist's words. Two nights before he died, our daughter, Loralyn, and I were sitting with him. I read the 23rd Psalm to him. When I came to "Even when I walk through the dark valley of death, I will not be afraid, for you are close beside me," he squeezed my hand, so I read it over again.

He whispered, "I'm not afraid, I'm just waiting—waiting!" He held my hand up to my chest and asked, "You are ready to let me go, aren't you?"

"Yes, my love you can go whenever you need to."

He held me close and told me, "You've been a good wife—the very best!"

Early in the morning of the fourteenth, I awoke to hear him enthusiastically say, "Yes, yes, yes!"

He was seeing something I could not. He squeezed my hand. I got up and called Loralyn and his sister Martha, because I felt the end was near.

A little later he began to whisper in delight, "Home, home," with each breath.

I assured him, "Yes, Norman, you can go home."

Into my mind came the hymn, "Lead me gently home, Father." I laid my head on the pillow beside his ear and sang the whole hymn to him. When I came to the last line, I repeated it several times—"Lead me gently, home, Lead me gently home."

By that time his breathing was extremely shallow and each breath far apart. We watched as the last few breaths came. Minutes before he quit breathing, I felt his spirit leave the body. In the moments after he quit breathing, I still felt his spirit in the room. The lines on his forehead disappeared, and he was at home and at peace. I could only cry, "Thank-you Jesus, thank-you Jesus!" What a precious moment! I felt a little like I did when I rocked the children to sleep, and then laid them in the crib, continuing to sing until I was sure they were completely at rest. The line between time and eternity seemed but a thin gossamer curtain. In death there is, indeed, victory!

Mental pictures often helped me in the crisis times of my life. Into my mind, now, came another. There stood my beautifully completed package of marriage to Norman. I saw it as having been an empty box at the beginning of our marriage.

We had carefully filled the space item by item. Everything was packed and neatly arranged; now the box was full. Those last months we had put in the last few thoughtful items, and worked at the wrapping to make it a beautiful package indeed.

The last hours were like the ribbon and bow and gift card. Now it was complete, beautiful and deeply satisfying, ready to give to our Maker. No regrets or might-have-beens, except perhaps a longing that it could have been a bigger package.

We called the doctor and funeral director. The rest of the family left the room as the doctor and funeral director prepared to take his body out. They asked if I wanted to leave, but I had to stay and accompany them to the door. I whispered, "Good-bye, my dear Norman!" as they carried him to the hearse.

How thankful I was that we had already chosen a casket and largely planned the funeral. There were only a few decisions left to make.

The funeral went mostly as planned. The burial took place first. We had a bunch of white daisies to hand out to anyone who wanted to throw one on the casket after it was lowered. He had chosen a song he wanted us to sing on the way into the church, but we had forgotten to ask someone to lead the song. One of the children reminded me, and we decided on the spot, to fulfill his request, that we, as a family, would begin singing together. The rest joined in as we walked into the church.

As we assembled, a few more of Norman's favourites were played—"'Till the Storm Passes Over" by the Niagara Community Male Chorus, and The Pachelbel Canon. The closing song was the Hallelujah Chorus for which everyone stood. What a wonderful send-off it seemed for our beloved. I felt quite satisfied that Norman would have approved and been happy with the focus of the day—that he was going home to his Saviour and the welcome was out for all to join him.

In the next few weeks I saw another picture—a room where Norman and I had spent years choosing colours, painting and papering, adding pieces of furniture, functional and comfortable and aesthetically pleasing—until we found the perfect combination to bring security and pleasure to us and to those who visited our lives.

When Norman breathed his last, it was as though we had left this room by separate doors—he, to leave for his heavenly mansion, I, to what felt like a big empty room. There were some familiar items, but the choosing of colours, many of the furnishings and special touches needed to be chosen all over again to make this new space one in which I could live. It felt very empty.

I was extremely thankful for the deep friendship and open communication, the wonderful affirmation and the accompanying spiritual growth which Marriage Encounter gave us. Because of that, there were no unresolved tensions and there was absolute security in each other's love.

People shared many books with me after Norman's death. Many, written by widows or widowers, recounted the deepest grief of not having been able to talk about death and not being able to share feelings, for fear of making it too difficult for the other—making each feel so alone in their grief.

There was no need for me to wonder what Norman was going through, or what he was feeling during the journey, because we shared those things freely. His care for me and for his family was evident in the way he made sure that we expressed our fears and anxieties to him. We shared our feelings of love and appreciation, too.

Many times he consoled us and seemed to find deep satisfaction in helping deal with our sorrow, even as we were able to understand his. When the final parting came, we had already dealt with much of the acute emotion. In the ongoing waves of grief, the consolation of hearing—in my mind, his words of encouragement—were solace like no other.

It still was, however, a whole new life. I sometimes surmised that, although it was the biggest loss in my life, letting go of Norman was much easier than going on without him. I had left home to marry him and, therefore, had no experience living alone. It was a whole new landscape. I often felt like one horse in a two-horse hitch. Everything seemed off-centre and odd. Nothing pulled even.

Added to all that, we were just coming up to retirement. Our whole lives together, we had ideas for what we could do with this time, thinking we could have *together* time unhindered by the demands of growing family, the need for making a living and a thousand other demands. Not once, had we considered what we would do if either of us was left alone.

The book, *A Grace Disguised,* by Gerald Sittser—who, in a moment, lost his wife, daughter and mother in one car accident—was a great help to me. He had a dream. He saw the sun setting in front of him, and behind him, the frightening darkness looming. He began to frantically run west, trying desperately to catch the sun, to remain in its fiery warmth and light. He was losing ground and found himself in the twilight with the darkness catching up behind him. He collapsed to the ground and fell into despair, feeling he would live in the darkness forever. (I could well identify with the desire to stay in the warmth and light of the love Norman and I shared, and the desperate feeling that the twilight was catching up with me.)

Telling the dream to his sister, she pointed out to him that the quickest way for anyone to reach the sun and the light of day is not to run west, chasing after the setting sun, but to head east, plunging into the darkness until one comes to the sunrise.

That insight confirmed the 'vision' I had experienced shortly after Norman's death. I found myself standing at a white gate, surrounded by banks of lovely flowers, bathed in light. It seemed to be like the gates to which I had walked with Norman in his final moments. I had felt the same glory there.

Now I felt God nudging me away from those gates onto a path that led into a huge, dark forest. As I stepped into that dense forest, I felt the coolness and shivered. It was so dark, I could not see. I dreaded, with everything in me, taking the path, yet knew in my heart I must go on.

As I groped my way along the path, I could barely see a step ahead. I had to test and feel the next step with my feet. Gradually, my eyes became accustomed to the darkness, and I could see some interesting patterns and fauna on the forest floor.

Inside, I heard a voice, "Do not hurry through, but learn to appreciate the darkness and the growth in this environment." So I did. I found some beauty and security there and became more at ease with the darkness. I could feel God's Spirit with me.

After a while the path started going upward, becoming rough and at times dangerous, with steep rocks on one side, a narrow path and sharp drop on the other.

Sometimes, there were tricky corners around rocky outcrops. Although I felt some fear and trepidation, I felt that an angel hovered over me and protected me from danger. Sometimes I had to climb over fallen trees or piles of rocks. The climb became quite steep.

Eventually, I became conscious that the trees were becoming less dense, when bits of light shone through, and the path a little smoother. After some time, the path was not so steep and, suddenly, I came into a clearing high on the mountain.

Looking back, I could see the tops of the trees through which I had travelled. I thought, *What a difference in perspective, when seen from the top instead of underneath!* The clearing was not large, and I could see valleys and other sizeable hills ahead, but for now, I rested in the sunny meadow, blue skies above, and watched eagles soaring among the scattered clouds. I felt at peace and somehow a different, more mature person—integrating what was and what is into a new whole.

This vision, indeed, was representative of the path my life took in the next few years. I determined to plunge into the darkness so that I could reach the dawn sooner.

Gerald Sittser's book imparted another piece of wisdom. He says, "All losses are bad, only in different ways. No two losses are ever the same. Each loss stands on its own, inflicts a unique kind of pain and is irreversible in nature."

I found out that it isn't a case of "getting over" the loss, as much as finding a way to go on and learning to live with it.

Loss of someone so close was a new experience to me. I am a talker and I needed to talk about it to process it in my own mind and life. But I soon found that there are very few people who are comfortable talking about death and its effect on the one who is left. It seemed they were afraid it may make it worse for me—and perhaps it would make me cry. I did cry easily, but as Shakespeare said,

"Give sorrow words: the grief that does not speak
Whispers to the o'er fraught heart, and bids it break."

So one of the most valuable gifts I was given by a few was the gift of truly listening and letting me cry if I needed to.

Fresh grief affected my every waking hour. There was such an aura of unreality and confusion. I felt so lost that it seemed that time had no meaning anymore. My memory was no longer dependable, and the configuration of my life was changed so drastically that there seemed to be no anchor posts from which to gain a sense of direction.

It felt a little like driving through a deep winter fog, a covering of snow blanketing the road, the ditches and fences. There was nothing to help me know where the road was, and yet I had to travel on and on.

## CONTINUING THE GRIEF JOURNEY

"How strange it is, you can resist tears victoriously, you can carry yourself very well at the most difficult moments. And then... you find a flower in bloom that was still closed the day before, — a letter falls from a drawer, — and everything falls apart."
—Sidonie-Gabrielle Colette

As time passed, there were glimpses of better times ahead, more acceptance of life as it had become. At first, those times are fleeting.

Eventually, they come for longer periods—however, it took only small happenings to crumble any progress I thought I had achieved. Each of these brought a fresh wave of grief washing over me, breaking down what seem like the sandcastles of new beginnings and fresh courage.

One friend seemed to sense when I needed support. Henny called one such morning and asked if I'd like to accompany her to the city to exchange a pair of pants that didn't fit her husband. It seemed to be just what I needed. We went into the men's department of the store totally unaware that there may be a wave ahead. She went to the desk to make the exchange. My eyes were drawn to the men's clothing and suddenly the thought came, *I'll never again have the joy of buying outfits for Norman.* Along with the thought, there arose, unexpected, a great, heaving sob. I covered my mouth and quickly hid behind a rack of clothing. I kept it quiet, but the tears came flowing in abundance as the wave of loss rolled over me once again.

When Henny found me after a search, she asked, "What's the matter, Ruth?"

I only needed to say a few words—she understood and gently led me back to the car, suggesting we drive a bit before going for coffee. Her kind understanding was like a soothing balm.

There is a saying I like: "Life is like an onion, you peel it layer by layer, and sometimes you weep." But I found that with each layer, I came closer to the centre that holds the real essence of life—the place where God dwells— and the real me could commune with him.

One morning, sometime after Norman's death, I was faced with several tasks for which he usually took responsibility. I felt so inadequate. At my age, the possibility of how many years I could have to live alone stretched stark and bleak ahead of me. In my morning quiet time, I called out to God. I told Him I trusted Him, but I just couldn't understand how He thought I could manage without Norman.

Tears, streaming down my cheeks, I cried, "I just don't understand, God, I just don't understand!"

Suddenly, I felt lifted up as though I had been put on the very lap of my Lord and held close in his arms. I heard a gentle, kind and loving voice.

"I know you don't understand."

Those words, even without answers, made such a difference. Somehow everything felt all right! Out of that moment, the following poem evolved.

## AFTER THE NIGHT

Life dealt
a crushing blow.
You picked me up
and held me close.
I felt your arms
but could not see
your face.

Where was your face
just when I needed
to see you most?
I cried
and lay exhausted
and cried again
until I was spent.

Finally,
my grief, poured out,
began to ease.

Like a child catching
a shuddering breath,
still wracked from sobs,
I raised my head
from the succour of your shoulder,
the warmth of your neck,

… and there,
so close to mine,
beheld
your loving face.

The grief journey was made more difficult, because, before my six month leave of absence was up, largely through a misunderstanding, my job at the Senior's Day Centre was also gone. Although I was given a job to do publicity and promotion for Craigwiel Gardens after Christmas, the demise of a job I so thoroughly enjoyed was another huge loss on top of the loss of my husband. The close association with the seniors that I so enjoyed was no longer a daily part of my life and I sorely missed it.

My life felt empty. Even though I was working in the same building in which I had worked for almost twelve years, I sorely missed working directly with the seniors who had become my friends. It didn't help that many of them missed me and couldn't understand why I didn't come back.

I finally asked permission to begin a weekly Brown Bag and Banter Lunch at the apartments—everyone brought a bag lunch and a few jokes or short stories to share— and I provided coffee and tea. I also planned monthly meetings that included entertainment of some sort and making an occasional evening meal for the seniors. That gave me involvement with apartment dwellers who had attended the Day Centre and also some new ones. Often, just being with those seniors, many of whom had experienced the loss of loved spouses, filled me with peace and comfort. Still, I felt a need for direction in my life that would give my existence more meaning.

One of the books given to me after Norman died was *Wife after Death* by Peggy Anderson from London. At the end of the book, it told about the 10-week "Alone and Growing" groups she ran a few times each year. I called and she set up an appointment for an interview. For ten weeks, three other women and a man met and grew together. That was a very helpful course where we talked about our spouses, the different areas of grief and the special ways we each experienced our personal loss. We then went on to explore ways of going on with our lives.

One of her assignments was to do something creative to express our growth. One night a picture came into my mind. It wouldn't leave and I couldn't sleep, so I got up and scrounged around until I found watercolours I had purchased for my grandchildren. I painted until the early morning hours and still didn't know what it meant. The next morning I kept looking at it. Finally, I went to the computer to put my feelings into words. I wrote and cried, and wrote and cried until it was done.

## OF BLOOMS AND BLOOMING ON

The colour in our life
together
had burst forth
in beauteous tones of bright splendour,
emerged from the dark earth of friction
that refines and breaks down
to productive nutrient.

The comfort and joy in our
togetherness
sent forth tangible perfume
that wafted through everything
we touched,
partook of,
enjoyed,
so that even others stopped
to sniff and smile in pleasure.

Came the call ending our
togetherness,
too soon,
far too soon.

Savouring the moments,
we clung to time for awhile;
blessing and being blessed,
loving and being loved
and in the end,
releasing.

From the purest centre of our love
together

we let go,
to go on blooming.
You to ethereal heights
and nebulous form,
I, taking on a darker hue
of muted beauty,
in a world bereft of you.

Still I try to let go,
still I seek to grow and bloom
to release the fragrance
of love once known
and still living in my heart.

Before our next meeting I had the picture and poem framed together as my project.

After Peggy finished with her usual course, the five of us continued to meet once a month for a meal and to keep up with our journey. We did so for five years before one and then another began to drop out for various reasons.

At the Marriage Encounter banquet in March after Norman died, I was given the privilege of sharing our journey toward death in a talk I called "When Comes the Parting." It was the beginning of a speaking career. I was even flown to Pennsylvania by the Marriage Encounter group there, to share my journey and how much Marriage Encounter had helped us in this crucial time of life.

Sharing my experience and finding the thrill of meeting the needs of others through the imparting of my pain, spurred me on to approach the REJOICE! Daily Devotional Magazine asking if I could be a contributing author. After sending a sample of my writing, I was accepted and given an assignment. I was somewhat apprehensive yet delighted as I thought of the many readers I might meet through this avenue.

## CHAPTER 39

## Steps Toward a Goal

> "Goals are not only absolutely necessary
> to motivate us. They are essential
> to really keep us alive."
> —Robert H. Schuller

M y friend Patricia, who had moved to Salt Spring Island off the coast of Vancouver Island, invited me to come for three weeks to get started on my assignment. She, too, was beginning to write. I had never done any travelling alone, but I packed my big suitcase on wheels, my computer, my assignment and clothes for the journey and flew from Toronto to Vancouver. From there, I took a taxi to the ferry that took me to Vancouver Island. I had made arrangements with Doug— who had been one of our volunteer drivers at the Day Centre—to be picked up there. I stayed with him and Barbara for the night then took a smaller ferry to Salt Spring Island where Patricia would meet me.

Patricia was very gracious in giving me space to write as she went on with her regular activities. I began with my assignment, thinking that when that was done, I would work at compiling worship materials I had written over the years.

On the third morning, I thought of the novel I'd had going around in my mind since interviewing Freda Litt at the Day Centre. On a whim, I decided to give it a whirl and see how it would go to write a book based on the life of her mother. I had a hunch I might have the story told in about ten pages and be left wondering how to flesh it out and make a book of it. I began at nine a.m. I thought of this woman I decided to call Ellie, and how it would feel to break an engagement to the man with whom I'd fallen in love, to marry a brother-in-law whom I had admired but without the kind of romantic love on which to form a marriage relationship.

I needed to set the scene a bit, so I began with that. Next thing I knew, Patricia was asking if I was going to stop for lunch. The day flew by. At nine o'clock, I thought I'd better give myself a break, but my mind kept going even after I went to bed. For the rest of the three weeks, my days, except for a few that I took off to go somewhere with Patricia, I sat at my computer from 9 a.m. to at least 9 p.m. Often scenes would come to me through the night and I'd get up to enter enough so that I could go on from there the next day. I felt as though the story was flowing through me rather than from me. Much of the story was written before my time was up. I flew home with a satisfied feeling.

My son's friend was involved in an organization that had annual workshops to encourage writers who are Christian. She asked if I'd be interested in going to a *God Uses Ink* conference. In June of 2002, I made plans to attend. By that time, Brenda was fighting cancer, so although I knew absolutely no one, I was determined to go. I felt like a naïve *newbie*, as I selected workshops and a continuing course, hardly knowing what I should choose. I knew nothing about publishing and was very conscious that probably most people attending were college or university graduates, and that I'd be going with only a Grade nine education. However, I was kindly welcomed.

Like a starving beggar, I guzzled up every opportunity that was offered. From the Early Bird reading sessions to the Late Owl readings, I was present. My head spun with all the new language, the intricacies of the writing worlds, the encouragement to write, the cautions about all the mistakes a new writer could make, the derision of editors and publishers directed at the 'rubbish' people expected to have published. I felt myself swayed from anticipation and determination to write, to dismay that I would think myself able to write anything of value, and back again, to wanting to try.

I had sent in the first few chapters of my book to be critiqued by a professional writer. When I met with her, she had no kind or encouraging words at all. She told me I was not ready to write a book and that my work was nowhere near the standards that would make a successful author. I don't think she had read the rules of critiquing that suggest that for every criticism, one should point out two strengths. I came away from that interview rather discouraged, to say the least.

The continuing class with Linda Hall was the highlight of the conference. We had been asked to write a short story before the conference, and then she sent copies to each member of the class and we all critiqued them before going. Through that I learned that what one person thought was the highlight of the story, or at least a very touching part, another would recommend leaving out. Each person's comments were important to consider—the more who agreed, the more seriously it should be taken—but in the end what felt right to you, the author, was the way to go. It made me value input from others that so improved my writing, but it also encouraged me not to be down-hearted at negative feedback or rejection letters.

I made new friends but still felt unsophisticated and amateurish beside all the seasoned writers. I still felt rather stupefied and definitely bewildered as I drove home, exhausted from two and a half long, jam-packed days. I fell into my bed with a sigh, letting my tired body and mind sink into the oblivion of a deep sleep.

As the sun arose and shone across my bed, I slowly emerged from sleep. Before I was fully awake, ideas for stories began to seep into my mind. It was only moments before I sensed an urgency to get up and get started. That thought first startled me and then filled me with exuberance. For so long, I had pulled the covers over my head when

I first awoke, dreading another day without my dear husband. Now joy filled my heart, and I literally sat up in bed shouted.

"Well, hello life! It is good to have you back." I felt as though I had quite decidedly turned a corner in my journey, not just a gradual curve but an actual corner! I could almost hear Norman say, "Good for you! Go for it, girl!"

Later that summer, asked to house-sit for Guelph friends who were going west for three weeks, I embraced the opportunity for uninterrupted writing time. I spent the time filling in details and descriptions, omitting parts that might not be needed or distracted from the story. Reading and re-reading the story many times, I kept finding mistakes and changes to be made, but those weeks greatly improved the project.

When I came home, there was a call waiting for me. A friend, who knew I had been looking at a different place to live, where there would be less outside care and maintenance, told me of a house in Ailsa Craig that I should look at. I had looked in London at a few places and also in Nairn and Ailsa Craig. Every single one seemed to have something that didn't suit. Many in Ailsa Craig were split level, and I already knew that when one gets a little disabled, having to go steps becomes a problem. I had my list of non-negotiables: attached garage accessible from the house, a wall large enough to accommodate the glass cupboard Norman had built for me, bedroom, bathroom, kitchen and laundry room all on the same floor, and the lot somewhere on the edge of town so I didn't have other houses on three sides of me.

I had almost given up, thinking I may have to build an addition on the house so I could at least have most of the required items I wanted in a house that would serve me until I was older. I wanted the laundry room, kitchen, bathroom and bedroom on one floor access to the garage from the inside of the house and have a view of open country. If I had that, I might be able to get help with the outside work if I couldn't do it. I almost didn't bother going to look at the house my friend suggested. But I felt inwardly compelled to do so. I decided I wouldn't bother asking one of my children to accompany me as I usually did, but just go have a noncommittal look at it. The moment I walked in the front door, the thought crossed my mind, *This is where I want to live.* The more I saw of the house, the more I was convinced. Everything on my list was available except the last, but the way the house was situated, the back windows overlooked the backs of the five or six lots on the streets north and south of this house, giving it an open feel. After another look, accompanied by my children, I decided to make an offer. What I really hoped for was to buy it with a closing date in the spring so that I'd have time to sell my three-acre lot, clean out the house and shop, sell the shop equipment and lumber and have time to paint the new abode before moving in. It seemed like a lot to ask for. I wondered if I could find buyers for my property who would be willing to wait that long.

Amazingly, God answered every one of those prayers. My house sold for more than the asking price and they were willing to wait. I got possession of my new house on April 25, 2004, and still had my other property until May 9. I immediately booked a painter to come in to the new house on April 26, so we could have the painting done and still have time to clean out the cupboards and start moving in the smaller things, so only the furniture and the appliances would be left for moving day.

My writing took a back seat as I sorted through the accumulation of the years, making piles to keep, sell, and give away or throw away. Room by room, I sorted through the accumulation of living in the same house for twelve years. Such activity took time, for as I handled everything, many memories were aroused.

When I first started selling the machinery in the shop, I felt as though I was having another funeral, as if I was selling the last parts of Norman—or at least his dreams. It was quite a struggle to get my gut to come along with my head and my heart, but I finally persuaded that part of my anatomy, too, that it was the right thing to do.

I was amazed and disheartened at how some people would try to take advantage of a widow. When I saw the name of a man who had been one of Norman's Fanshawe instructors advertising for wood, I called thinking I could trust him to evaluate the piles of lumber Norman had ready to make furniture. When he came, I saw that although the name was the same, he was someone different. He took a look at the lumber and declared, "I know it's not what you want to hear, but this is just left-over junk. No good lumber here!"

"There is quite a bit of walnut here," I said. "That certainly isn't junk. I find it hard to believe that even the rest is junk. Norman was still making nice furniture from this wood until he got too sick to do it."

"That's just it. He has used all the good stuff, and it's only the worthless stuff that's left. The walnut may not be junk, but you can hardly give walnut away these days. Nobody wants walnut anymore."

After a few more moments of looking through the racks of lumber, he jotted some figures on a pad he had, and then looked up.

"I know with your husband gone, you'll want to clear things out of the shop." He scratched his head. "I'm very busy, but for $200 I could load it up and haul it away for you, to take the load off your shoulders."

I was appalled! I could hardly believe what I was hearing. I took a deep breath and said as kindly as I could, "Oh, I wouldn't dream of imposing on a busy man!" I said, trying to keep the exasperation from showing. "I'll find someone to do it for me, don't worry."

"Are you sure? I can perhaps do it next week."

"No, no. Thanks for offering, but I won't burden you with it."

I thought he looked a little disappointed as he walked away, but I watched him leave, locked the shop door and went to the house with a distaste and disillusioned feeling.

A week later, a man I trusted took a look at it. When I told him what had happened, he pointed out three pieces of cherry and said, "These pieces alone are worth $100. Walnut, too, is very desirable!"

Often, I felt inadequate as I was forced to put a cost on equipment I wasn't that familiar with pricing. I didn't want to take advantage of anyone, but neither did I want the buyers to take advantage of me.

On the Thanksgiving weekend—the third anniversary of Norman's death—our whole family rented a few condos in Collingwood and spent the weekend together. We had a good time and spent some of it reminiscing as well as connecting on a deeper level. Somehow that weekend and the remembering we did helped me to feel at peace about moving from the house we shared for the last years of Norman's life.

In spite of a prolonged bout of bronchitis, I kept packing all winter. As soon as I got possession of my new house, I washed out the cupboards, then started taking carloads from my cupboards and placing things in my new kitchen. The painter was a little delayed, but he did come and started in the upstairs so I could continue moving things in. The carpet cleaner also came and got all the carpets done. The big garbage bin we had ordered began to fill up as we discarded what we no longer needed. When we started on the garage, it filled up even faster.

I was so glad for help from my families and friends. I don't know how I would have managed without. Besides my own children, Menno and Earl came to help with the things in the shop, and Vern and Joyce Gingrich took many items from the garage to sell at an auction.

The moving van arrived on the last day and made short work out of moving the heavier furniture and appliances, saving the backs of my own family.

I felt absolutely at home from the first day. There were changes I wanted to make—more flowerbeds, and I needed to fill in around the edges of the house where it had settled and could cause water problems, but it seemed much more manageable on such a small lot. My friend's hired man built a small storage shed behind my house which gave me more room in the garage. Although I still remembered Norman, there was some relief at not having every square inch of the house and lot continuously reminding me of what was. The move gave me a fresh start.

CHAPTER 40

## *Happy Surprises*

> "There rose up within me
> a profound sense of being loved.
> I felt 'gathered together' and encircled by a Presence
> completely loving, as if I were enveloped by the music
> of a love song created just for me.
> … Just a warm knowing that I was in
> God's loving embrace...
> centered and unified there."
> —**Sue Monk Kidd,** *God's Joyful Surprise: Finding Yourself Loved*

During that busy year, I kept contact with other writers through The Word Guild listserv on the Internet. That helped my confidence grow, and my desire to write, flourish. By June, I was settled enough to return to the God Uses Ink writer's conference now reinvented to become Write Canada. Again, I was inspired to keep writing and to get *Not Easily Broken* ready for publishing.

At the conference, I made an announcement after one of the meals. "If there are any here from the London area who would be interested in forming a writer's group, please come and see me after the meal.

Mary Haskett approached me. She lived in the south part of London, but we agreed that we would find a place to meet. She, of course, had more contacts in the city, so by the time we had our first meeting in her home, we had probably ten people. That group, *Ready Writers* changed my life. What a support, inspiration and encouragement they became. Not only did we spur one another on to better writing, but we helped each other to find places to share the fruits of our labour. Many of us were published as a direct result of our times together.

It was also at that 2003 conference that I approached Ray Wiseman who along with his wife, Anna, did editing for others. He agreed to take my manuscript and gave me invaluable advice to make it a better book. He freely pointed out the mistakes he found, brought to light my over-use of a few favourite words. I was totally unaware and horrified at how often I used them—*some* and *just* seemed to be in almost every other sentence, and most places were entirely superfluous. But one thing Ray and Anna also did for me; they gave me encouragement and gentle and wise advice.

## HAPPY SURPRISES

April 11, 2005, I was nicely settled in my new home. That evening I celebrated Norman's birthday by getting out the cards he had given to me over the years. I settled down on my recliner and read his messages of love. He always carefully chose cards with verses that expressed what he wanted to say and wrote a personal note at the end. Memories of his love and support that grew over the years we shared, came flooding over me. I was filled with thanksgiving for the gifts we had been given. It was then that I remembered the wish he had expressed a few nights before he died—that I could get married again.

"Well, Norman, I don't think that's going to happen. It's been six years now and I haven't met anyone I'd want to share my life with. But that's okay. I'm learning to live by myself, and I am enjoying life as it is." My heart glowed within me, but then I thought of getting old alone, so I continued my prayer, "But Lord, if that is what you have planned for me, to live alone the rest of my life, please don't make it too long before I can come home to you."

During my last sentence, the phone began to ring. I waited until I was finished then picked up the phone. "Hello?"

"Hi! This is Paul Meyer."

*Paul Meyer! What does he want?*

"Hi Paul, how are you?"

"I was just looking through the cards I got when Marion died. I found your card and note with your telephone number and decided to give you a call."

Paul and I had grown up less than a mile from each other. We swam in the same swimming holes in the creek, skated together on the pond between us and tobogganed down the hills together. When we first were married, we visited each other and were involved in some of the same community activities. Now we caught up on each other's lives as we chatted together about all the people and experiences we had in common. I had always thought of him as being quiet, but it felt so comfortable talking to him. Two hours after his first "Hello," I hung up with a grin on my face.

Suddenly, I felt as though a smiling God was nudging me saying, "There you go!"

"Oh, just a minute, God, he said he was calling to get Dad's address so he could stop and visit him on the way west this summer." But it seemed God only smiled more.

The next morning, I thought I should have asked Paul for his sister Ruth's address too, because I often sent my Christmas letters to her, but they had moved and the last one had been returned. I wrote a short note to Paul, asking if he could send it to me.

The next Friday night he called again and we talked another two hours. The following week, I was having a little nap in readiness for a busy evening when the doorbell rang. I raced up from the family room. There was no one on the verandah, but I saw a truck in the driveway, so I went out past the corner to see who it was. There was Paul! I invited him in and we had a nice little visit. He said he was looking for a truck cap in Strathroy, so he thought he'd stop in.

When he left, my heart was singing. I could scarcely believe what I was feeling, but it felt strangely like love. With each phone call and each visit, the song grew in exuberance and with harmony I could not have imagined.

When I told him that I was invited to Floradale to a concert, he said, "If you come up to Listowel, I'll take you out for a meal before the concert."

My heart sang all the way to Listowel. He showed me through the house that he and Marion had planned and then we went to Clifford for an early evening meal. I almost asked if he'd like to come to the concert with me but didn't know how he'd feel about it. My heart was full of thanksgiving and I sang all the way home that night.

On the next call, he asked, "Do you have a "boyfriend?"

"No, I don't, Paul."

"Would you consider having me take that place in your life?"

"With pleasure!" I said. My consent was all it took to make the visits more frequent.

Paul was scheduled to go on a fishing trip with Bob Lewis and his friends in the last part of May, after which he was to travel on west to visit his son Jeff and family. We worked in as many times together as possible before his departure.

The last evening together was sweet, but also agony in knowing it would be several months before we'd see each other again. As I mulled over in my mind how my life had changed in the matter of a few weeks, I penned another poem to send with him.

## SURPRISE

Nothing through the dullness quite broke through.
Cloudy skies, lacklustre days,
Learning to live without special love,
trying to find joy in smaller ways.

Life settled down—hopes not so high,
Leaning hard on God's great grace
Letting it go, depending on Him
To bring me to His own best place.

Then a few night calls a sensed intent
a gift straight from God's hand,
My spirit rose up in hymns of praise
I felt my heart expand.

When he had made the purpose clear
I was full blessed indeed!
I felt as though my heart came home-
God hears our every need.

Tears of thanksgiving, bursts of joy,
This dear one brought to me,
The more I hear the more I see,
I feel it's meant to be.

When together, there's a sense of bliss,
The epicentre sure
Of God's good will, His intended way,
Something that can endure.

Paul, oh, dear, dear Paul, so gentle, calm.
In your voice, growing fire
That echoes, too, deeply in my heart,
A shared intense desire.

The telephone kept us in touch through the fishing, the trip west, and his visit there. I posted my letters regularly. When he told Jeff and Sheri about our relationship, they were anxious to meet me, so I made plans to fly to Winnipeg first, and then to Barwick to visit my sister and

Dad, who had been asking when I was coming to visit him. The plan was to stay there almost a week before I would fly on west to Calgary to spend several weeks there, and then we'd travel back to Ontario together.

He called every day. One evening a few weeks later, the doorbell rang. When I got there, a man said, "I'm looking for Ruth Smith."

"That would be me!"

"Well then, I have some flowers for you." He went back to his van and came back carrying a dozen long-stem roses. "These must be from your son or grandson"— then he looked at my face, "Or maybe it is from your boyfriend!"

"Maybe it is!" I smiled.

On the tag were the words, "To my girlfriend, from your boyfriend, Love Abie." (A nickname he'd had since grade school.)

By that time, I think the delivery man knew it was from this old woman's boyfriend—whether he wanted to believe it or not!

A dozen long-stemmed roses—six deep red, three deep pink with white, and three yellow. What lovely specimens and sentiments! I spent some time just praising God, crying and laughing in the delight He sent me in Paul. I felt so blessed. I felt as though I was drinking from the cup of God's pleasure. I also called Paul that night to thank him and smiled at the enthusiasm and delight in Sheri's voice as she told me she'd take the telephone to Paul.

When we talked about what we could do while I was out there later in the summer, Paul asked, "Would you like to go to the Edmonton Mall?"

"Oh, Paul!" I cautioned, "There is something I need to tell you about myself. I'm not like most women." I could hear a sharp intake of breath. "I really don't like shopping at all. I'd rather take a walk in the out–of-doors or go see some nice scenery." There was a pause then a long "Whew!"

"I thought you were going to say if I took you to the mall, that I'd never get you out. I don't think I mind at all having you just the way you are."

He immediately began planning to show me some of the countryside, to take me to places like Drumheller, and to see the mountains in closer range, although we could see them from the other side of the road at Jeff and Sheri's.

Often through the years, my dreams have given me direction and assurance. With all that was happening in my life at this point, it wasn't surprising that once more my night-time ruminations would produce confirmation. One night I dreamt that as I walked along a path beside the woods, I saw Marion ahead of me holding out a large white, embroidered cape. She was smiling broadly, her eyes twinkling as though she was pleased to be surprising me. Two more times the dream was repeated, and each time Marion was closer. I woke wondering what the dream meant. The next time the dream was repeated, Marion smiled even more, and I heard the words as though they came from the clouds, "Like Elijah's mantle." They descended on my heart like a blessing. I awoke with tears running down my cheeks. I felt so blessed. I had known that Norman would be pleased, but now I felt we also had Marion's blessing.

Another night my dream showed that I was driving a school bus through a lovely, wooded, hilly area, when the engine got hot. I thought I had better stop for a while to let it cool. Later, I tried again. It thought I drove through a place where on either side of the road, there was a school bus that had been cut through, leaving the front and back parts separate. There was a sense of acceptance that some buses end that way. To me, those decimated buses were representative of Paul and Marion and Norman and my marriages—cut off before the expected destination could be reached.

Finally the time came for my flight. My heart was set on seeing Paul again and rejoicing in being with him, but before that happened, I was to experience another unexpected blessing. Two single women from the Barwick area were going out to Winnipeg for supplies. They picked me up at the airport, but it was almost nine before we got to the Nighswander home. I knew Dad often was in bed by eight, so didn't expect to see him until morning. When Martha met me at the door on our arrival, she said, "I couldn't get Dad to go to bed. He doesn't remember much for very long these days, but he remembered you were coming today, and he wanted to stay up until you came."

I walked into the room where he sat in his rocking chair. "Hello, dear Papa!"

"Ruth! You finally came!"

"Yes, I did." I walked over to him as he rose from his chair and I gave him a hug.

"I love you!" I whispered in his ear.

In the next moment, something happened that I had given up all hope of ever experiencing. I was astounded—he hugged me closely to him and replied with warmth and assurance, "I love you too!"

Tears filled my eyes and joy filled my breast. I had resigned myself to the fact that I probably would never hear those words from my dad's lips. It was a moment that is deeply imprinted on my mind and in my heart. Years of longing and uncertainty fell away as we clung together for several moments. I felt an inner medley of emotions. Simultaneously, I was my papa's little girl again and yet more mature and whole than I had ever felt in my life. How precious!

The next day as I sat holding his hand, I told him that I was seeing Paul Meyer and that we were discovering a deep love for each other.

"That is nice," he told me. "I was so sorry you had to lose Norman when you were still young. I hated thinking of you going through the separation I was feeling after your mother died."

After a while he nodded off to sleep. He hadn't slept long when he awoke and said, "Ruth, I don't think it will work."

"What won't work, Dad?"

"You and Jake Meyer. I think that's too great a difference in age."

"Oh Dad," I hastened to assure him. "It isn't Jake I'm seeing, it's Jake's grandson, Paul."

"Oh! I thought you and Jake would be too far apart."

When I was about to leave, he wished I could stay longer. I told him that Paul and I would stop in on the way back to Ontario and we'd stay a day or two.

"Once I see him, if I still think he's too old for you and I tell you, what will you do about it?" he asked.

"I guess I'll have to tell you that you made a mistake in marrying Mom."

"Why do you say that?"

"Well, Mom was four years older than you, and Paul is only three years older than me." I smiled.

"Oh, you always have an answer for everything!" he said, but he, too, was smiling.

## CHAPTER 41
## New Love and Life

Just when I thought that love
could never be a part of me,
that's when you came along
and showed me happiness!
—by Elvin

My heart sang all the way to Calgary and as I came down the escalator, I saw Paul standing at the bottom with love shining in his eyes. With a welcoming hug, he whispered into my ears, "I love you so, and I'm so glad you're here!"

"I love you too," I whispered back.

He picked up my luggage and we headed to the parking lot to his truck. There, he presented me with a jewelry box that contained a little gold heart with a diamond inside. He fastened the chain around my neck as he, again, declared his love for me.

That was the beginning of a lovely visit. We spent many of our days with his family. Often his granddaughters, Deandra and Caitlynn, visited with us in the trailer that Paul had bought to put on Jeff's property, so they'd have a place to stay when they visited. Of course, getting to know Jeff and Sheri was a great experience too. We also went to visit places of beauty and some of the neighbours with whom he had become acquainted. Sometimes in the evening we sang along to cassettes he had in the trailer. That felt good too.

On our way back, when we stopped in to visit my father, Dad's heart was quickly won over as Paul talked about the old neighbours in Altona. They visited all afternoon and when Enos and Arlene's family planned a wiener roast out on the bank of the river, he willingly came and sat there enjoying the supper and further visiting. When he finally was persuaded that it was time for bed he said, "I hate to spoil the visit. It's the best day I've had in a long while!"

After our return home, we travelled the road between Listowel and Ailsa Craig quite often. I got to meet his daughters and their families. During September and October, Paul had been invited to an anniversary of friends, a wedding of Marion's great-niece and a wedding reception of his brother-in-law and new wife, so I quickly became acquainted with many of his friends and relatives. Everywhere, people told me what a good man I would discover in Paul. I also realized that Paul had only a year to mourn Marion's death, so I hoped I could be of help in that adjustment.

He joined my family for our annual Thanksgiving weekend at the Bayfield cottage and he quickly fit right in. We attended each other's churches and soon realized our union would more than double our support structure. Soon after Thanksgiving, Paul took me shopping for an engagement and wedding ring. Our wedding date was set for December 3.

At a routine examination, in November, Paul's doctor noted a small rise in his p.s.a. and suggested he see a specialist to make sure all was okay.

"I don't think it's anything to worry about," Dr. Donald assured him. "Your count isn't very high, but since it's been up a bit the last few times, I think we'll send you to a specialist just to make sure."

The specialist said almost the same words. "It's highly unlikely that it's anything, but we'll do a biopsy to be safe."

That evening when he told me about his visit, Paul asked, "Should we postpone the wedding until we know for sure?"

"Sorry, Paul, it's too late. I love you already, and if it happened to be bad news, I'd rather be with you than let you go through it yourself."

"Are you sure?"

"I am very sure."

The biopsy was scheduled for the week after our marriage.

## PLANNING FOR A WEDDING

My good friend, Henny, went with me to Michigan to shop for a wedding dress. We searched and searched for the ivory dress I had in mind. That year, it seemed there were very few dresses at all. Pant suits were all in, but I wanted a dress and black was almost the only colour available. I began to despair. On a sale rack, Henny spied a red full-length dress.

"Try it on!" she urged.

"Red—for a wedding dress?"

"It's almost Christmas and you look good in red."

It fit, it felt good, and the price was definitely a plus!

"I'll get it and keep looking to see if I can find something more like what I had in mind.

We looked in more stores on the way home, but nothing turned up.

There was no other opportunity, because the next morning, two weeks before the wedding—it was a Tuesday morning—I woke with a black curtain over a third of my left eye. I went right to my optometrist.

"Do you have anyone to drive you home?" she asked. "I'd like to put drops in your eyes so I can examine you better."

"No, I don't. I drove out by myself."

"Could you have someone bring you back on Thursday?'"

"Isn't that too long to wait?" I asked her.

"I think Thursday will be okay."

I left with an uneasy feeling. On Thursday she sent me straight to emergency at St. Joseph's in London. There I learned that it was a detached retina, and that I needed immediate surgery. However, the surgeon said he already had four scheduled that night, and I didn't want to be the fifth. It would be better, he said, if I came back on Friday night. I was nervous about the delay, but the surgery was done late Friday evening.

The doctor pronounced the surgery as being effective, but because it was so long since the retina had detached, there were some "wrinkles" they couldn't smooth out. Immediately, I was concerned because of the way my eyes work.

When I expressed my concern, the doctor said, "Your overall sight may be a little less, but you won't be able to discern it, because you will see with both eyes, and the difference will be negligible."

"But my eyes are different than most people's, because I can see with either eye independently and also with both eyes. I'm afraid this will make it impossible for me to look with both eyes."

"No, no!" he assured me, "The brain doesn't let you know the difference."

I tried again to explain, but he didn't seem to comprehend. When I went back for my follow-up visit, I wrote my history out and handed it to him. "Before you start with your examination, will you please read this?"

He read it with great interest, sometimes nodding, sometimes shaking his head. "This is very interesting!" he remarked. "Can I keep this in my files?"

"Please do!"

"This could make a difference in your sight," he conceded.

And so it did. I essentially became a one-eyed person again. Although I can see with my left eye, the image is very wavy. Seeing at a distance isn't too bad, but reading any fine print is impossible.

My eye was still rather red and a little swollen on our wedding day, December 3, 2005, but it did not hinder our joy in becoming one. What a difference forty-five years makes! There was such a calm assurance in both our hearts—although they fluttered, it was because of thankfulness and anticipation, rather than a case of nerves. We had no unrealistic expectations of marriage—we'd both been through it before. We had no need of changing each other to meet our expectations or needs—God had so wonderfully made it clear that it was his idea and we were ready to accept the gift he gave, just as we were. We were in the right place at the right time.

Jeff was best man for his dad and Loralyn stood by my side as bridesmaid during the ceremony. We had planned the ceremony and the vows we wanted to make to each other—vows that acknowledged our previous mates and included our families and friends. The Nairn ladies catered a beautiful reception before we went to Grand Bend for our wedding night.

We didn't stay longer than the next day, for we wanted to see Jeff and Sheri and their family while they were in Ontario; they only had a few days.

Paul's biopsy came during the next week. At the follow-up appointment with the specialist two weeks after the wedding, we were told that all 12 specimens taken at the biopsy were cancerous, and ten of them were a very aggressive kind. There was no alternative; he needed to have his prostate removed as soon as possible. The surgeon said hopefully they would be able to get all the cancer along with the prostate, and that it hadn't spread as the doctor seemed to think; but if it had, he would need radiation and perhaps chemo. "If that doesn't work, get ready for a long, slow, painful death."

What a verdict! It seemed a little like déjà vu. Seven years prior when we heard the Big C, Norman and I had only seven months left together.

My feelings of the moment can be summed up in a poem I later wrote:

Unbidden thoughts push
into crevices of my mind
—the last race
with undesirable end.

Determined, I thrust aside
all thoughts but this alone
—the goal before me.

Breathing deep,
lungs fill with air,
ears listening,
alert for the starter's gun
signalling the beginning
of this Olympian challenge.
I'm ready to go.

If this was what I was called to do, I'd run the race before me as well as I could. Even seven months with this wonderful new love in my life would be worth it! Any more would be a bonus. Even the Big C could not dim the joy I felt at God's gift.

Paul made it much easier—he was unfazed by it all. He must have been born with an attitude of acquiescence. He so readily accepts whatever comes his way and trusts God to give him strength and courage, and even joy, for the moments as they come. What a pleasure to walk with him and support him.

Surgery was scheduled for February and was successful, but it was going to require radiation because his p.s.a. had not come down very far. For some reason the appointment at the cancer clinic kept being put off. We couldn't understand the reasons. Since Paul had been scheduled for April knee replacement surgery, that went ahead. The knee surgeon recommended it be done with an epidural, but I was apprehensive and expressed it. "Oh, please not an epidural!'

"Why would you say that?" he asked.

"I just know too many cases where an epidural had lasting ill effects."

"Oh, those were probably long ago. We have better ways of doing things now," he said. "It's so much nicer than waking up after anesthesia."

"Well, I'll leave the decision to Paul."

The surgery went well, and it was nice not having the after effects of anesthesia. Paul was faithful in his exercises, and it wasn't long until he was walking with only a cane and then even without that aid.

I had my house in Ailsa Craig, Paul had the house he and Marion had built in Listowel, and he still owned his two farms at Teviotdale. We thought we would take our time to decide where we wanted to live.

During that summer, we spent time at Paul's farm. Paul worked outside and I set up a desk in the house where I could work on my writing. It was a lovely place with a good view out the window, but no telephone to interrupt the process. We often went for walks in the woods and had picnic lunches. It was a nice way to get in touch with that part of Paul's life.

That summer was also a time of getting to know Paul's daughters. When I married Paul, family increased more than two-fold. I had a son and three daughters—he had three daughters and a son. He also had thirteen grandchildren. It was a pleasure to get to know them all. Paulette, even though she lived in Port Elgin with Dean and daughters Laura and Melanie, had taken some responsibility in helping her dad adjust to living alone, so she still stopped in frequently. Julie and Bruce lived near Palmerston with their children, Andrew, Josh, Amanda, Joel and Amelia, and Dianne and Murray and children, Kyle, Lindsay, Alyssa and Cole, near Mount Forest. They all were a delight to get acquainted with and brought me much pleasure.

I was conscious of living with their mother's things and wanted them to have what they would like. Marion had a great collection of dishes, mugs, tea cups and dolls. Since I am not a collector, I gradually got all the dishes from the cupboards and five china cabinets and set them out on tables. Paulette, Julie and Dianne all came with their daughters. We drew names, then, in turn, they chose one item from the tables and repeated the turns until the girls had all they wanted. After that, in the same order, their daughters could choose from what was left. The mothers took some items for their sons as well. When that was done, I selected what I wanted to keep and boxed up the rest for a garage sale or thrift store. That day proved to be a satisfying one of getting closer in touch and proving to them that their desires meant a lot to me. It also deepened our relationship.

In September and October, Paul had 35 radiation treatments. Most of them went alright, but the last few caused some burning, and an infection set in, causing a lot of pain and discomfort, before we found the correct solution.

The doctors okayed the second knee replacement for November. Again, I was uneasy about an epidural, but Paul's comment was, "The first knee went well, and it was a nicer way to go."

This time, too, his recovery and mobility came soon, although he complained almost from the first of a stretching sensation from his back to knee. He wondered if, somehow, they had put too big a part in his knee.

It wasn't quite the year we had anticipated, but we still thoroughly enjoyed our life together. We joked that we got married for better or for worse, and we were just getting the worse out of the way at the beginning.

That next spring, we travelled to Northern Ontario to my nephew's wedding. Before we returned home, Paul was walking across the lawn when he fell. I asked if he had tripped on something. "I don't know what it would have been," he said.

When he got up, he realized his left foot hung down and he was unable to lift it up into a normal position. It was numb as well. Investigating on the Internet, I discovered drop-foot can be the result of nerve injury or pinched nerve. It stressed that the only hope of reversal was if it was attended to within the first six weeks after it began. The trouble was that there wasn't a neurologist we could see before November.

He was sent to get a brace so at least his foot would be held up. He also was referred to a physical therapist for exercises the therapist hoped would help.

The worst seemed to be continuing, for through the next years Paul would suffer a prolonged time of pain in his back as he waited over a year for an appointment with a back surgeon. An MRI showed tumours growing in his spine. Immediately the doctors said, "That will be a different kind of cancer, since prostate cancer goes to the bone, but not inside the spine."

Surgery was planned for April 2012, to try to remove some of the growth, to relieve the pain, and to take a biopsy to find out what kind of cancer it was. It turned out to be prostate cancer after all—the first time that occurred in the experience of the hospital. His case was written up in the medical journals because of the phenomenon. The doctor said he had done nothing to relieve the pain, but the agony he had experienced for so long was gone. Both the doctor and we acknowledged it as a gift from God.

The oncologist decided to give him five radiation treatments, and then chemotherapy for nine months. Because the tumours were non-secreting, p.s.a. levels didn't reveal what was happening—he needed MRIs with contrast dye in order to see the tumours and their growth or shrinkage. When the growth continued in spite of the chemo, it was decided to quit that and try a new prostate cancer drug. That, thankfully, began to shrink the tumours and gave Paul a new hope and greater level of health.

We also experienced a lot of *best* even through the *worse* of life, for through it all, our love just grew and became more and more satisfying and such a great source of blessing.

## CHAPTER 42
## Back to Writing

"Have faith in your abilities
and stay committed to your goals."
— Lailah Gifty Akita

My writing and effort to get published had taken a back seat for a while, but at the next Write Canada conference, I had an interview with writer Keith Clemmons whose works I'd read and admired. After taking a look at my book, he recommended that I self-publish. He said that at my age, I didn't have time to wait for mainline publishers to find a place and time for me. I came home and acted on his advice, researching self-publishing companies. Word Alive in Winnipeg had a distributing arm as well which was attractive to me, and so I contacted them. I was inexperienced, but they encouraged me along the way. Because I didn't know all the terms and didn't even know what questions to ask, I made mistakes. However, plans were put in place, the book edited again by their editor and finally went to print in the summer of 2007.

By the end of September, 200 books arrived on our doorstep. Another 500, thankfully, came a few weeks later since I was asked to be speaker for the Palmerston Evangelical Missionary women's retreat on October 12–13, and most of the 200 were already sold by that time. I had a book launch at Nairn Mennonite one Sunday and another at Ailsa Craig Library the following Friday night, and soon after at Palmerston Evangelical Missionary Church.

Immediately, opportunities for speaking engagements arose. Of course, I took my book along and I signed and sold many at those occasions. By January, I had sold over 800 copies of *Not Easily Broken*, and I was gratified to hear positive comments from the readers. Most satisfying was hearing that readers were helped in some way by reading the book.

The grandchildren of the main character (the woman I called Ellie), were quite happy with the story of their grandparents. The granddaughter I knew best called me one day.

"Ruth, our family is wondering if you would consider writing a sequel to *Not Easily Broken*—a story about our mama. She had quite an interesting life too."

"In fact," I said, "I have already started. But if you work with me, more of the book can be true. Would you do that?"

"We'd be happy to do that," Donna said.

Soon after that, three of "Rina's" daughters and I met for one full afternoon of reminiscing that I recorded. At the beginning of that meeting, Donna spoke up.

"Before we start on the new book, we'd like to ask when Mama told you so much about her family. We were surprised at how much you knew. "

"I only had the bare bones of the story. Your mother told me about how her mother was engaged to be married when her sister died in childbirth, leaving two daughters. Her parents insisted she break her engagement and marry the brother-in-law so the girls would stay in the family. She told me of the birth of their own son, and that when he was eight, his father died. After that her mother married her husband's cousin and had her. She said her dad used to call her his favourite daughter, and it would make her feel so good. It was years before she realized that she really was his only daughter."

"But you knew the full names of her husbands."

"No, I just chose names for them. I didn't know their real names."

The women looked at each other in disbelief. "The names you chose for both of them were actually their second given names."

They said the prayers of Ellie and John sounded just like they remembered their grandparents, and they marvelled how I had accurately caught the spirit of the family. Even some of the incidents that I had just made up were actually true. We all agreed there must have been another Spirit at work.

By the time I had several further meetings with more members of the family, I felt like part of the Litt clan and had mounds of material for *Not Far from the Tree,* my second book. The writing brought me much joy, and after its publications, more speaking engagements. The openings included Sunday morning sermons, women's meetings, service organizations, family history groups, weekend retreats, workshops and many more. In the next few years, I had at least twenty engagements a year. Through it all, Paul gave me his full support and usually accompanied me and gave me positive feedback—he even glowed with pride at my accomplishment.

My next project brought to fruition another goal—that of painting pictures. When Veronica Arnel died at 39 of breast cancer, I looked for a book about death that I could give to her niece and nephew. There were quite a few about the death of pets, and a very few about the death of an old grandparent, but none that seemed to answer the need I felt. Through one night, a poem came to me. I got up and wrote it down so I wouldn't forget it. I was motivated to get it printed so children experiencing the death of a loved one would have something to help them deal with it. I tried several artists to get it illustrated, but none were what I had been imagining. I had done drawing all my life, but I was never very good at depicting people accurately. However, I decided to try it. I used watercolours and began to experiment. I needed a sad boy for the front cover. It took me a long time before I realized that the shape of the eyebrows had a lot to do with it. Picture by picture, I got it done and *Tyson's Sad Bad Day*, too, went to Word Alive. It wasn't long before I began to hear stories of how that book helped little ones deal with death. One woman, who had bought the book for little girls in her family after their grandfather died, told me, "They wanted someone to read your book every night for weeks. It brought them a lot of comfort."

It wasn't only Paul's positive support through all my book signings and speaking engagements that made me feel gratified—after every one of those events, I had the feeling that the yearnings of my childhood were being fulfilled. The significance came into sharp focus when I was asked to speak at the annual service at the Altona Meetinghouse. I used to sit in that church, in the back seat with my friends, and wonder why I had such a strong, deep God-given desire to be a minister—why then had I been born female instead of male?

Much of my life moved in the direction of allowing God to use me as he wanted, however, Norman's death was a huge upheaval that turned into a catalyst in my life. It propelled me to move forward, to open myself to growth and to blessings God had in store for me. It seemed that I was being given a chance to accomplish things of which I'd dreamed, to bring to resolution relationships that had hurt, to spread my wings and fly to freedom, to add to my years of marriage in a new setting.

Although I felt much more at ease, I still struggled to put into words the direction my life had taken and the significance of the differences throughout my life from the very beginning.

When I read *Holy is the day, Living in the Gift of the Present*, by Carolyn Weber, (InterVarsity Press), a few paragraphs suddenly made sense of my journey and tied together the loose strings that had dangled before and around me for years. What sense did all these *out of the ordinary* things in my life make? What purpose have they had in my life, and how should I evaluate the effects on my life?

Here is what popped out as I read Carolyn's book.

Craig Goeschel points out in his book, *Weird: Because Normal Isn't Working,* "Christians should strive to not be normal, to not settle for the stress, exhaustion, despair, fear and frayed relationships that a world without God upholds as the "norm."

As Christians we are anything but normal, because our god is anything but ordinary.

...Because we serve such an extraordinary God, we are called to live in *difference*: "Do not conform to the pattern of this world, but be transformed by the renewing of your mind. Then you will be able to test and approve what God's will is—his good, pleasing and perfect will" (Romans 12:2). Others who do not believe *should* look at us and not only wonder why we are "different" but also be led to crave being in that "difference" too.

I read that, then read it again and cried out to my husband who was in the room at the time, "Aha! That's it! That's what ties my life together and makes sense of it all!"

The difference I sensed between my life and others, the discrepancy in the way my body was made and performed, often presented a challenge. There was, however, a positive side. They were good reminders not to expect to be ordinary. Not only did those variations engender creativity and resourcefulness in meeting the complexities, but they also made me conscious of choices to be made and accepted.

Vivid memories from such an early age prove to be a blessing every time I am tempted to doubt the existence of God—the certainty of his presence as I felt it in my crib doesn't leave room for more than a momentary doubt, and even that is soon dispelled.

Growing up in a home and church that was distinct in appearance was also a benefit— it helped me understand that one doesn't need to be the same as everyone else. Even though my outer appearance no longer is so different, I still know that inside I need not be conformed to this world, but transformed by God's dwelling in me.

Even having peculiarities in my physical makeup kept me conscious of the fact that we are not carbon copies of one another, but individuals carefully planned by our maker.

Many people, as I, experience tragedies—fire, accidents, broken marriage relationships and early death of partners. I believe that my understanding of being out of the ordinary assisted me to look for the opportunities for personal growth and progressive faith development in each of those watershed points of my life in a way I may not have otherwise seen.

Being out of the ordinary helped me, with God's assistance, to forge my own path in life and made me more conscious of my dependence on God, led me to more readily accept others who were out of the norm, and to carefully evaluate by whose rules I wanted to live.

As I get older, I am even more at ease with walking close to my Lord and Saviour, allowing him to work in and through me, in and through others, and in our world. Although I continue to lift people and situations up to God in prayer, and contribute if he leads me that way, I am content to let him shine his love on their lives and do what he knows is best.

In my life, too, things that at one time would have caused me concern, and a felt need to do something about it, do not cause me to rush into helping. I am more content to let God make the first move and to let me know if he needs my help. I've learned to listen more than talk.

Life may be summed up in the following poem I wrote.

## OUT OF THE CHRYSALIS

A soul is born —
birthed from protective womb—
yet still cocooned
in parental love.

Grasping life,
we struggle to be free,
to separate,
to stretch our wings,
to be ourselves.

Growing slowly,
wisdom seeks entry,

until in the end we concede,
beautifully content
to be part of the cycle of life
and we let go—
freed to fly home.

I hope to hover here awhile, but I, too, am getting ready to fly home to where it will be anything but ordinary!

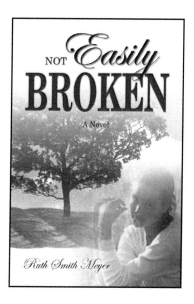

## *Not Easily Broken*
Word Alive Press, 2007
1-897373-10-4

Ellie is a strong young woman faced with circumstances that are not her choice. When Ellie's older sister Regina dies at the birth of her third child, her parents request that Ellie break off her engagement to the man she loves and marry their son-in-law, John, so the children will stay in the family.

Ellie reluctantly agrees but determines in her heart to give it her all to make it a good marriage. She and John begin life with a somewhat contrived feeling to their relationship, but love grows because they are both committed to it.

Come to a deeper understanding of the process of grief as you live through the joys and sorrows of the characters in *Not Easily Broken*.

Based on a true story.

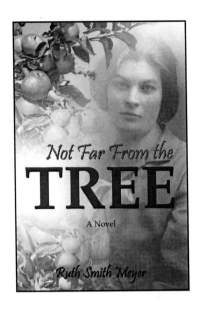

## *Not Far from the Tree*
Word Alive Press, 2008
978-1-897373-59-0

Those who lived in the twentieth century saw more rapid changes than to any previous century. Born at the beginning of this era, to a family that had already faced dramatic change and challenge, Rina seemed to come into the world with a zest for the revolution the century would bring.

When she is barely a grown woman, marriage to an imaginative and sometimes impractical dreamer husband, the arrival of babies, the great depression and life in general take over, molding her into a strong woman not unlike her parents. The unbelievable twists in the lives of Rina and her beloved David will keep readers fascinated with the indomitable strength of the human spirit when there is a solid foundation of love and faith. In this sequel to *Not Easily Broken*.

Based on a true story.

## *Tyson's Sad Bad Day*
978-1-926676-43-2
Word Alive Press, 2009

*A little boy named Tyson*
*was feeling very sad,*
*It was one of the worst days*
*that he had ever had.*

And so begins this delightful story that leads children through the honest feelings of confusion, fear and uncertainty with the death of someone dearly loved.

In this day and age with so many suffering from cancer and other diseases, it isn't always grandparents and older people who die.

It is the author's hope that this book will help ease frank discussions and provide the means of comfort on a child's level that will help both child and parent.